101 DEFENSES

101 DEFENSES

How the Mind Shields Itself

Jerome S. Blackman, M.D., F.A.P.A.

BRUNNER-ROUTLEDGE

New York and Hove

Published in 2004 by
Brunner-Routledge
29 West 35th Street
New York, NY 10001
www.brunner-routledge.com

Published in Great Britain by
Brunner-Routledge
27 Church Road
Hove, East Sussex
BN3 2FA
www.brunner-routledge.co.uk

10 9 8 7 6 5 4 3 2 1

Library of Congress Cataloging-in-Publication Data
Blackman, Jerome S.
    101 defenses : how the mind shields itself / Jerome S. Blackman.
        p. ; cm.
    Includes bibliographical references and index.
    ISBN 0-415-94694-8 (hardback : alk. paper) — ISBN 0-415-94695-6 (pbk.
: alk. paper)
    1. Defense mechanisms (Psychology) 2. Mental illness. 3. Diagnosis,
Differential.
    [DNLM: 1. Defense Mechanisms. 2. Mental Disorders—diagnosis.
3. Mental Disorders—therapy. 4. Psychotherapy—methods. WM 193 B629z
2003] I. Title: One hundred and one defenses. II. Title.

    RC455.4.D43B534 2003
    616.89—dc21

                                                    2003010499

Contents

Preface

Steve, 26, wanted testosterone shots so he could function sexually with his wife. He had a good reason for the shots; he had undergone surgical removal of his pituitary gland several months earlier[1] and now needed hormone replacement therapy.

I was an intern at the time, on the internal medicine service in the hospital where Steve had been admitted for monitoring and adjustment of his replacement hormones. I didn't know much about psychology or defenses at the time, but one day on rounds, when I had a few moments alone with Steve, I mentioned my interest in his need for the testosterone shots. He explained that testosterone relieved his impotence with his wife. His embarrassment lessened as we talked, and I was able to complete the sexual history by inquiring if his sexual problems included lack of morning erections or inability to masturbate.

At that point, Steve sighed. He looked over at the door to his room, making sure it was shut, and said, "Well, since we're talking about this honestly, there's something I should tell you. The truth is, I only need the shots to have sex with my wife. I have a girlfriend I don't need the shots for."

Steve complained that his wife had never enjoyed sex. She had been a virgin at marriage. Since the birth of their two-year-old son, sex had been relatively infrequent. He said his surgery didn't have much to do with the problem. Although he loved his wife, he could not think of a way of solving the problem, which, he said, she acknowledged was hers. He expressed a fervent desire to be able to enjoy sex with her; she had been a good wife in many other ways—helping him through his illness, for example.

The following day, when I made rounds, Steve's wife was at his bedside. They apparently had discussed the situation. She expressed a wish to get over her serious sexual inhibition and asked whom she might consult for help. I obtained some referrals for her in the community from the internal medicine resident who was my immediate supervisor.

Years after completing my psychiatric and psychoanalytic training, I was able to formulate about what had occurred in my interactions with Steve. By asking about other areas of sexual difficulty, I had actually "confronted" (chapter 5) Steve about various defenses he was using, including: *prevarication (lying) (23)*[2] about his impotence; *displacement (19)* of his sexual wishes from his wife to his girlfriend; and *rationalization (42)* and *concretization (52)*—finding an excuse by seeing his sexual problem as having a purely medical origin. In a supportive way (chapter 7), I also had expressed enough interest that Steve trusted me and turned to me with his maladaptive compromise formation (see chapter 1)—*avoiding* his wife and *lying* to her to avoid guilt, *suppressing* his frustration, and *displacing* his sexual wishes elsewhere.

In other words, Steve knew that he was physically capable of sexual performance even without the testosterone shots, as evidenced by his activities with his mistress. However, he had convinced himself that he needed the shots in order to perform with his wife; they were like Dumbo's magic feather (Aberson & Englander, 1941).

Steve's favorable response to my confrontation of his defenses had led him to reveal his conflicts. Rather than take testosterone shots the rest of his life and depend on destructive extramarital contacts for sexual gratification, he and his wife now could face their psychological problems and resolve the conflicts that were interfering with their ability to enjoy sex within the marriage.

Thirty years later, Dr. C asked me, "Would you really say that? It's so aggressive!" He was a U.S. Navy lieutenant finishing his psychology internship at the Naval Medical Center in Portsmouth, VA. I had just explained to his class that when they could see, during evaluation, that someone was *lying* about suicidal intentions in order to get out of the service, they could say to the person something like, "My impression is that you're not being truthful with me" and could add, "And you're trying to manipulate me into going along with you. So you also are not treating me as your therapist; you're basically attempting to use me."

After Dr. C's interjection about how "aggressive" these interventions sounded, I pointed out that *lying (23)* and *devaluation (50)* are *defenses*. If Dr. C confronted the defenses, as I suggested (see chapter 5), perhaps a sailor would admit to using them and then elaborate on the conflicts he had been avoiding. In other words, some of the interns' cases, who secretly carried the sardonic diagnosis of "WOOTEN" (Want Out Of The Navy), might actually be treatable with dynamic psychotherapy, and not be just a pain in the neck. In addition, confrontation of the defenses could help in diagnosis: the psychopathic (antisocial) types would probably persist in lying, and the grandiose psychotic ones would probably verbally attack Dr. C for daring to question their motives.

In any case, Dr. C could prevent himself from hating his work because he was being used; at least he would not just *passively (62)* sit there, allowing the sailor to *intimidate (83)* him. Dr. C liked my suggestion and reported thereafter that he enjoyed employing confrontation of defenses with some of his WOOTENs, occasionally finding a treatable one. He commented to me that he realized he had somehow equated being empathic with being passive, so that he had felt some guilt about being direct in his approach to people he evaluated or treated.

The human mind has an amazing capacity to invent mechanisms that shield a person from becoming aware of unpleasant emotions. These mechanisms often are disguised and operate outside of a person's awareness. Because of the stealthy quality of defenses, uncovering them and understanding their potentially detrimental effects can be useful. For example, a person who is unable to recognize anger toward a loved one may feel intense self-loathing instead. When that person shows up in the ER for severe depression, the ability to discuss the defensive operation of *turning on the self (15)* can be extremely helpful in preventing a suicide attempt or other self-destructive conduct (see chapter 8).

Understanding defenses is also valuable in other life situations. Recognizing a teenager's use of *minimization (75)* and *counterphobic behavior (44)* can be helpful to parents trying to steer their child away from dangerous activities. Understanding a rival's *grandiosity (63)* may enable an executive to gain the upper hand in a competitive business situation. Confronting *denial (6)* and *rationalization (42)* is important for family members who are concerned with a loved one's alcoholism. Noticing *identification with the lost object (37)* is helpful when comforting a grieving relative. Last but not least, the detection of *distancing/avoidance (61)* mechanisms in a romantic relationship can clue you in that someone is not inclined toward the fidelity and constancy required for a long and happy marriage.

In clinical situations, mentioning defenses to the wrong kind of person, or at the wrong time, can also be counterproductive. That's if you can even find the defenses, since they are so often unconscious. Intervening in a therapeutic way can be even more daunting.

In this book, I have tried to provide a framework that explains the origination, properties, and causes of defensive activity, and have included a chapter on differential diagnosis that describes who should be treated with interpretive techniques and who should not. There is a section on how to decipher the pathological defenses being used. I have included separate chapters on how to zero in on defenses, and then intervene supportively versus interpretively, depending on which techniques are indicated. And finally, I have included a chapter to demonstrate how to use confrontation of defenses as an adjunct to other techniques used in assessing suicidal propensities.

Acknowledgments

This book is dedicated to the many students, from many disciplines, that I have enjoyed teaching over the past 28 years, who encouraged me to organize my handouts in one place. I hope that others will also find it a user-friendly discussion of defenses, along with some ideas about how defenses can be used in diagnosis and treatment.

As with many important ideas about the mind, Sigmund Freud was the first to mention defenses, in 1894 (!). But his daughter, Anna Freud made the first list, in her pioneering study, *The Ego and the Mechanisms of Defense* (1936), utilizing material from adults and children she treated. I am likewise indebted to Percival Symonds, who authored a voluminous compilation of about 25 defenses: *The Dynamics of Human Adjustment* (1946). From his students at Columbia Teachers College, he gathered mountains of examples and commentaries about defenses.

For their many editorial criticisms and corrections of my manuscript, many thanks go to Cecilio Paniagua, M.D., psychoanalyst in Madrid, Spain; Janet L. Schiff, L.C.S.W., psychoanalyst with the New York Freudian Society; William R. Goldman, Ph.D., Director of Psychology Internship Training at Eastern Virginia Medical School; Steve Brasington, M.D., Chair of Child Psychiatry at Portsmouth Naval Medical Center; Dr. George Zimmar of Brunner-Routledge; my office manager, Jean Broughton; my wife, Susan; and my son, Theodore.

Introduction

The term *defense* refers to the way the mind shuts feelings out of consciousness.[1] It's common knowledge that therapists try to understand the feelings of people they treat. But in practice, understanding feelings usually isn't enough to help people overcome their problems. It's also necessary to explain how and why unconscious *defenses* are keeping people from knowing about their unpleasant feelings. In actuality, most emotional difficulties result from a combination of problematic defenses and affects.

With adequate insight into their pathological defense mechanisms and feelings, people can more clearly understand the meanings and origins of their irrational behaviors, symptoms, and attitudes. That knowledge often relieves painful psychiatric symptoms (such as depressions and phobias), and enables people to make salutary changes in their lives.

There are probably an infinite number of defenses—not only the 101 I've listed. Two of the greatest psychoanalytic theoreticians, Anna Freud (Sandler & Freud, 1983) and Charles Brenner (2002a), have emphasized that almost anything can be a defense. Looking away can be a defense (Renik, 1978, p. 597). Screaming at someone can be a defense. Playing golf can be a defense. So can saving money. Or, at least, all these activities may involve defenses. Whatever the mental activity or behavior, if it shields you from experiencing unpleasant emotion, it is *defensive*.

Emotions can be pleasant or unpleasant. In general, it's the unpleasant ones that cause people the problems brought about by maladaptive defenses. More specifically, **unpleasurable affects** are defined as possessing two **components**:

> an unpleasurable **sensation** plus a **thought** that something terrible is going to happen ("anxiety") or that something terrible has already happened ("depressive affect") (C. Brenner, 1982a).

We can therefore expand the definition of defense:

Defenses are mental operations that, as a rule, remove some component(s) of unpleasurable affects from conscious awareness—the thought, the sensation, or both.

Diagnostically, we use these concepts of affects and defenses to explain, for example, the phenomenon of forgetting something that's important to remember, perhaps an appointment. The thought content gets shut out of consciousness. You may remember it an hour later when something "jogs" your memory; then you realize you didn't really want to meet with the person anyway. In other words, the thought content (one part of the affect) was *stored* and could be *retrieved* from storage. But your mind switched off the thought to relieve you of the unpleasantness (the other part of the affect) of the memory.

An analogy might be made to an electric circuit—where the potential for a current is present, a lightbulb is intact, and the circuit has no damage. However, a switch has been thrown that breaks the circuit, so that the lightbulb does not work. The switch would be like a conscious defense—"I'll put it out of my mind" or "I don't want to go there!" If the switch is thrown without your conscious intent, you have an unconscious defense.

Unconscious defenses actually operate more like circuit breakers. When the current gets too great, the increase in amperage trips the circuit breaker, which breaks the circuit, and the light goes off. Analogously, when the intensity of affects (emotions such as anger, anxiety, depression, and guilt) threatens to melt down the functioning of the mind, a mental circuit breaker is thrown: certain thoughts are switched out of consciousness: forgotten. As with a circuit breaker, this type of forgetting occurs automatically.

Diagnostically, we also have to consider that there may be primary defects in the bulb. Attempts to repair it lead to the construction of a delicately balanced bulb, with faulty elements, that at best blinks erratically (as in schizophrenia). The person's own attempts to repair the bulb or the wiring defects (like the defense of *reconstruction of reality* [78] after a break in reality testing) may lead to short circuits (delusions).

In a different set of patients—those with borderline personality organization (Kernberg, 1975)—it's as though the circuits are connected and the lightbulb and power source are intact, but the wiring isn't strong enough to handle heavy amperage without melting the wires or tripping a circuit breaker. The weakness of the circuit may have been caused by the heat of chronically high amperage, much as some adult victims of child abuse had their "circuits" for affect management damaged by chronically inflamed rage and anxiety during long stretches of their upbringing. As a result, at times of power surges, the circuit with the wiring of a lower gauge will become overwhelmed and trip the circuit breaker. In adults with borderline personality, the analogy is that their limited affect-tolerance can lead to a tendency to utilize defense.

Finally, those people analysts refer to as "neurotic" have everything in the circuit intact, but the circuit breaker was placed there from a different circuit years ago and is no longer necessary. The wiring has since developed and is much stronger than it was in childhood, but that old circuit breaker may shut down the circuit even though there's no real, present-day danger of overload.

The therapist's job is to determine the kind of problem in the circuits. Then, we either reconstruct the bulb, enhance the wiring, provide new circuit breakers, or, when neurosis is present, find the faulty, unnecessary circuit breakers and allow placement of new switches more realistically commensurate with the needs of an adult.

To complicate matters, some mental problems are not primarily due to defenses, but to a lack of functioning of other parts of the mind. For example, people's feelings can also *overwhelm* them, melting down their abilities to organize thoughts and to concentrate. Erosion of functions like concentration and organization of thought is not caused by defenses (see chapters 4 and 6 and, as an exception, *ego regression [28]* as a defense). But if people are late to a class they really hate, and the professor ridicules them, it's likely they were *avoiding* class, and perhaps even *inviting punishment (41)* to defensively relieve their guilt.

When you treat someone, it's a good idea to be familiar with common defenses so you can, first, find them. Next, you'll need to make decisions about whether to explain how problematic defenses are working—dynamic therapy (see chapter 5), or to suggest new defenses—supportive therapy (see chapter 7). It's also a good idea to know what induces defensive activity. We will examine this in chapter 1.

1

General Concepts about Defenses

Let's recap the definitions of defense and unpleasurable affect. Then we can go further in describing a host of properties and functions of defenses.

DEFINITIONS OF DEFENSES AND UNPLEASURABLE AFFECTS

Defenses are mental operations that remove components of unpleasurable affects from conscious awareness.

Unpleasurable affects include anxiety, depression, and anger. Anxiety is composed of an unpleasurable sensation plus a thought that something terrible is going to happen. Depressive affect is an unpleasurable sensation plus a thought that something terrible has already happened (C. Brenner, 1982a). Anger involves an unpleasurable sensation plus a thought of destroying someone or something (C. Brenner, personal communication, 1990). The thought content for each of these affects may derive from perceptions or memories *from any developmental stage through the present*, and may be reality based, fantasy based, or some admixture of the two.

TRIGGERS FOR DEFENSES

Normal or "Average-expectable" People (Hartmann, 1939)

In normal people (E. Jones, 1942), a very intense affect may threaten to melt down (or overwhelm) the mental functions of thinking, organizing, and concentrating. Freud (1926), more technically, called affects "traumatic" if they interfered with the ego functions of thinking, organizing, and concentrating (Hartmann, 1939).

Ms. AB, a 39-year-old woman, was in treatment with me for marital problems. She reported discovering that her husband was hiding marijuana in the medicine cabinet in the master bath. She *suppressed* (consciously put out of her thinking) her anger until her 13- and 15-year-old children were sleeping, and then expressed her multiple concerns to her husband: worries about his health, the kids' well-being, his arrest or prosecution, the danger of him committing foolish acts while stoned, and the risk of public humiliation. She also objected to his setting an immoral and illegal example for the children. When he defended his right to smoke pot, she "lost it." She began crying, but stopped herself.

The next day at noon, while she was at a garden store picking out flowers for the front yard, Mr. AB called her on her cell phone. He was at home, waiting. They were supposed to have met for a "hot sex date" while the kids were at school. She had completely forgotten, and felt guilty that she had disappointed him.

In this situation, Ms. AB at first *suppressed (31)* her anger (consciously), but when her husband was unreasonable in his reaction to her concerns, her anger and depression became "traumatic" due to their intensity. She then instituted several other defenses without being aware that she was doing so. She *repressed (25)* the "hot sex date"; this both relieved her of her anger and simultaneously expressed it (a compromise formation). She used *projective identification (4)*—creating severe frustration in her husband to relieve her own frustration about him not being more attentive to her wishes. She *identified with the aggressor (35)* by doing to him what he had done to her (ignored her wishes). She rejected his sexual overture and *displaced (19)* her attention onto feminine elements (flowers for her garden), *symbolically (20)* reaffirming her femininity. She thereby *repressed (25)* the insult she felt because he had disregarded her concern. She also *isolated (13)* (shut off) the sensations of her depression regarding the marriage.

When I pointed out to her that forgetting the date with her husband and focusing on the flowers apparently had the above meanings, she became more aware of her anger at him and her guilt. Her conflict between anger and guilt had also caused her to become *passive (62)* when he had argued with her. In her follow-up session a few days later, she reported that she had explained to her husband that she felt angry and discouraged about the marriage because of his stubborn insistence on committing illegal, self-destructive drug abuse. Her confrontation led him to rethink his obstinacy, especially in light of the potential impact on their teenage children. He apologized and threw out the marijuana.

Psychosis & Borderline Personality

In people with psychosis or borderline personality, on the other hand, even mild affects may melt down ego functions. In those illnesses, affect-tolerance, an ego strength (Kernberg, 1975), is minimal to begin with.

> Mr. DB, age 25, had been severely neglected by his mother throughout his childhood. She allowed his older brothers to beat him up. In addition, he witnessed his adolescent sister's prostitution when he was in junior high school. Since age 15, he had been a binge drinker. All of these factors (i.e., the overwhelming rage at his brothers, the sexual overstimulation caused by seeing his sister's sexual activities, and the interference with the development of ego strength by his use of alcohol as an affect-neutralizer throughout adolescence) had led Mr. DB to develop a serious weakness in affect-tolerance.
>
> Now in graduate school, when asked to do an extra assignment, he felt enraged to the point where he was not able to concentrate and organize (integrate) his thoughts. He couldn't study. To handle his overwhelming anger and depressive affect, he defensively blamed his girlfriend (*projective blaming*) (5) for having encouraged him to go to graduate school. He also became *grandiose (63)* (thought that he would report the professor for unfairness), and he drank (*substance abuse as a defense*) *(69)*.

In other words, due to (ego) damage in affect-tolerance, a normative stress like an extra homework assignment (causing anger) led him to become overwhelmed by rage. Pathological defenses were then brought into play to assuage his shame over experiencing breakdown in his (ego) functions of concentration and integration.

Neurotic Illness

In people with neurotic illnesses (including phobias, conversions, panic, obsessions, compulsions, some impulsivity, some depressions), ego strength (see Appendix 2) may be adequate. But even if an affect's intensity is only mild, a small amount of the affect acts as a signal (Freud, 1926; C. Brenner, 1982a). This **signal affect** triggers defenses in situations that remind the person, usually unconsciously, of prior situations when they actually had been overwhelmed.

> Renée, age 34, felt panicky. Her thoughts about her anxiety ran to her recent wish to bear children. She was afraid to tell her husband, since they initially had agreed not to conceive. In addition, Renée didn't want to become "dependent" on her husband's income. She noted

how, as a teenager, she had had to beg her father for her allowance and how she hated it.

I pointed out that she seemed to expect her husband to be as parsimonious as her father had been. Renée realized that this was an unfair characterization of her husband, who had always been generous with her. Following a course of brief psychotherapy (a few months), Renée broached the subject of children with her husband, who, it turned out, was excited and happy about the idea. (For a fuller description of this case, see Blackman, 2001, pp. 174–177.)

Renée had been using the defenses of *reticence (59)*, *avoidance (61)*, and *pseudoindependence (72)* to shield herself from *transference (79)*-based anxiety with her husband. In other words, her signal anxiety, not over-whelming in nature, had generated the pathological defenses.

CONSCIOUS VERSUS UNCONSCIOUS DEFENSES

Shutting off affects is like breathing. People usually are not aware of the regulation (unconscious defense), but they may purposely take control of the regulation (conscious defense). In fact, defenses operate consciously and unconsciously; people can use them on purpose or without being aware of it.

In analytic nomenclature, the distinction between conscious and un-conscious employment of a defense is sometimes made by using a differ-ent term. *Suppression (31)*, for example, indicates purposeful forgetting, whereas *repression (25)* means unconscious forgetting. Similarly, *prevari-cation (23)* means purposeful lying, whereas *confabulation (24)* suggests falsification that occurs without the person's awareness. Note that Ms. AB (above) had initially suppressed anger; later she repressed angry thoughts of leaving her husband.

BASIC VERSUS ANCILLARY DEFENSES

In adults, the primary defense mechanisms are usually *repression (25)* and *isolation (13)* (of affect). According to C. Brenner (1982a), all affects have two components: sensations and thoughts. The sensations may be plea-surable or unpleasurable, and the thoughts conscious or unconscious. *Repression* is the term given to the phenomenon where a person's mind automatically shuts the thought content (of an affect) out of conscious-ness. *Isolation* refers to the mind shutting the sensation out of awareness, but not necessarily the thoughts. Other defensive operations, in general, are helper defenses that support repression, isolation, or both. Kernberg

(1975) has taken exception to this general rule, theorizing that some people, whom he diagnoses with borderline personality, use *splitting (8)* as a primary defense.

ADAPTIVENESS VERSUS MALADAPTIVENESS

Most defenses can be used adaptively or maladaptively. In fact, a therapist should probably only mention a defense to a person in treatment if the defense seems maladaptive. Maladaptive defense constellations are responsible for obsessions, phobias, and disturbed coping with external situations ("fitting in" [Hartmann, 1939]). The therapist, upon deciphering the culpable defenses, will usually consider bringing them to the attention of the person in treatment—a technique analysts call "confrontation" (see chapter 5).

> An accountant experienced no trouble at work due to her perfectionism, *intellectualization (45)*, and insistence on *ritualistic (12)* management of details. However, her husband's frustration with her perfectionism was disrupting their marriage. The therapist therefore brought those obsessional defenses to her attention and suggested that she was thereby protecting herself from some unpleasant feelings.

EMERGENCY VERSUS CHRONIC DEFENSES

Defenses are commonly used in emergency situations. The person experiences a threat of overwhelming affect (whether that threat is real or not) and then tries to derail the affect. Some people, however, experience defensive operations chronically, always blaming others or constantly talking too much.

> Emergency defenses developed in parents when their son accidentally got his finger cut off in a storm door. His parents experienced severe anxiety, guilt, and depressive affect. Their emergency defenses prevented those intense affects from interfering with their judgment, anticipation, reality testing, and psychomotor activity. The father *isolated (13)* unpleasant sensations while planning a course of action. The mother considered the prognosis *(intellectualized) (45)*. They both *suppressed (31)* fear. The father calmly drove the child to the emergency room, with the mother calmly *(counterphobic) (44)* holding the severed finger on ice. [1]

They couldn't indulge their feelings of panic and terror until their son was safely delivered to the care of the ER doctor. Their defenses protected their autonomous ego functions so that a decision (judgment, anticipation) regarding the hospital (reality testing) could be made expeditiously and the child could be protected while being transported (psychomotor). The finger was saved.

Preconscious automatisms (Hartmann, 1939) are groups of defenses that chronically arise in symbolic situations.

> Mr. J, an electrical engineer, consulted me as he was about to lose his job. He complained that his colleagues were lazy and flaunted rules. He felt he had to report even minor transgressions against unimportant regulations. I soon understood that he did this in a vociferous, obnoxious way. When I pointed out that his style of complaining provoked others to dislike him and that he spoke obnoxiously, he recalled witnessing his mother tolerate verbal abuse from his father (which he considered a transgression). She had told Mr. J that she wished she could have confronted his father.

Mr. J had *identified with the victim (36)*, leading him to behave in a way his mother had wished for herself (to actively confront wrongdoing). At the same time, he *disidentified (53)* from her passivity, becoming active *(turning passive to active [64])*. He had developed a *transference (79)* to the company (unconsciously seen as an abusive father), which prevented him from remembering the rage and fear he had felt toward his father. In addition, he defended against his anger at his father by using *identification with the aggressor (35)*: now Mr. J verbally abused people. Moreover, he *displaced (19)* his anger toward his father onto others.

His chronic preconscious automatism of obnoxious confrontation, which operated when he saw a rule being bent, included his defensive operations of *provocation (41), impulsivity (68), disidentification (53), identifications with the victim (36) and the aggressor (35), transference (79), displacement (19)*, and *turning passive to active (64)*. After a series of confrontations and interpretations of his defenses and affects, he better understood his misbehavior, could desist from it, and was ultimately able to obtain and retain a new job.

DEFENSE MECHANISMS VERSUS DEFENSIVE OPERATIONS

Anna Freud (Sandler & Freud, 1983) defines a "defense mechanism," such as projection, as a mental tool used against an affect, akin to using a hammer to hit a nail. "Defensive operation" is a broader term that includes any other mechanism so employed, such as using a shoe to hit a nail. Masturbation, for example, a sexual pleasure-related activity, may be used defensively to relieve depression or anxiety (Marcus & Francis, 1975).

Even more complex behavior may be used defensively. For example, after Theodore Roosevelt's wife and mother died on the same day in 1884, he left New York City to live as a cowboy in the Badlands of the Dakotas for over two years (White House, 2002). This sudden change in behavior seems to have been, at least in part, his conscious attempt to relieve (defend against) severe grief.

In another example, antidepressant medication was requested by a philanderer, in spite of the fact that he knew it interfered with his sexual performance. After he badgered his female therapist to prescribe it, she came to realize—and interpret to him—that he wished to have her punish him to relieve his guilt over infidelity (Blackman, 2003). In other words, his wish for and use of medication was defensive.

SIMPLE DEFENSE VERSUS CHARACTER DEFENSE

Some defense mechanisms are simple and stand alone, such as *intellectualization (45)*: at a party, a person talks about a recently read book to relieve social anxiety (Slavson, 1969).

Character defenses are more pervasive, chronic, and complex. They often involve other aspects of mental functioning. An example would be condescension, which includes *projection (1), self-aggrandizement (63), devaluation (50), identification (34),* and *splitting (8).* A more subtle character defense is the assumption of the role of disciple. Many people will attempt to treat their therapists as omniscient gurus as a way of avoiding painful affects.

CONFLICT-RESOLVING VERSUS DEVELOPMENTAL PROPERTIES OF DEFENSES

Most defenses are used to manage affect generated by intrapsychic conflict. But some seem to be building blocks of normal psychic structure and are not just used to ward off affects. *Introjection (2)* of parents' soothing ministrations early in life, besides calming (defending against) the infant's emotional storms, also seems necessary for the child to develop the ego strength of affect tolerance (Lustman, 1966; Tolpin, 1971; Kernberg, 1975).

Identification with parents' value systems during latency (ages 6 to 10 years), doesn't only protect the child from fear of parental punishment. It also helps establish an important structure: the superego (C. Brenner, 1982a). In fact, values, ideals, and critical capacities (superego) are highly influenced by identifications throughout life. In childhood and adolescence, identifications with idealized teachers, coaches, and media figures have a powerful effect. In adulthood, identification with the values of mentors, employers, and organizations can affect people's values. John Dean (1976), in his autobiography of his role in the Watergate scandal, details the deterioration of his value system, as an adult, via his *idealizations (49)* of and *identifications (34)* with Nixon, Haldeman, and Ehrlichman.

DEFENSE VERSUS DEFENSE

Defenses, in addition, may shut out of consciousness any mental content or function including sexual and hostile wishes, conscience pangs, and reality perceptions. Sometimes, a defense may even prevent another defense from becoming conscious, as in a man who minimized his chronic *joking (51)*, which in turn had prevented him from becoming aware of sad feelings.

Greenson (1967) has pointed out that although some people experience resistance to treatment, they won't admit it. He called this "resistance to resistance," usually caused by defense.

> A 35-year-old man was 20 minutes late for his first appointment, and apologized, saying he had forgotten about it until the last minute. When I tried to interpret that his forgetting might indicate that he had some second thoughts about even consulting me, he insisted that it was a "meaningless mistake." Later in the consultation session, after he had recalled his criticism of and frustration with prior therapists, I was able to successfully point out that he had preferred to think his forgetting his appointment with me was meaningless so that he would not have to face his fear that I would be as disappointing as his previous therapists had been.

FLYING IN FORMATION

Defenses usually occur in groups, or constellations. (Also see chapter 4). Typical defense constellations occur in the following pathological states:

1. Criminal psychopathy (criminals and other antisocials): *prevarication (23)*, *projective blaming (5)*, and *rationalization (42)*:

> "I didn't kill her. I didn't even know her. The district attorney said if I admitted to it, I would serve time and not get the chair—that's the

only reason why I confessed. Also, I was so upset about being arrested, I didn't know what to say. . . ."

2. Borderline personality organization: *denial (6a), projective identification (4), idealization (49), dedifferentiation (7), devaluation (50), grandiosity (63),* and *splitting (8):*

> "My husband's an idiot! Not like Steve. He's wonderful. He understands my need to have two men in my life. Steve tells me what to do, and I do it because I agree with him. My husband can kiss my ass! I'm staying with Steve this weekend, and my husband can take care of the children! Why shouldn't I be in control for a change? Why do I want to die?"

3. Hysteria
    a) Histrionic subtype: *repression (25), one affect versus another (57), socialization (46), dramatization (67), transference (79), inhibition of ego function (48),* and *garrulousness (60):*

    > A new consultee opens her first appointment saying: "It's so wonderful to meet you, Dr. C! I know your husband's an accountant with Anderson. It must have been so hard to go through the scandal! Well, what about my problem? It's so embarrassing. . . . Do we really need to talk about it? I'm sure you've heard worse. . . . You seem so stable and so worldly!"

    b) Conversion subtype: *repression (25), symbolization (20), somatization (65):*

    > After a heated argument with his wife, a man loses strength in his arms.

    c) Phobic subtype: 3a or 3b plus *projection (1), displacement (19), symbolization (20),* and *avoidance (61)* (see chapter 4):

4. Obsessional disorders: *projection (1), displacement (19), symbolization (2), concretization (52), isolation (of affect) (13), reaction formation (11), undoing and rituals (12), perfectionism, hyperpunctuality, parsimoniousness, intellectualization (45), rationalization (42), hypercriticism of the self or others (15),* and *inhibition of critical judgment (48).*

5. Depressions: *turning on the self of rage and/or criticism (15), reaction formation (11), oral libidinal regression (27), inhibition of ego functions* (psychomotor and speech) *(48), provocation of punishment (41),*

identification with the victim (36), and *identification with the lost object (37)*.

APPEARANCE DURING DEVELOPMENT

Many defense mechanisms initially appear during a specific phase of childhood development. In adults, most defenses can be used together, regardless of when they originated. In other words, an adult may use *garrulousness (60)* and *intellectualization (45)* (which began in latency), sexual intercourse (adult genital), *identification with the ideal object (34)* (adolescence), and *projective blaming (5)* (anal) together, as follows:

> A depressed man sweet-talks (*garrulousness*) a woman into bed (*sexual intercourse as a defense*), the way his "cooler" older brother used to do (*identification with the idealized object*), and thereby feels less depressed. Later, when the woman wants to stay overnight and have breakfast together, he accuses her of being pathologically dependent (*projective blaming* and *projection*).

COMPROMISE FORMATION OR THE "PRINCIPLE OF MULTIPLE FUNCTION"
(Waelder, 1936; C. Brenner, 1982a, 2002)

Although a defensive operation prevents some aspect of mental functioning (usually an affect) from becoming conscious, the *defense itself* may take on other meanings and serve other functions as well. For example, if you *identify* with someone you admire (an idealized object), you relieve guilt over competitive hostility and at the same time gratify a wish to be like that person. Therefore, theoretically speaking, besides the defense being *part of* a compromise formation (a complex mental formation that simultaneously expresses and defends against affects), the defense, itself, is a compromise formation.

Keeping this principle in mind helps in treating people. For instance, you interpret to a woman that her silence is an identification with her mother that helps her avoid anger at her mother. She responds, "Is my not talking bothering you, too?" Here, her *identification* (silence) not only avoids her hostility, it simultaneously is designed to provoke you, which expresses her hostility.

SUMMARY

Defenses are mental operations that usually prevent various ideas, urges, emotions, and even other defenses from reaching consciousness; at times, certain defenses, such as identification, can also be employed for the development of psychic structure. Defenses are triggered by normative affects when people have limitations in ego strength, as well as by signal affects and traumatic affects. Defenses can be used consciously or unconsciously, and may be adaptive to the environment or highly maladaptive. They are typically used in emergencies but may also be chronic, as in neurotic (anxiety and depressive) symptoms. When they fly in formation, constellations of defenses explain the causation of many psychiatric disturbances, as per the principle of multiple function: the defenses are part of the solution to intrapsychic conflicts; at the same time defenses are themselves compromise formations.

Keeping in mind these general concepts regarding defensive operations, we can now move on to the definitions of 101 common defenses in chapters 2 and 3. Following that, we'll address how defense theory is used in diagnosis, in assessment of treatability, in supportive and dynamic technique, and in determination of suicide risk.

Quick Definitions of 101 Defenses in Approximate Order of Their First Appearance During Development

Oral Phase (0 to 3 years)

1. **Projection** (Freud, 1894; Willick, 1993)—You attribute your own stuff to another person.
2. **Introjection** (Freud, 1917; A. Freud, 1936, 1992; Sandler, 1960; Meissner, 1970; Volkan, 1976)—You form an image of another person.
3. **Hallucination** (Garma, 1969; Arlow & Brenner, 1964)—You see or hear what you are trying not to think about—wishes, comments, fantasies, or criticisms—with no reality testing.

Anal Phase (1.5 to 5 years)

4. **Projective Identification** (Kernberg, 1975)—Three common ways this term is used:
   a. Projecting so much of yourself onto someone else that you massively distort him or her.
   b. Stimulating in someone else your unpleasant affects ("misery loves company").
   c. Stimulating in someone else your unpleasant affects, plus acting like the person who had made you feel so bad.
5. **Projective Blaming** (Spruiell, 1989)—You unfairly blame somebody else for your problem.
6. **Denial** (A. Freud, 1936; Moore & Rubinfine, 1969)—Assumes you've perceived reality (reality sense is functional):
   a. *Denial per se*: Disavowal of a reality in spite of overwhelming evidence of its existence.
   b. *Denial in deed*: *Behavior* that symbolically says, "That nasty reality isn't true!"
   c. *Denial in fantasy*: Maintaining *erroneous beliefs* so you won't have to see the reality.
   d. *Denial by words*: Using *special words* to convince yourself of the falsity of a reality.
7. **Dedifferentiation (Self-Object Fusion)** (Mahler, 1968)—You become whatever someone else wants you to be.
8. **Splitting** (Kernberg, 1975)—You see certain people as purely hostile (McDevitt, 1985), and others as purely loving. Or, you now hate the devil you loved.
9. **Animism** (Freud, 1913; Mahler, 1968)—You give human qualities to nonhuman entities.
10. **Deanimation** (Mahler, 1968)—The person you see isn't human, so you don't have to worry.
11. **Reaction-Formation** (A. Freud, 1936; Gorelik, 1931)—You feel opposite (e.g., so nice you can't tell you're angry).
12. **Undoing and Rituals**—You go against your conscience (superego). Or you do what you feel guilty about and atone by punishing yourself in another symbolic act.
13. **Isolation (of Affect)** (C. Brenner, 1982a)—You are unaware of the sensation of affects.
14. **Externalization** (Glover, 1955)—You think "Society" will criticize you, but actually *you* feel guilty.
15. **Turning on the Self** (Freud, 1917; A. Freud, 1936)—You're angry at someone, but attack/kill yourself instead.
16. **Negativism** (Levy & Inderbitzin, 1989)—You refuse to cooperate, and treat other people condescendingly.
17. **Compartmentalization** (Freud, 1926)—You inhibit yourself from making connections.
18. **Hostile aggression** (Symonds, 1946; McDevitt, 1985)—You get into fights to hide unpleasant feelings.

First Genital Phase (2 to 6 years)

19. **Displacement** (Freud, 1900a; Arlow & Brenner, 1964)—You feel one way toward a person, but shift it to another person or situation.

20. **Symbolization** (Freud, 1900a; Arlow & Brenner, 1964)—You give irrational meaning to some aspect of mental functioning.
21. **Condensation** (Freud, 1900a; Arlow & Brenner, 1964)—You weld together disparate ideas that are contiguous.
22. **Illusion Formation or Daydreaming** (Raphling, 1996)—You consciously visualize a scene that is upsetting or pleasant, and know it's a fantasy.
23. **Prevarication** (Karpman, 1949)—You lie on purpose, for a reason.
24. **Confabulation** (Spiegel, 1985; Target, 1998)—You lie without knowing it, to relieve lowered self-esteem.
25. **Repression** (Freud, 1923; Arlow & Brenner, 1964)—You forget thoughts without wanting to.
26. **Negative Hallucination** (Wimer, 1989)—You don't see something upsetting that's right in front of you.
27. **Libidinal Regression [Psychosexual Regression]** (Freud, 1905, 1926)—You are afraid of sex and assertiveness, so you become dependant (oral) or stubborn (anal) instead.
28. **Ego Regression**—Three ways this term is used:
    a. *Interference with a function:* Your ego function or ego strength stops working, so you can't feel something unpleasant.
    b. *Reversion to earlier defense mechanisms:* You start using defense mechanisms that arose in an early stage of development.
    c. *Inefficient defensive operations:* Your defenses fail to shut off affect, and the failure relieves guilt by punishing you.
29. **Temporal Regression**—You focus on earlier times to not think about current conflict.
30. **Topographic Regression** (Arlow & Brenner, 1964)—You dream to avoid painful reality.
31. **Suppression** (Werman, 1985)—You purposely try to forget.
32. **Identification with a Fantasy**—You act like your favorite hero or heroine.
33. **Identification with Parents' Unconscious or Conscious Wishes/Fantasies** (Johnson & Szurek, 1952)—You do as your parents forbid, act out their corrupt wishes, and get punished.
34. **Identification with the Ideal Image or Object** (Jacobson, 1964)—You think and act like someone you think is great.
35. **Identification with the Aggressor** (A. Freud, 1936)—You act abusive to a person because someone has acted abusive to you. This protects you from feeling angry.
36. **Identification with the Victim** (MacGregor, 1991)—You act like someone else by either allowing or seeking victimization. You do this as a rescue wish or to fight off your own anger or guilt.
37. **Identification with the Lost Object** (Freud, 1917)—You act like a lost loved one. If you keep souvenirs and never grieve, you've got "established pathological mourning" (Volkan, 1987a).
38. **Identification with the Introject** (Sandler, 1960)—You make an introject part of your superego.
39. **Seduction of the Aggressor** (Loewenstein, 1957)—You seduce someone sexually or sycophantically to relieve fear.

Latency Phase (6 to 11 years)

40. **Sublimation** (A. Freud, 1936)—You engage in an activity that symbolically represents a fantasy.
41. **Provocation** (Freud, 1916; Berliner, 1947; C. Brenner, 1959, 1982a)—You get other people to have sex with or punish you, or both.
42. **Rationalization** (Symonds, 1946)—You make excuses to relieve tension, usually after denying some reality.
43. **Rumination**—You "overanalyze" and "spin your wheels" trying to solve problems.
44. **Counterphobic Behavior** (Blos, 1962, 1979)—You do exactly what scares you.
45. **Intellectualization** (A. Freud, 1936)—You get cranked up about a peculiar theory of behavior.

46. **Socialization and Distancing** (Sutherland, 1980)—You use your social ability to distract yourself from painful thoughts.
47. **Instinctualization of an Ego Function** (Hartmann, 1955)—You attach symbolic meaning to an ego function (e.g., "Washing dishes is women's work" irrationally equates a certain type of work with gender).
48. **Inhibition of an Ego Function** (Freud, 1926)—Your instinctualized ego function clashes with guilt, so you shut off the function (e.g., you can't read because reading is equated with forbidden sexual activity [Anthony, 1961]).
49. **Idealization**: (Kernberg, 1975; Kohut, 1971)—You overvalue someone because of:
    a. narcissism (Freud, 1914a): to relieve shame over your inadequacy
    b. narcissism (Kohut, 1971): you fuse the person with your overestimated self-image ("selfobject")
    c. love: to not experience disappointments
    d. transference (Freud, 1914b): they're like a wonderful parent, when you were little.
50. **Devaluation**—You look down on someone to preserve your own self-esteem.

Adolescence and Later—Second Genital Phase (13 to 20 years plus)

51. **Humor** (Zwerling, 1955; Vaillant, 1992)—You use kidding around to avoid painful feelings. If you get extremely wound up, you're *hypomanic* (Lewin, 1950; Almansi, 1961).
52. **Concretization** (Blos, 1979)—You stop using abstract thinking (which you have); you blame a "chemical imbalance" or look for a virus to avoid thinking relationships make you upset.
53. **Disidentification** (Greenson, 1968)—You endeavor not to be like one of your parents.
54. **Group formation** (Freud, 1921)—You surround yourself to guard against sexual impulses.
55. **Asceticism** (A. Freud, 1936)—You avoid contact with humans.
56. **Ipsisexual Object Choice**—Your same-sex "buddy" allays fear of heterosexual stimulation.

Assorted

57. **One affect versus Another** (Ackerman & Jahoda, 1948)—You focus on one emotion to avoid another.
58. **Hyperabstraction**—You abuse theories. If you also deny and reconstruct reality, you're probably psychotic.
59. **Reticence**—You stop speaking to avoid being found out.
60. **Garrulousness**—You're talking too much, but aren't circumstantial or tangential.
61. **Avoidance**—You stay away from situations due to the conflicts they generate.
62. **Passivity**—You automatically adopt a compliant or submissive attitude in the face of aggression.
63. **Grandiosity/Omnipotence** (Freud, 1913; Kohut, 1971; Kernberg, 1975; Lachmann & Stolorow, 1976; Blackman, 1987)—You are God's gift to earth, have special powers.
64. **Passive to Active**—"You can't fire me; I quit!" You control your own victimization.
65. **Somatization** (Kernberg, 1975; Deutsch, 1959)—You focus on your body to avoid conflicts with oral, sexual, or hostile impulses.
66. **Normalization** (Alpert & Bernstein, 1964)—You convince yourself you are normal despite obvious psychopathology.
67. **Dramatization**—You inject emotion into your speech to relieve conflict about being noticed.
68. **Impulsivity** (Lustman, 1966)—You use sex, eating, or hostility to relieve tension or an unpleasant affect.
69. **Substance Abuse** (Wurmser, 1974)—You use a concoction to quell unpleasurable affects.
70. **Clinging** (Schilder, 1939)—Clutching onto a person who rejects you.
71. **Whining**—Complaining, you don't see the infantile quality of your wish to be taken care of.

72. **Pseudoindependence**—You become the Lone Ranger, not allowing anyone to help you.
73. **Pathological altruism** (A. Freud, 1936)—Actually projection and identification with the victim: you deny oral urges, project them onto the needy, then vicariously feel nurtured.
74. **Gaslighting** (Calef & Weinshel, 1981; Dorpat, 2000)—You cause people to be mentally disturbed or to believe they are.
75. **Minimization**—You are conscious of a painful reality but give that reality little weight.
76. **Exaggeration** (Sperling, 1963)—You make too much of a deal over something.
77. **Generalization** (Loeb, 1982)—To not hate someone, you see him as part of an evil group.
78. **Reconstruction of Reality** (Freeman, 1962)—You reinvent a situation after denying the reality.
79. **Transference** (Freud, 1914b; A. Freud, 1936; Loewenstein, 1957; Marcus, 1971, 1980; Blum, 1982)—You shift memories of past situations and relationships onto a current person. You then use old defenses to forget the past or to master it by living it again symbolically or changing the ending.
80. **Dissociation**—(1) You forget a whole aspect of yourself. If you name it Butch, you are probably psychotic (Frosch, 1983; Gardner, 1994). (2) You get someone to define you, then reject his or her ideas (Whitmer, 2001).
81. **Photophobia** (Abraham, 1913)—You avoid the light to avoid your scoptophilic (voyeuristic) impulses.
82. **Apathy** (Greenson, 1949)—You have no particular interest in engaging in an activity.
83. **Intimidation of Others—Bullying** (Knight, 1942; Blackman, 2003)—You put others on guard to relieve your own anxiety.
84. **Compensation for Deficiencies** (Ackerman & Jahoda, 1948)—You ostracize those who are more integrated than you are.
85. **Psychogenic Tic** (Aarons, 1958)—Twitching to relieve tension/anger.
86. **Introspection** (Kohut, 1959; Fogel, 1995)—You preoccupy yourself with inner musings to relieve tension or to sidestep external realities.
87. **Qualified Agreement** (Abend, 1975)—You partly agree as a way of avoiding rebelliousness.
88. **Instinctualization of an Ego Weakness** (Blackman, 1991a)—You give a gender connotation to your weakness in affect-tolerance or impulse control (masculine or feminine).
89. **Inauthenticity** (Akhtar, 1994)—You fake it, perhaps habitually.
90. **Hyper-Rationality** (Spruiell, 1989)—You use secondary process to avoid affects.
91. **Vagueness** (Paniagua, 1999)—You hide details.
92. **Hyper-Aestheticism** (Paniagua, 1999)—You get into beauty and truth, avoiding reality or affects.
93. **Glibness**—You speak readily but don't mean much of it.
94. **Physical Violence** (Glasser, 1992)—You "nullify the object," halting your hatred.
95. **Identification with the Injured Object** (Kitayama, 1991)—You model yourself after wounded birds you've known (and sometimes, loved).
96. **Formal Regression** (Freud, 1900a; Blum, 1994b)—You stop using logical, time-oriented thought.
97. **Hypervigilance**—You keep an eye out all the time, even when it's entirely unnecessary.
98. **Temporal Displacement to the Future** (Akhtar, 1996)—You imagine "if only . . ." or "someday . . ."
99. **Fatigue**—You feel tired, but you're not physically ill.
100. **Frankness** (Feder, 1974)—You're honest and blunt, but this covers up your actual thoughts and feelings.
101. **Turning Self-Criticism onto the Object**—You criticize somebody else instead of berating yourself.

2

Defenses That Arise in the Oral, Anal, and First Genital Phases of Psychosexual Development

Let's restate the general rule: **Defenses are mental operations that re-move components of unpleasurable affects from conscious awareness.** (Affect is the psychoanalytic term for an emotion.)

In looking through the following definitions, remember that *any defense can act to relieve any affect* by making some part of it unconscious. In addition, most of the time you will find *groups of defenses acting together.*

Also keep in mind that to get a complete picture of mental functioning, areas other than defenses need assessment, such as: drive activity (eating, sex, and aggression); affective experience (anxiety, depression, guilt, shame, joy, anger); superego activity (self-punitive trends, values, ideals, reliability, punctuality, responsibility); autonomous ego functioning (integration, logical thought, speech, perception, reality testing, abstraction, self-observation, judgment, avocations and skills [ego interests]); ego strength (affect-tolerance, impulse control, containment of fantasy) (see appendix 2); and object relations capacities (empathy, warmth, trust, identity, closeness, and stability in relationships) (see appendix 3).

Pathological mental symptoms (such as hallucinations, phobias, compulsions, and conversions) occur because of the ways drives, affects, superego, autonomous ego functions, ego strengths, object relations, and defenses conflict with each other. The final common pathway for resolution of the various conflicts is called a "compromise formation." In the case of mental problems, we discuss "pathological compromise formations" (C. Brenner, 2002). We'll study more about compromise formations in later chapters (also see chapter 1).

In many of the clinical examples[1] that follow, more than one defense is involved; nevertheless, I have tried to choose examples that highlight the defense under discussion. In the following list, defenses are arranged by the approximate psychosexual phase in which they first appear. But defenses don't necessarily disappear after the close of the psychosexual phase in which they first occurred. In fact, adults can use any combination of these defenses. I have elected to describe the defenses using a casual style and, often, second-person voice (e.g., *identification with the aggressor* means **you** do to others what has been done to **you**), as I have found that generally to be easier on both the reader and the writer.

ORAL PHASE (AGES 0 TO 3 YEARS)

1. Projection (Freud, 1894; Willick, 1993)

You attribute to (your mental representation of) another person your own affect, impulse, or wish, distorting the manner in which you see that other person.

If there is a defect in reality testing, too, the result is "psychotic projection." Projection is aggravated by deficits in self–object differentiation. Prejudice results, in part, from people projecting, onto a group, traits they don't like in themselves.[2]

> Ms. D reported that she thought her boss was angry at her the day before. She explained that he had asked her to prepare a memo and get it to him right away. This was difficult because of other commitments she had that day. She turned it in later in the day than she had hoped to. While her boss did not expressly indicate any displeasure over her untimeliness, she was up all night worrying that she had made him angry.
>
> After brief discussion, it was evident that *she* was the one who was angry at *him*, because she felt it was unreasonable for him to expect such a fast turnaround on the memo, when he knew she had other duties to tend to. She had *projected* her anger onto him and imagined that he was mad at her.

Tip.

> It's usually best to confront projection early in people's treatment so they can see how it works. Otherwise, massive distortions may persist in their minds, especially about you, the therapist. To someone who begins a session by asking you, "Had a bad day?" for example, you might respond, "Maybe *you* have, but would rather think it was me."

Even more importantly, if the person queries, "Why are you look-ing at me funny?" your immediate response should be something like, "Not at all. However, I notice you're looking at me kind of strangely. Seems like you're attributing something to me that you're actually think-ing or feeling." A person with the ability to understand this type of con-frontation will be far more amenable to insight-directed treatment.

2. Introjection (Freud, 1917; A. Freud, 1936, 1992; Sandler, 1960; Meissner, 1970, 1971; Tolpin, 1971; Volkan, 1976)

You construct an image of another person, using the ego functions of perception, memory, and integration; that is, you see the person, remem-ber what you've seen, and then organize the perceptions and memories. The "mental representation" (also called "the introject" or the "object representation") so formed may be used as a target for fantasies and affects.

The introject is often considered a component of "psychic structure." We think that the soothing ministrations of the mother[3] during the first year of life are somehow incorporated by the baby (*introjected*), and that thereafter the baby continues to gradually introject the mother to develop its own self-soothing capacity. Therefore, theoretically speaking, introjects contribute to development of control and delay capacities (ego strengths), especially affect-tolerance and impulse control (Lustman, 1966). (See ap-pendix 2.)

If you are using introjection as a defense (to ward off affects), you become something like your image of another person. Some analysts de-fine *identification* as a more permanent agglomeration of introjects (Meissner, 1970, 1971). Schafer (1977) explores the vicissitudes of these processes as *internalization*.[4]

Mr. Z. repeatedly felt suicidal after his father sadistically criticized him. I had interpreted to him that he was actually feeling murderous toward his father, but due to his dependency on his father, he *turned the rage on himself*; this caused him to think of killing himself. Mr. Z relished the fantasy of destroying his father's political career by committing sui-cide and thereby creating humiliating headlines. But he agreed with my interpretations that killing himself would punish himself and would not even give Mr. Z the satisfaction of witnessing his father's demise, since Mr. Z would already be dead.

A couple of Monday mornings later, on arriving in my office after the weekend, I found that Mr. Z had left a message on my answering machine. It said: "Dr. Blackman, it's your fault that I'm alive. My fa-ther put me down again, so I got in the car in the garage, and was starting to turn the key. But then I thought you would say it was 'stu-pid' to hurt myself just because I was mad at my father. See you later."

In this situation, my dynamic interpretation of Mr. Z's defense of *turning on the self* had only been partially effective. He had not entirely integrated my interpretation. Instead, he had maintained an *introject* of me and my words to him concerning the futility of killing himself. My introject apparently admonished him not to do anything "stupid" and reaffirmed for him that his own life was worthwhile to someone (me), unlike to his father. It was that positive affirmation of caring (as opposed to the dynamic interpretation) that apparently impeded his suicide attempt.

3. Hallucination (Garma, 1969; Arlow & Brenner, 1964)

Psychotic people see or hear thoughts that are not only unreal but that represent things they are trying not to think about—wishes, comments, fantasies, or criticisms. And they can't tell that what they see and hear are their own thoughts because their ego functions of reality testing, reality discrimination, abstraction, and containment of primary process (Kernberg, 1975; Holt, 2002) are not working. If those ego functions were operating, and they were not psychotic, we'd use the term "illusions" or "daydreams" to refer to their perceptions (visual, auditory), sensations (gustatory, olfactory, tactile), thoughts (commands, condensed fantasies), conscience pangs (criticism), and memories (auditory, visual).

ANAL PHASE (AGES 1.5 TO 5 YEARS)

4. Projective Identification (Kernberg, 1975)

There are three ways this term is usually used:

a. Seeing so much of yourself (character traits and defenses) in someone else that you massively distort him or her.
b. Stimulating in someone else, through behavior or attitudes, affects you don't like in yourself ("misery loves company").
c. Stimulating in someone else, through behavior or attitudes, affects you don't like in yourself, plus acting like the person who had stirred up your unwanted affects.

> Ms. UU, a 23-year-old depressed single woman, described problems in her relationship with her father, where he constantly attacked her irrationally. During one session, she proceeded to criticize me for being one minute late. She said, "You treat me like I'm an invertebrate! You know I can't stand waiting because of the way my father treated me, and then you keep me waiting! I don't like you manipulating me with your psychological technique! I demand an apology!"

> Throughout her diatribe, I felt unfairly accused, but also felt that
> defending myself would be fruitless, since she seemed so irrational.
> Fortunately, I suspected that my emotional reaction indicated a response
> to her use of *projective identification*. I therefore said to her, "I now
> feel like I've met your father."

My comment was based on my realization that she had managed *to
get me to feel* pretty much the way she used to feel when he was irrationally
angry at her and she could not defend herself. Later analytic work demonstrated that one of her motives for doing this to me was to allay (defend
against) fear that I would never understand how she felt. By injecting into
me a state of helpless anger, she could feel that at least someone knew
what she had gone through. Other defenses were also present, such as
identification with the aggressor (she acted toward me the way her father
had acted toward her) and *displacement* (shifting of anger at her father
onto me). But the projective identification seemed the most noxious, since
it fostered mistrust, and therefore I decided to interpret it first (see chapter 5).

Tip.

> Some people in therapy behave or express themselves in such a way
> that you find yourself disliking them. Akhtar (2001) includes this in his
> list of danger signs in suicidal people—see chapter 8. You can figure
> they're probably getting you to feel the way they do, but you have to
> test your hypothesis, since it's based on inductive reasoning. A good
> way to approach the problem is to say something like, "I have the im-
> pression that you are somehow trying to control yourself so that you
> won't be critical or irritated. Any truth to that?"

5. Projective Blaming (Spruiell, 1989)

You are responsible for something that's upsetting, but you blame someone else instead of feeling irresponsible or neglectful yourself.

> At 9:30 p.m., a father comes out of his study where he was using the
> Internet and realizes his school-age son has been playing Nintendo and
> has not done his homework. The father declares accusingly at the mother,
> "Why hasn't Jimmy done his homework?" The mother, who has just
> gotten off the phone after a lengthy call with a client, shoots back, "I
> was busy! Why didn't you get him to do his homework?!"

This mechanism occurs frequently in many households, where it is
often dispelled by the blamed person restating a reality and then adding,
"So, don't blame me!"

6. Denial (A. Freud, 1936; Moore & Rubinfine, 1969)

This is the way the mind has of not paying attention to reality. To say people are *denying* a reality, you are implying that if it were not for the defense, they would see the reality. There's an important diagnostic distinction between people who have a defect in their ability to test reality (who may be psychotic) and those who can see and understand reality but avoid doing so to resolve conflict (usually not psychotic).

There has been a plethora of psychoanalytic and psychological literature on denial, as well as country music songs.[5] Anna Freud described four subsets of this defense:

Denial per se. The disavowal of a reality in spite of overwhelming evidence of its existence. For example, even after being presented the evidence of the German atrocities against 6 million Jews, Catholics, and Gypsies during World War II, some authors still claim that the Holocaust never occurred (Holocaust Educational Research, 2002).

Clinically, the defense of denial is a common finding. Severe alcoholics often not only minimize how serious their addiction is, but they may not allow themselves to even recognize that they are addicted at all. Alcoholics Anonymous (AA) utilizes the theory of unconscious defense in their initial approach to alcoholics (which AA calls an "intervention"), where they bring in all manner and means of evidence to convince the alcoholic that he is not only addicted, but that he is *denying* the reality of the addiction.

Bornstein (1951) first pointed out how latency-age children deny the reality of their own affects. They may be crying, for example, but when asked if they're upset, they say no.

Denial in deed. Behavior that symbolically says, "That nasty reality isn't true!" For example, an American couple sailed their boat to the island of Grenada (their "deed") just after hearing the Reagan administration's warning regarding the presence of bellicose Cubans there. The couple was shocked to find armed Cubans waiting for them. They then realized the warning had been "real" and escaped just before the U.S. Marines landed.

Denial in fantasy. The maintenance of erroneous beliefs to avoid facing, often, a terrifying reality. For example, "Everyone has some good in them. Even though he raped and killed a 5-year-old girl, he can be helped."

Denial by words. The use of special words to magically convince yourself of the falsity of a reality. The following clinical vignette, I believe, illustrates how this defense was used by a prescreener employed by a state mental health clinic in a commitment situation. Usually, prescreeners are brought in for a second opinion regarding the necessity of involuntarily hospitalizing a psychiatric patient, after a mental health practitioner has made an initial determination that the patient is dangerous to self or others.

The prescreeners were, years ago, brought in by the states to protect the civil rights of mental patients. However, as many of us know from experience, one unintended consequence of this system is that it gives the person being examined time to retract prior statements of suicidality or homicidality. If the prescreener applies the commitment criteria too literally and does not seriously consider the evaluating practitioner's assessment of the patient's defenses, the true danger posed by the patient may be missed. The legal and procedural emphasis on "imminent dangerousness" can lead a prescreener to institute the defense of *denial by words.*

> Mr. Y, a 48-year-old man, was admitted to a mental hospital just after he strangled his wife during sexual intercourse to the point where she lost consciousness. Upon awakening, still in her nightgown, she escaped to a neighbor's house and called the police, who picked up Mr. Y and brought him to the hospital.
>
> During evaluation, Mr. Y said he was sorry he had attacked his wife but was angry that she had removed her wedding ring. He then insisted on leaving the hospital, claiming no further intent to harm his wife, since he believed she would return to him. But his wife had left him, and the evaluating psychologist foresaw the return of Mr. Y's homicidal rage once the *denial in fantasy* (that his wife would return) broke down. A nurse who was witness to the evaluation filed a temporary detention order on Mr. Y to keep him in the hospital.
>
> When the state screener saw him later that day, Mr. Y refused to say the magic words, "I want to kill my wife imminently," instead claiming he was sorry he had done something so "silly." The prescreener used *denial by words,* paying no attention to the written psychological assessment that spelled out the evaluator's opinion regarding Mr. Y's *denial in fantasy,* and refused to approve a detention order for preliminary involuntary hospitalization of Mr. Y.
>
> Mr. Y, therefore, went home. He later drove to his mother-in-law's house, where his wife was staying. He accosted his wife as she was walking her dog and tried to persuade her to come home with him. When she refused and started running away, he shot her in the back, killing her. Later, alone in a motel room, he shot and killed himself.

7. Dedifferentiation (Self-Object Fusion) (Mahler, 1968)

You become whatever someone else wants you to be in order to avoid problematic affects, commonly fear of loss.

In *West Side Story* (Laurents, Bernstein, Sondheim, & Robbins, 1956), the protagonist, Tony, uses this defense. Although he initially knows better, after falling in love with Maria, he learns she is against the "fair fight" he had arranged between the rival gangs instead of a rumble. To avoid losing her love, he gives up his identity to become like her—to idealistically believe love can conquer all violence. His use of this defense leads him to cancel the "fair fight" in favor of trying to get the rival gangs to love one another. His unrealistic attitude, ironically, leads to the death of his best friend, and later, his own.

Dedifferentiation can operate in conjunction with *passivity* (versus aggression) and *identification with the aggressor.* When this happens, a person will tend to be vulnerable to manipulation by a cult's guru.

8. Splitting (Kernberg, 1975)

People suffering with psychosis or borderline personality organization tend to see some people as purely hostile (McDevitt, 1985) and others as purely loving. (Psychotic people have more damage to reality testing, relationship to reality, and integration than borderline individuals.) These disturbed people "split" each introject in two—a purely loving half versus a purely hateful, destructive half—and then experience the other person as containing only the *split* loving or hating portion. Therefore, the splitter usually attributes only love or hostility to a particular person, not seeing that most people potentially possess both loving and hostile qualities.

Splitting and *projection* contribute to the child's poem:

> What are little girls made of?—Sugar and spice and everything nice!
> What are little boys made of?—Snakes and snails and puppy-dogs' tails!

In another variation, some borderlines and psychotics will *split* the so-called "good" and "bad" introjects of a single person, and see the two extremes in the same person but at different times—one day as wonderful and angelic, the next day as demonic and vicious. Kernberg (1975) describes how people with borderline personality organization use splitting to defend against anxiety generated by recognizing the (integrated) "whole object" qualities and complexities of another person.[6]

Tip.

Beware of splitting in people who compliment your therapeutic ability before you've even made a therapeutic intervention (*splitting* + *idealization*). Soon afterward you'll become a mean ignoramus who duped them (*splitting* + *devaluation*). When you encounter these defenses, it's best to interpret them as soon as possible, for example, "You're hoping I'm as great as Dr. Smith said I was because, I think, perhaps you're a bit nervous that I'm not."

9. Animism (Freud, 1913; Mahler, 1968)

Giving human qualities to nonhuman entities, to guard against demoralization about humans. The person bathes his pet rock, sweet-talks his plants, argues with his stove, and hides from his T.V.

Although this is a prominent mechanism in psychotic adults, it is also common in normal children, who ascribe living qualities to their dolls or stuffed animals. Many religions, over thousands of years, have assigned living qualities to nonliving objects and icons. To this day, even in western civilization, many people visit mediums, and believe, as a defense against grief, that the crystal ball "communicated" with a lost loved one or spoke with the voice of the lost loved one.

10. Deanimation (Mahler, 1968)

If people don't see you as human, they don't have to worry about trusting you.

> A man in treatment with me reported that he disliked seeing me outside my office because it made him think of me "as a real person," which meant, to him, unpredictable and demanding. He preferred to see me "more like just a doctor-thing. Not like a real person who has a life."

This mechanism is common in psychosis and in severe narcissistic personality disorders.

Interestingly, deanimation of enemies also occurs during war. In World War II, the Allies referred to the Japanese as the "Yellow Peril." The vicissitudes of this defense—seeing the enemy as inhuman—were artfully depicted in the classic movie, "A Majority of One" (LeRoy, 1961), in which, soon after the end of World War II, a Jewish-American widow, who had lost a son in the war, is courted by and eventually falls for a Japanese man who also had lost relatives in the war.

11. Reaction-Formation (A. Freud, 1936; Gorelik, 1931)

You turn something into its opposite. Commonly, you're so nice you can't tell you're angry.

A man laughed as he described a childhood memory of his mother chasing him around the house to beat him with an extension cord. As he was describing this physical abuse, he was unaware of any anger toward his mother or any guilt.

He had felt angry toward her, and later came to realize he had also felt guilty about that anger because he knew his mother had tried to raise him to know right from wrong. Due to his conflict between anger and guilt, he had instituted several defenses, including *isolation of affect* (not feeling the anger or guilt), *humor* (laughing about the abuse), and *reaction-formation* (feeling love toward his mother instead of anger).

Perfectionism, hyperpunctuality, and parsimoniousness involve *reaction-formation*. Obsessional people with such traits often harbor unconscious rebellious urges (discourteousness), oral-dependant wishes (laziness and greed), and harsh self-criticism (irascibility). The reaction-formations cause them, contrarily, to act in a manner that is overly courteous and punctual, workaholic and stingy, and overly calm, respectively.

Because of their conflicts between anger and self-criticism, some obsessional people can be duped by psychopaths who "play the game" of timeliness and courtesy. Honest, affectionate friends who are late or imperfect may be rejected because the perfectionist becomes angry (and insulted) when the defenses are disrupted.

Being "nice" to patients may also involve a reaction-formation, especially if the therapist should be aware of irritation.

Defensive niceness turned out to be a prominent mechanism in a therapist, Dr. X, who went along with the demand for antidepressant medication by Mr. A, a man in treatment with her. Although she was irritated with Mr. A's demandingness, Dr. X had not become aware of this during her sessions with Mr. A. During supervision, Dr. X realized she had been using *reaction-formation*, as well as a number of other defenses, and that acceding to Mr. A's request for medication, which had caused Mr. A some sexual dysfunction, was not really so "nice" (Blackman, 2003).

In fact, Dr. X's accommodation of Mr. A's demand had guarded her against knowledge of retaliatory hostility she felt toward him.

12. Undoing and Rituals

Undoing can mean you go against your conscience (superego) to relieve yourself from feeling controlled by your own morality. For example, a freshman college girl has sex with a guy at a fraternity party to prove she's not the goody-two-shoes she was in high school.

Undoing can also occur in obsessional rituals, where you fight your conscience by symbolically doing what you feel guilty about, and then atone by punishing yourself in another symbolic act. It's sometimes said that the second act magically "undoes" the first.

> A 9-year-old boy insisted on wiping the faucets clean after washing up before bed. He then rechecked the faucets to make sure they were not dripping. When I pointed out, during session, that he seemed to be protecting himself from something, he responded that actually he was protecting his family, especially his mother, who could not swim, in that the dripping faucets could cause a flood that might drown everyone in their sleep. We were able to figure out that when he cleaned and double-checked the faucets, he was trying to avoid guilt by "undoing," symbolically, his murderous feelings toward his harshly critical mother and passive father.

13. Isolation (of Affect) (C. Brenner, 1982a)

You remove from conscious awareness (without knowing you are doing this) the sensation of affects. (The thought content may remain conscious.)

> A woman tells you matter-of-factly that her husband has not made love to her for more than three years. He leaves the house at 5:00 A.M. daily and returns after 11:00 P.M. and has a martini. He does not see the children, or her, but just goes to sleep. Although she blandly describes feeling "a little bothered," she is unaware of unpleasant sensations over the insults and the deprivations she had so succinctly summarized.

14. Externalization (Glover, 1955)

A special form of projection where you experience a part of your mind as "external" to yourself. You might think someone or "society" will criticize you, when actually *you* feel self-critical.

Clinically, this is extremely common as a resistance to treatment. Many people entering therapy feel guilty about something. They will often use a phrase like, "You'll probably think I'm a terrible person," or "you'll probably tell me I'm crazy," and then reveal part of some embarrassing behavior. The therapist's responses should be along the lines of, "Sounds like you expect me to be a harsh conscience. Perhaps you're feeling self-critical, so you also expect me to be critical of you."

Tip.

> People in treatment often *externalize* before they become *reticent* (59) in initial sessions. They may believe that you will be, or already are, critical of them; their fantasy is based on *externalization* of their super-

ego onto you. It's a good idea to look for this defense whenever it appears in early treatment, since it causes a powerful, but highly interpretable and resolvable resistance to treatment (Glover, 1955).

In addition, when people are self-critical, be careful not to immediately try to relieve their guilt by *reassuring* them or *persuading* them that they should not feel so self-critical (supportive techniques); in other words, it may not be such a good idea to say, "Well, you really shouldn't feel so guilty about that!" Remember, it's possible that what they're feeling guilty about is some dastardly action—the guilt doesn't have to be an overreaction.

Interpretation of the defense of *externalization* may help people understand how they've been *warding off awareness* of their guilt. This understanding, when integrated consciously, may lead them to decide to stop doing whatever it is they're feeling guilty about. Alternately, they may decide that their guilt has been irrational and that they should allow themselves to indulge in the activity that was causing guilt.

15. **Turning on the Self** (Freud, 1917; A. Freud, 1936)

Suicidal people don't like themselves for feeling violently irate toward someone else. Instead, they take it out on themselves.

Once, in interviewing a suicidal woman from Mexico (in Spanish), I interpreted to her that her suicidal ideation represented a defensive turning on herself of anger she did not allow herself to feel toward her ex-husband, to wit: "Creo que usted quisiera matarse a sí mismo porque no quiere pensar en estar enojado con él." She responded, "No, Doctor. Estoy más que enojada (I am more than angry). Estoy furiosa; no, enfadada; no, ¡encolerizada! (I am furious; no, enraged; no, [a superlative having to do with the archaic concept of the "ether" of "choler"— no equivalent in modern English])".

Tip.

Turning on the self of anger is implicated in almost all suicide attempts, and many cases of suicidal ideation (see chapter 8). It's a good idea to try to discuss this mechanism with anyone harboring suicidal thoughts.

16. **Negativism** (Levy & Inderbitzin, 1989)

You refuse to cooperate, which keeps you from having to get close to people.

A 42-year-old man consults you because his mother "forced" him to come and even drove him to the consultation appointment. He feels he will kill himself sometime "soon" but won't say when or how. When you recommend psychiatric hospitalization, he refuses. When you point out that he just threatened to kill himself, he now says he didn't really mean it and doesn't think it will happen "today." You suggest some medication, but he says he doesn't want any medicine, and doesn't want to see any psychiatrists or other therapists.

17. Compartmentalization (Freud, 1926)

You inhibit yourself from making connections (don't integrate) because putting things together symbolizes something awful. This *inhibition* of integration (a defense, see 48) is different from an integrative defect but can look quite a bit like one.

Ms. W, a 28-year-old woman with problems in heterosexual relationships, reported in session that she invited a date to go skinny-dipping at midnight. She was appalled, on returning to her apartment from the pool, that the man attempted to make love to her. She "felt good" that she "expressed her feelings" by refusing sex and that he left her apartment without a hassle. She now expected her therapist to be pleased with her for standing up for herself.

The therapist, concerned about how Ms. W was approaching men, but not sure how to handle this technically, presented the case to me in supervision. I advised her to bring to Ms. W's attention the non-integration of swimming naked with a man with whom she did not plan sexual activity, since a man is likely to interpret this conduct as a prelude to lovemaking. I felt this confrontation should clarify whether Ms. W had a defect in integration or was using compartmentalization.

I felt that if Ms. W responded by attacking the therapist for being just like the man she had dated, "always thinking everything is sexual," Ms. W probably had an integrative defect. In that case, a supportive therapeutic approach of expressing understanding of her confusion and anger about men and sex, without further interpretation, would probably be best. The therapist could also praise Ms. W for her assertiveness and then advise her not to go skinny-dipping again if she wasn't interested in seducing the man.

However, I felt that if Ms. W was shocked by the confrontation, did not understand why she would have done something so foolish, further questioned her motives, and could see that she was not behaving in an organized way, the therapist was probably dealing with a *compartmentalization* defense.

A week later, the therapist reported in supervision that her confrontation led to an increase in Ms. W's observing ego. Ms. W saw that she felt so guilty about her own sexual urges that she only partially acted on them (by swimming naked). Simultaneously, she relieved her guilt by *compartmentalizing*: separating her behavior from her sexual wishes, which also helped keep her sexual wishes *repressed*. In addition, they figured out that Ms. W had *projected* blame for her own sexual desire onto the man.

Over time, the therapist reported that Ms. W's insight into these compromise formations led to a dramatic improvement in Ms. W's judgment.

18. Hostile Aggression (Symonds, 1946; McDevitt, 1985)

Frustration of "purposive directedness" (McDevitt) generates hostile aggression. The hostility can then be used to ward off unpleasant sensations and thoughts.

> A 29-year-old man sheepishly admitted, in session, that when his wife had worn a sexy negligee to bed, he angrily ridiculed her for "wearing your whore outfit." This comment upset her so much that she walked off and slept alone in their guest bedroom.
>
> We analyzed that his hostile approach to her sexual invitation was unconsciously designed to push her away. In other words, his *hostility*, which, in fact, did drive her away, had acted as a defense to ward off his multiple anxieties over closeness and over sexual performance.

FIRST GENITAL PHASE (AGES 2 TO 6 YEARS)
(Galenson & Roiphe, 1971; Parens, Pollock, Stern, & Kramer, 1976; Parens, 1990)

19. Displacement (Freud, 1900a; Arlow & Brenner, 1964)

You're having a feeling toward one person but actually experience it toward someone else.

> A woman's 11-year-old son left his history book in school. She immediately screamed at him, "You're just like your father, always forgetting things!"

She had a chronic buildup of frustration with her husband's inattentiveness, which she *displaced* onto her son.

20. Symbolization (Freud, 1900a; Arlow & Brenner, 1964)

You give special (sometimes irrational) meaning to some aspect of mental functioning. For example, you are actually afraid of driving over bridges because they represent both your wish to leave your husband and your guilty fear of punishment (death) for that hostile-abandoning wish. Then you dream you are naked on the French Riviera, having a tug-of-war over a pair of pantyhose with a donkey. The dream contains in its symbolism your warded-off thought that your husband is a stupid ass about sex.

21. Condensation (Freud, 1900a; Arlow & Brenner, 1964)

You illogically weld together disparate ideas, images, object representations, or mental functions that are contiguous or symbolic.

> Mr. V sees a Lexus in his therapist's parking lot, and assumes it belongs to the therapist. When he sees the therapist, Mr. V says, "I like your car. It's the Lexus, isn't it?"

This is a condensation. Mr. V thought the therapist was wealthy, due to a negative (hostile) *father-transference (79)* (Mr. V's father was greedy). Mr. V also believed that people who own Lexus automobiles must be wealthy, since a new Lexus is expensive. He then welded together those two thoughts and came to the conclusion that the car belonged to the therapist. Mr. V approached the matter using, besides condensation, *socialization (46)* (discussion of automobiles) and *reaction-formation (11)* (friendly rather than competitive about the car), shielding himself from awareness of his negative *transference (79)* to the therapist.

22. Illusion Formation or Daydreaming (Raphling, 1996)

You consciously visualize something, but know it's a fantasy. This fantasy (or daydream) may gratify wishes, take you away from painful reality, or relieve guilt.

> A woman reported a repetitive "vision" of a pleasant, "fresh" green field in the springtime. She turned out to be defending against shame over having had a child out of wedlock, which she considered her "dirty little secret." She hated feeling so ashamed and angry that she had gotten pregnant during unprotected intercourse in a meadow.

Renik (1978) reports on Weinshel's case of a woman who developed an illusion that a Japanese print on the office wall had an area of protuberance in the crotch area. This illusion guarded her against shame over her curiosity about her male analyst's penis.

23. Prevarication (Karpman, 1949)

Consciously calculated lying. This very common mechanism is often underassessed by mental health practitioners. Lying is characteristic of felons, in whom it customarily is accompanied by *projective blaming (5)* and *rationalization (42)*.

In addition, we routinely see defensive lying in prelatency children, in adolescents, and in embarrassed adults. Certain social fibs (for example, "Sorry we can't make the party; we couldn't get a babysitter") are often deemed morally proper and even taught to children to protect them from social ostracism. If people expressed their "real feelings" (i.e., their negative thoughts and opinions) socially, they might cause narcissistic injury to (insult) others. In other words, lying may be a highly pathological or a "normal" (adaptive) defense, depending on the circumstances.

The French playwright Molière (1666/1992), in *The Misanthrope*, plays with these distinctions. After Philinte has just stated that you should be polite to people who are polite to you, Alceste, his friend, argues, ". . . I decline this overcomplaisant kindness, which uses no discrimination . . . the friend of all mankind is no friend of mine" (Molière, 1992, p. 2).

Philinte responds, ". . . But when you live in a society, it's best to exhibit politeness as common usage demands." Alceste comes back, ". . . our feelings should never hide themselves under vain compliments." Philinte then lectures him: "There are plenty of places where plain frankness would become ridiculous and would not even be permitted . . . it's a good idea to hide your heartfelt feelings. Would it be appropriate and thoughtful to tell a thousand people everything you think about them? And when you meet someone you hate or dislike, are you going to tell it like it is?" Alceste answers, "Yes!" (Molière, 1994, p. 24, my translation).

Tip.

> Sometimes people who lie experience virtually no shame or guilt (superego functioning). If this is the case, they are usually not treatable. However, in people who have superego functioning, prevarication may be a defense *against* superego anxiety that may be interpretable. The superego distortion may be remedied thereby.

> I once confronted a 10-year-old boy I was evaluating by telling him I knew he was lying about doing well in school (his divorced mother had already informed me otherwise). He smiled, acknowledged that I'd "got" him, and admitted he was just like his father, who, it turned out, was in jail for white-collar crimes involving aliases. The boy proceeded to understand, with my help, that his lying—associated with identifications with his father—defended him against feelings of loss and anger at his father for being "put away."

In other words, he had not faced his anger at his father for committing acts that took the father away from him. Instead, he had identified with his father and become a liar.

24. Confabulation (Spiegel, 1985; Target, 1998)

Blatt (1992) defines this mechanism: ". . . an initially accurate perception becomes lost in extensive, unrealistic, grandiose, personal elaborations and associations" (p. 704). He is describing confabulation as it occurs in relation to ego defect ("unrealistic") and defense ("grandiose").

More specifically, confabulation as a defense shows up as automatic lying (unconsciously motivated), usually to relieve the lowered self-esteem associated with having forgotten the details of something. Narcissistic characters, including "as if" types (H. Deutsch, 1965), can confabulate notoriously. Certain impostors' phoniness is quite automatic. However, most commonly, *confabulation* occurs in states of brain damage, such as Alzheimer's, where there are orientation and memory defects.[7]

> An 86-year-old woman with Alzheimer's Disease was brought by her minister for consultation because she had been letting pots boil over on the stove in her house, where she was living alone. She also got lost on her own block. When I discussed these orientation and memory lapses with her, she said, "I don't get lost. Most of the time I'm just walking. Sometimes I forget little things because I'm upset."

Her interesting use of the psychoanalytic theory of *repression* (that she forgot upsetting things) was actually a combination of *confabulation* (making up a false answer, which she believed), *intellectualization* (using a false theory), and *rationalization* (making excuses).

25. Repression (Freud, 1923; Arlow & Brenner, 1964)

You make the thought content of an affect unconscious. (Remember, affects have two components—sensation and thought.) You don't know you are *repressing* things. Contrarily, if you forget something on purpose, you are *suppressing* it.

During a panic attack, people feel jittery, they perspire, and their heart pounds, but they often don't recall the thoughts that started the reaction. However, they complain of feeling "nervous." The unpleasant sensation of anxiety, in other words, has remained conscious, while the triggering thought has not.[8]

Freud, early on (1900a), concluded from his data on people with conversion symptoms and sexual disturbances that *repression* caused socially scorned sexual thoughts to be forgotten, which in turn resulted in the sexual urges being changed into anxiety. In other words, he first theorized that repression caused anxiety. Later (1923, 1926), he realized he had the order backward. Anxieties were actually caused by intrapsychic conflicts involving sexuality or aggression, and *repression* was one of many defenses the mind could then institute to relieve the anxiety (Arlow & Brenner, 1964). Today, we know that *repression* can be used to ward off the thought content of any affect, including depressive affect (C. Brenner, 1982a) and anger.

26. Negative Hallucination (Wimer, 1989)

You don't see something right in front of you, because it's upsetting or symbolic of something upsetting.

> A 39-year-old man who had been in treatment for several months asked, "Is that map on the wall new?" When I clarified that it wasn't, he said, "Funny. I never noticed it before." He later associated to how he hated going to his mother-in-law's house, a day's drive away. I could show him that not "seeing" the map was connected with avoiding his hostility toward his mother-in-law.

27. Libidinal Regression [Psychosexual Regression] (Freud, 1905, 1926)

Due to neurosis, you can't stand thinking about sex and assertiveness—they make you feel guilty. So, instead, you act childish, and avoid being sexual or aggressive.

There are essentially five types of libidinal regression: to the oral, anal, first genital, latency, and adolescent (early second genital) phases. Children in any one phase can shift in their functioning to an earlier one—like a toilet-trained 4-year-old (in the first genital phase) who suddenly begins soiling again and getting stubborn (anal regression) just after the (upsetting) birth of a sibling.

> A narcissistic man having a "middle-age crisis," in an effort to relieve highly unpleasurable affects associated with aging and sexual worries, began thinking like a teenager—a regression to early second genital phase functioning. He bought a "cool" phallic-looking car, took up with a young girlfriend, and got his ear pierced to please her.

Adults who slip into wishing for oral gratification (holding, feeding, or petulantly demanding anxiety relief), and complain of feeling "helpless," dependent, and disorganized (all of which could suggest borderline personality organization), may be using *libidinal regression* to oral phase functioning in order to avoid guilt over sexual or hostile wishes.

> A 31-year-old married homemaker consulted me because she was critical of herself for eating too much. She had gained about 60 pounds, was uncomfortable, and her clothes did not fit. She spent quite a bit of time explaining her various diets, clinics, and exercise routines, all of which had been unsuccessful. When I mentioned to her that I noticed she had told me quite a bit about her eating habits, but nothing of her life with her husband, she became quiet. Further exploration of her quietness led her to say she was ashamed to admit that she and her husband slept in separate bedrooms. Lately, she had been masturbating, which made her feel "weird" and guilty.

In other words, her focus on oral level conflicts had shielded her from her guilt and shame over sexual and interpersonal conflicts with her husband.

28. Ego Regression

There are three ways this term is used:

Interference with a function. An autonomous ego function (like intelligence) or an ego strength (like impulse control) stops working so that you can't tell you are feeling something unpleasant.

> A 25-year-old married woman complained of being "tired and confused" just after criticizing her husband. I formulated that her "confusion" was a regression in integrative functioning. Therefore, I pointed out to her that "confusion" might feel more comfortable to her than anger. She agreed and then expressed more anger and criticism of him.

Renik (1978) describes *depersonalization* and *derealization* as defenses where the sense of reality between self and the environment is transiently lost: *regression* in the ego function of relation to reality (Frosch, 1964).

Reversion to earlier defense mechanisms. You start using many defense mechanisms that arose in the early stages of child development (such as denial, projection, projective identification, splitting, and dedifferentiation).

> Ms. U, a 45-year-old successful businesswoman, consulted me because of relationship problems. In one session, after describing a difficult interaction between herself and a man she was dating, she asked in

desperation, "So what do I do? You must have answers to these problems."

I told her that she seemed to want me to be a sort of guru, and that she seemed to wish to be my disciple. Ms. U then recalled how she had always enjoyed following her mother around the kitchen, doing what her mother had told her to do: "I felt like I was part of her, that she couldn't do anything without me. It was fun. My mother was a saint—very religious. She didn't know how much of a devil I was—I think you have a little devil in you, too!"

I was then able to demonstrate to her that she first had wanted to be part of me, as she had felt, at times, with her mother (*dedifferentiation* and *transference*) when she was a little girl. Then she imagined I thought exactly the way she did (*projective identification* and *splitting*), where I was unlike her mother, and so was she (*disidentification*).

Vaillant (1992) considers these "primitive" defenses. In that sense, Ms. U had regressed from her more mature functioning in business. The defenses seemed to be triggered by her (*transference*) conflicts about me.

Inefficient defensive operations. Your defense mechanisms fail to stop horrible thoughts, and the failure relieves guilt by punishing you with suffering.

A 27-year-old single man from a family of "achievers" still had not finished college, after nine years. He often masturbated while thinking about blind José Feliciano having sex with Britney Spears. He opined that this fantasy represented his own "oedipus complex" with his sister. I didn't challenge his *intellectualization,* but I pointed out to him that by allowing himself to drift into reveries about such things, he distracted himself from studying; at the same time he didn't have to face shame over his penchant to be lazy. Excitedly, he responded, "That's why I can't get my work done! Maybe I should stop thinking about those things so much!"

29. Temporal Regression

You think of earlier times in your life, to circumvent thinking about current conflict. Alternately, you begin thinking, talking, or acting like you did at a previous stage of development. (In the latter definition, the term is virtually synonymous with *ego regression* accompanied by *libidinal regression*).

Temporal regression in its simplest form shows up occasionally in people who begin their initial evaluation interview by focusing on childhood traumas.

A 21-year-old depressed sailor, hospitalized for suicidal ideation, at first claimed he had been depressed since childhood. I opined that his explanation seemed a bit pat and that he seemed to be avoiding telling me about any recent happenings. He responded by recalling how a young woman he had dated a few nights before not only drank him under the table at a bar, but danced with his friends and then stole his car! We could further elucidate that he hated being angry at anyone, and that he had therefore turned his anger at her onto himself, causing the suicidal ideation. (For more detail, see Blackman, 1997.)

At the start of the consultation interview, he had defensively clung to the notion that his depression had begun in his childhood (which later turned out to be partly true).

30. Topographic Regression (Freud, 1900a; Arlow & Brenner, 1964)

You go to sleep and dream instead of facing the music. You move from consciousness to unconsciousness as a defense.

For example, during a spirited discussion with four psychiatry residents regarding violence and homicidal acts, one of the residents fell asleep! He later told me he had difficulty "dealing with death."

31. Suppression (Werman, 1985)

You purposely try to forget:

a. the thought content of an affect, or
b. the affect's thought content and sensation.

Vaillant (1992) considers this a "mature defense" because it is often adaptive.

Tip.

> Many people in treatment say they "don't want to go there" regarding painful or embarrassing thoughts. Their suppression prevents them from addressing their conflicts and, in interpretive therapy, should be interpreted. In supportive therapy, this defense may be encouraged by the therapist.

32. Identification with a Fantasy

You start to act the way you imagine you want to be, maybe based on a hero or heroine.

I had just explained to an attractive, 37-year-old woman in treatment that she minimized her sadistic, anti-male retaliation and simultaneously punished herself as she tortured her husband by depriving him of sex. She then remembered that, as an adolescent, she had admired Cleopatra and Désirée, Napoleon's mistress. It was startling to her to realize that in her marriage, she at times acted the part of the controlling, dominating Queen, and at times behaved like the jilted, punished mistress.

She had *identified* with her fantasies of these adolescent idols. The identifications had been enhanced by the reality of her adolescent "good looks," which gave her a certain kind of control over boys. That control, during adolescence, had been sociosyntonic and pleasurable for her. In her marriage, however, her oscillation between regal demandingness (like Cleopatra) and petulant deprivation[9] (like Désirée) was maladaptive and disruptive.

As a child, Sigmund Freud idolized Hannibal (AROPA, 2002), the Carthaginian general who had courageously taken on the Roman Empire.[10] Interestingly, as an adult, Freud also took on an overwhelming adversary. In the late 1800s, on returning from his studies in Paris with Charcot, he lectured to physicians about the latest in mental illness. He described how he had viewed conversion symptoms in men as well as in women (Breuer & Freud, 1895). Although Freud was right, his observations challenged the prevailing medical view that hysterical conversion was an illness only of women. The other doctors were incredulous of Freud's claims, and ostracized him professionally for many years.

33. Identification with Parents' Unconscious or Conscious Wishes/Fantasies (Johnson & Szurek, 1952)

Instead of doing as your parents say, you act the way they told you not to. They then see their (sometimes warded off) corrupt wishes in you and secretly get a kick out of your misbehavior. When they criticize you (instead of themselves), your guilt is relieved, and you keep acting up.

Johnson and Szurek first described this interesting defense in teenagers, and various forms of "acting out" and "acting in" have been elaborated on quite a bit since then (Rexford, 1978; Paniagua, 1997).

In Wagner's (1870) opera, *Die Walküre*, the god Wotan commands his favorite divine daughter, Brünnhilde, to cause the death of Siegmund, his beloved half-human illegitimate son. Wotan has been forced into this decision as a punishment by his wife, Fricka, because he had raised Siegmund to be rebellious and incestuous (Siegmund has just had sex with his married twin sister, Sieglinde). However, Brünnhilde senses that Wotan would have preferred for Siegmund to live, if it were not for Fricka's threat of punishment. Brünnhilde therefore proceeds to try to save Siegmund in battle. Because of her "acting out," Wotan punishes her with loss of divinity and with sleep until awakened by any man.

Brünnhilde *identified* with her father's wishes, which he had been forced to give up due to (*externalized*) punishment. She acts out the father's suppressed wishes, and then he punishes her, instead of him being punished by his wife. Interestingly, Brünnhilde points these dynamics out to Wotan before he consummates her punishment. He acknowledges the correctness of her interpretation, and then punishes her less severely.

34. Identification with the Ideal Image or Object
(Carlson, 1977)

You pattern yourself after someone you think is great. (The person is either great or a projection of your own imagined omnipotence.)

Blos (1979) found that career choices in males are influenced by the separation of late adolescent boys from their (normatively) loved father. The transient depressive affect produced by this symbolic loss leads boys to use this identification defensively. They will then tend to incorporate into their ego ideals the aspects of the fathers' value systems that they had (at least partly) rejected during mid-adolescence.

This defense is also implicated in people drawn to cults. They model themselves after the leader in order to avoid facing a variety of unpleasant affects.

35. Identification with the Aggressor (A. Freud, 1936)

After the fact. You act abusive toward a person because someone has been abusive to you. This shields you from feeling angry. If your abusiveness is chronic and generalized, you are a sadistic character, a *bully (83)*.[11]

Tip 1.

Look for this defense after you've been on vacation or otherwise been out of the office, or even if you've just been a few minutes late. The people in treatment with you may now miss a session or be late themselves. If and when they do, you can attempt to show them this defense as a guard against shame over missing you, or as a guard against their anger at you for leaving them (which may be based on transference).

Tip 2.

If you are a teacher who notices bullying behavior in a child, you have to worry that the kid may be experiencing physical or emotional abuse at home.

Before the fact. You anticipate hostility and get hostile first. This is a tremendous problem with children who have been physically abused, discovered by the authorities, and then placed in a foster home. Such children may use a large number of defenses, but attacking the new caretaker before they get attacked is often one of the problems.

On the other hand, children normally identify with the aggressor to resolve anxiety produced by projection of competitive hostility onto parents, who become the "aggressors" during disciplinary activities. The children's absorption of their parents' attitudes aids in superego formation (Sandler, 1960).

> For example, when my son was 4 years old, I instructed him not to take drinks into the family room, because he'd had some spills on the carpeting. Later, when I carried a cup of coffee into the family room to join him in playing blocks, he said, "Daddy, no drinks in here! Put your drink back in the kitchen."

36. Identification with the Victim (MacGregor, 1991)

You act like someone else by allowing yourself to be hurt or by getting yourself hurt. You do this as a rescue wish or to fight off your own anger or guilt.

> Mr. S, a 35-year-old assistant pastor, was constantly allowing himself to be bullied by the minister of the church. Analysis revealed that Mr. S seemed to be behaving similarly to a younger brother who had been the main target of his father's raging corporal punishment. Mr. S's mother had protected Mr. S.

Mr. S's guilt over his competitive feelings toward his brother and his guilt over his murderous rage toward his abusive father caused him to allow himself to be victimized currently by the minister, who had taken on the unconscious *transference* significance of his father. At other times, the assistant pastor provoked punishment from the minister—the defense of *masochistic provocation*. (See also Freud, 1919, 1923.)

In other words, Mr. S had identified with his brother in allowing himself to be unfairly punished. He did this mainly to relieve intense guilt.

37. Identification with the Lost Object (Freud, 1917; Volkan, 1987a)

So you won't feel the pain of grief, you pick up some attributes of the lost loved one. If you also keep souvenirs and never grieve, you've got "established pathological mourning" (Volkan, 1987a).

The same clergyman (as in #36, above) revered his "saintly" mother, who had died from cancer when he was 17. He had never grieved over her loss. Instead, he took punishment the way he had seen her suffer at the hands of his father; that is, he used identification with the lost object as well. He became saintly and took punishment to keep his mother symbolically "alive" (i.e., to not grieve over her loss).

38. Identification with the Introject (Sandler, 1960)

In latency, after you form an image of someone, you wind up making that image part of your superego.

In pathological adult situations, if people incorporate a deceased but unconsciously hated loved one's character traits into their self-image, they may then turn the unconscious hate on themselves, creating a reactive depression (Freud, 1917; Volkan, 1987a).

Further, when a therapist's self-image transiently "absorbs" aspects of a patient's (already introjected) image, the therapist can develop countertransference (what Racker [1953] calls a "concordant identification"). The therapist has developed a "complementary identification" after unconsciously adopting the view of a person who has been important to the patient.

A 30-year-old woman suffering with marital problems and depression complains that her husband does not speak to her, express love verbally, or seem interested in her except for sex. If you experience a concordant identification, you might ask her why she tolerates this. If you've developed a complementary identification (with her husband), you may ask why she blames her husband for everything.

Tip.
Questioning patients during therapy can be dangerous (Dorpat, 2000). Try clarifying defenses instead. Or wait for more data if you can't figure out what to interpret.

39. Seduction of the Aggressor (Loewenstein, 1957)

When a person is scary to you, you seduce that person sexually or sycophantically, to prove you are not afraid.

People who seduce the aggressor are probably also using *reaction-formation, inhibition of judgment, counterphobia*, and *minimization*. These defenses can create havoc in a person's choice of mate (e.g., a woman who believes she will reform a "bad boy" through her love for him).

Mr. JE, a 30-year-old plumber's assistant, was upset with his current relationship with a woman, and depressed. He reported that his wife had left him to help her new lover set up pornographic websites. Mr. JE now was dating a woman who plied her trade as an astrologer and palm reader. He *rationalized* that she would not need to engage in these scams if he married her and supported her. He had already bought her a new computer and a new refrigerator.

Among the many dynamics involved in Mr. JE's problems, I advised his therapist to interpret his *seduction of the aggressor* mechanism (as well as Mr. JE's *minimization* of his new woman friend's apparently antisocial traits). When the therapist did so, Mr. JE responded with relief. Mr. JE began to see that he picked out troublesome women and then tried to overcome his fear of them by being "sweet and supportive."

It would seem self-evident that it's best for a therapist to avoid unconsciously employing *seduction of the aggressor*, but certain people can stimulate this defense by threatening to leave treatment. They can mobilize the therapist's defenses through the use of *projective identification*, where they create anxiety over object loss in the therapist.

Dr. C presented a case of an adult analysand, Ms. R, at a psychoanalytic meeting. Ms. R canceled many appointments. Dr. C described how she found herself looking out the window to see if Ms. R was walking in, wondering whether Ms. R would show up for her appointments.

In response to a conferee's question, Dr. C reported that she had not confronted Ms. R about the missed sessions but had simply charged her for the appointments. Ms. R had paid without objection.

Based on the past history of the patient, a discussant asked Dr. C if she had interpreted Ms. R's attempts to get Dr. C to experience what Ms. R, herself, had experienced as a child: longing and insecurity regarding a mother who took care of her financially but was frequently gone on trips. Dr. C responded that she had not thought of this; she had felt it best to "contain" Ms. R's striving for independence. Dr. C did not want the patient to quit because she felt Ms. R needed the treatment.

My impression was that, by being an understanding "container," Dr. C had unconsciously *seduced the aggressor* (Ms. R) to avoid anxiety over Ms. R possibly quitting treatment. Dr. C's anxiety was apparently stimulated by Ms. R's hostile, rejecting behavior.

Tip.

When, during consultation or treatment, people try to use you for something other than psychotherapy, they are often symbolically attacking you. Be careful not to become accommodating ("nice") to people who make outlandish or unrealistic demands, or who miss many appointments.

3

Latency, Adolescent, and Assorted Other Defenses

LATENCY PHASE (6 TO 11 YEARS)

40. Sublimation (A. Freud, 1936)

Because you're having a shocking sexual or destructive fantasy, you defend by engaging in a productive activity that, in part, symbolically represents the fantasy. No one will know about the fantasy, including you, and you'll usually get a healthy interest out of it.

Parents and teachers strive to interest grade-school children in activities—art, music, athletics, collecting—that common sense tells us is "good" for children. It is. All of these activities channel both sexual and aggressive fantasies.

> I was consulted by a large Catholic girls' home because they had had a spate of suicide attempts. The home housed more than 200 girls from grade school through high school, most of whom had been the victims of their parents' physical or sexual abuse.
>
> After evaluating over 30 girls from the home who had attempted suicide, it became clear to me that there was an institutional problem, aside from some of the girls' individual differences. The problem seemed to be that the main punishment used to discipline the girls was removal of activities, such as after-school sports, dances, and artistic lessons.
>
> I pointed out to the administrator of the home that, particularly in girls who are angry about how they have been previously treated, it is extremely important to allow them healthy outlets for aggression *(sublimations)*. Otherwise, hostile-destructive aggression[1] will get *turned on themselves,* and suicide attempts will follow. I recommended that punishments be more focused on extra duties or chores, and that healthy sublimatory channels be preserved for the girls.

41. **Provocation** (Freud, 1916; Berliner, 1947; C. Brenner, 1959, 1982a)

You behave to make other people do something to you. If they sleep with you, you've induced sexual fantasy. If they hurt you, you've incited them to make you suffer, possibly to *punish you* to relieve your own guilt.

During my general psychiatric training, some residents sometimes disparagingly referred to sexually provocative people as "id-ticklers." Sexual predators, for example, have discovered various manipulations that may induce certain vulnerable persons to engage in sexual activity with them.

We usually presume that sexually alluring or seductive people are quite aware of what they're doing and have a definite motive in mind. But sometimes the provocateurs (or -euses) are relatively unaware of how stimulating they are—due to several unconscious defenses, including *provoking* the sexual interest in the other and, at times, *denial* of the reality of the effect of their behavior.

> In 2002, a male colleague reported an unusual consultation with a striking young woman who complained that all the men she met seemed preoccupied with quickly having sex with her. What was unusual was that the woman, in his office, was wearing a see-through blouse and no bra. At some point, he gently introduced the idea that she seemed unaware that the way she was dressed might be contributing to her problems. She was at first defensive, *rationalizing* that see-through blouses were "in style." However, she quickly realized she had been rationalizing, as well as unconsciously *provoking* sexual interest by others, while not noticing her own exhibitionistic wishes. She grabbed her jacket and for the rest of the consultation sat covered.

Masochists, who provoke their own suffering, may be attempting to relieve guilt, although their motives for self-punishment can involve other dynamics (Novick & Novick, 1996). Masochists can bring suffering on themselves for many reasons, including the following:

- to control the timing of a feared unpleasurable experience (*turning passive to active*)
- to prove to themselves, through procrastination, that they can repetitively live through painful situations where someone must wait for and then get irritated with them
- to keep their own rageful impulses toward a victim out of conscious awareness—*identification with the victim* (MacGregor, 1991)
- to unconsciously repeat, in symbolic form, previous traumata, in an attempt to reify magical thinking and make those traumas turn out differently (*"acting out" of transference conflicts*)

- to *provoke*, against themselves, hostility or criticism they actually feel toward others
- to unconsciously imagine they are disarming a frightening figure (Loewenstein's [1957] *seduction of the aggressor*)
- to *cling to* a narcissistic or sadistic lover, in order to feel in control of anxiety and depression over loss of that person
- to provoke power struggles in order to avoid conflictual sexual urges (*anal libidinal regression*)
- to appease authority figures in order to magically obtain their "phallic power" (*identification of the idealized object*, involving what Greenacre [1956] called pathological "*penis awe*")
- to unconsciously create or disrupt a fusion of identities (i.e., of self and object images), associated with weakness in self-boundaries and conflicts over distance (Akhtar, 1994)
- to alter drive functioning, so that suffering takes on symbolic sexual significance (Freud, 1919)
- to obtain, *symbolically*, oral or genital gratification from a person who inflicts pain, associated with the thought that that person must care (defense versus loss of love)
- to relieve guilt over sexual matters so that sexual excitement can be enjoyed

42. Rationalization (Symonds, 1946)

You make excuses. (You're not "overly rational," which is the lay meaning). If you're obsessional, you *rationalize* along with *isolation, reaction-formation, undoing,* and *intellectualization*. If you are a probation officer, you may see rationalization along with *projective blaming* and *prevarication* in criminal psychopaths. If you treat people in the hospital, you'll find borderlines and psychotics use rationalization along with *denial, projective identification,* and *splitting*.

> Ms. LM, 37, brought a lawsuit for mental anguish against a man who had rear-ended a car in which she was a backseat passenger. She claimed her emotional damages included sleeplessness and severe anxiety. Her only physical injury from the 3-miles-per-hour accident was a bruise on her right index finger. During a forensic psychiatric examination related to her lawsuit, she admitted to hearing voices from outer space and from the past; they dictated "automatic writing" to her.

She *rationalized* that her schizophrenic symptoms had been caused by the bruise on her index finger, which in turn had been caused by the accident.[2]

43. Rumination

You "overanalyze," trying to solve a problem, but you're actually avoiding awareness of other thoughts and sensations by revisiting the same thoughts. Essentially, you spin your wheels mentally.

> A 35-year-old divorced woman spent weeks in therapy trying to "figure out why" her recent boyfriend had broken up with her. Eventually we could see that she was *ruminating* to avoid her grief (depressive affect) over losing him.

44. Counterphobic Behavior (Blos, 1962, 1979)

You do exactly what you're scared of, to prove to yourself that you're not frightened.

> An analyst colleague felt, after careful evaluation, that her narcissistic male patient would probably benefit most from intensive psychoanalytic treatment. She therefore recommended he increase his session frequency to four times a week, which is standard. His first response was to accurately list all his problems and conflicts by way of agreeing with her that intensive treatment would allow him to focus more on himself. However, in the subsequent session, he claimed he could not take the time off from work to handle the increased frequency of sessions.
>
> His analyst confronted his excuses as protecting him from anxiety over depending on her. He then revealed a wish, since his school-age years, to "remain invisible." He described his relationships as having an "elaborate network of levels and doors," to which only he held the keys—to let people get close, or not.

His initial agreement to increase frequency of sessions was successfully interpreted by his analyst as a *counterphobic* response defending him against his conflicts over closeness and its attendant self–object fusion anxiety and castration anxiety.

Tip.

Look to interpret this mechanism to adults who immediately request intensive treatment but then get cold feet.

It is also imperative to quickly confront life-threatening, counterphobic behavior in adult risktakers and daredevils. Their behavior can be compared to average-expectable latency and adolescent children, who allay their social, castration, and identity diffusion anxieties by taking risks.

To complicate matters, we encourage our children to master fears of new situations by urging them to "try it." So if used in conjunction with judgment, a bit of counterphobic defense may be adaptive. However, if your teenage son adds *denial in deed, rationalization,* and *inhibition of judgment* to counterphobic behavior, you may be holding your breath while he attempts to jump his motorcycle over your new SUV.

45. Intellectualization (A. Freud, 1936)

You become immersed in a fallacious theory of behavior. This helps you not face feelings (aids the *isolation* defense in preventing sensations from becoming conscious).

> A 42-year-old male college professor confessed during evaluation that he was cheating on his wife. When I pointed out his hesitation in describing this (*suppression*), he began crying over hurting his wife. Suddenly, he asked if his depression might not respond to Prozac. He had read that depressions were due to a "chemical imbalance." When I interpreted that I thought he'd feel less guilty if he could draw me into a discussion of brain chemistry, he agreed, and then admitted to more history of guilt-ridden infidelity.

Tip.
> Since *intellectualization* involves the use of an autonomous ego function (intellect) for defensive purposes, be careful not to misinterpret healthy intellectual activity as a defense.

46. Socialization and Distancing (Sutherland, 1980)

You use your social skill (an autonomous ego function) to distract yourself. If you're depressed, you bury yourself in social activities to relieve the unpleasant sensation. If you have self-esteem problems, you try to convince yourself that people like you.

Some people with object relations anxieties (over self–object fusion) use variable distancing as a defense. They're what I have sometimes referred to, figuratively, as "comets." "Comets" essentially have a type of borderline personality organization. Like actual comets that first orbit close to the sun (warmth) but then swing back out into (cold) space, human "comets" cycle in and out of close, warm relationships. Comets *socialize* to experience periodic warmth, along with narcissistic and sexual gratification (like a comet entering orbit around the sun), and to avoid loneliness. However, sooner or later they escape (into the coldness of space) by leaving someone intimate behind, at least for a while; they may circle back sometime later. (Balint [1955] called such people "philobats." The term never caught on.)

Other people are more like moons: they have a more schizoid type of borderline personality organization using *fixed distance* mechanisms. They remain more consistently emotionally distant from others. *Socialization* keeps them "in orbit," which provides some satisfaction of object hunger, but from a distance. (Balint's [1955] term was "ocnophil." This also never caught on.)

Comets and moons both tend to use *socialization* to

- circumvent the self–object fusion anxiety that develops with consistent, intimate emotional contact (Akhtar, 1992a), and
- relieve the depressive affect (loneliness) that occurs once they've established distance.

47. Instinctualization of an Ego Function (Hartmann, 1955)

You attach a sexual or hostile meaning to an ego function to avoid thinking about your conflicted feelings about the drive wish. If you turn the function into something sexual (e.g., "She's bending over; she must want sex") you're using "sexualization" (Coen, 1981), also called "erotization" or "libidinization." If you turn a function into something hostile ("judging people is mean"), you're using "aggressivization."

High school class clowns sexualize speech by finding sexual meanings in otherwise nonsexual expressions, such as a girl's complaint on a warm day, "I'm hot!"

Men who think auto mechanics is a "guy subject," and are good at it, may consider themselves "one of the guys," relieving anxiety about their masculinity. The movie *My Cousin Vinny* (Launer, 1992) highlighted the irrationality of cars taking on masculine symbolism: Vinny's girlfriend saves his legal case and his legal career by serving as a surprise expert witness on automobile traction controls.

48. Inhibition of an Ego Function (Freud, 1926; Anthony, 1961)

Once you've attached a sexual or hostile symbolic meaning to an autonomous ego function (such as intellect, abstraction, or speech), that function may clash with your superego, creating guilt, anxiety, and depressive affect. Your mind may then shut off the (instinctualized) ego function to defend you from the affect. Because this defensive activity is so important, I will describe how it operates against many autonomous ego functions.

Psychomotor control.

A 25-year-old woman who lived with her mother developed severe arm weakness. During analytic psychotherapy, we realized that she had felt guilty about angry wishes to hit her mother. Her arm weakness had prevented her from acting on her hostile wish and from even knowing she harbored any hostility toward her mother.

The arm weakness, aside from punishing her, stopped her from using her psychomotor function. In other words, the conversion symptom (weakness) resulted from inhibition of her aggressivized ego function of psychomotor control (i.e., strong arms = hit mother and feel guilty; therefore, weak arms = punishment and *not* hit mother).

Speech.

In a case involving speech inhibition, a 67-year-old physician, Dr. O (also see Cath, 1986), referred himself for consultation due to an acute problem with stuttering, after possible organic etiologies had been ruled out. He noted that the stuttering had begun a couple of months previously, during a meeting, though he had forgotten exactly about what.

When I tentatively interpreted to him that the stuttering must have had some symbolic meaning in the setting of that meeting, Dr. O chuckled ironically. His thoughts ran to his dissatisfaction with the profession of medicine, but he immediately attempted to find excuses for (*rationalize away*) the government's interference with his practice. When I further interpreted the *rationalization* (excuses) as a defense, he expressed intense angst and anger. He had planned on retiring some years before, but a younger physician colleague, of whom he was quite fond, had convinced him to take a senior role in the medical group. Dr. O realized he felt ashamed of his wish to leave the practice and guilty that he would let his mentee down. I suggested that these thoughts and feelings might be connected with the stuttering, which wound up limiting his speech. He responded, "Yeah. So I couldn't say the words I wanted to say: 'I quit!'"

When he returned for a follow-up session the next week, the stuttering had disappeared, and he had made plans for his retirement in the next month. He reported feeling slightly depressed but was relieved to be getting out of active medical practice.

For Dr. O, the act of speaking had taken on the symbolic aggressive meaning of quitting (an action due to his frustration and anger). His aggressivized speech function had then come into conflict with his guilt (superego), and the result had been an acute *inhibition of his speech function* (stuttering).

Perception. Inhibition of looking, a defensive restriction of an aspect of perception, can occur in children who have been repeatedly exposed to adult sexual intercourse. For them, the act of looking takes on sexual symbolism. In preschool children, stimulation of sexual thoughts threatens to overwhelm the mind (ego-fragmentation anxiety); in school-age children, conflict between the sexualized function and the conscience produces superego anxiety (guilt); in either case, the anxiety can cause the mind to defensively shut off the looking function. Then, in other situations of looking, such as reading, sexually overstimulated children may refuse or be unable to read because of the symbolism of looking (looking = getting overwhelmed or = being "bad"). These children need to be differentiated from neurologically damaged children and those with idiopathic developmental delays (Marcus, 1991).

Inhibition of seeing is usually considered the mechanism in psychogenic (or "hysterical") blindness—where looking has taken on a hostile or sexual meaning and then been turned off. ". . . Such a formulation may be related to the mechanism of actual neurotic blindness outlined by Freud (1910). Instinctualization or reinstinctualization may hinder or foster ego development" (Barglow & Sadow, 1971, p. 438).

Memory. Sometimes, remembering something is so conflictual that simply repressing it is insufficient. Instead, the person may inhibit the memory function. This produces such states as the "absent-minded professor."

> Ms. N, a 32-year-old, divorced, educated woman, requested insight-directed therapy for anxiety and depression. In her first interview, she could not recall how long her marriage had lasted, the date of her anniversary, or the IRS due date (April 15). I referred her for neurological workup and neuropsychological testing, both of which were negative. When I then presented Ms. N the likelihood of her memory problem being due to some protective mechanism, she cried and shamefully admitted to murderous, sadistic thoughts toward her ex-husband, her father, and all men.

The conflict between Ms. N's memory (now symbolic of the rage) versus her shame had created superego anxiety, which she had unconsciously defended against by shutting off her memory. As such conflicts were interpreted to her, her memory functioning improved markedly.

Intelligence. Defensive restriction of this function due to symbolic meaning is common. If academic subjects take on a gender connotation, for example, they may become impossible for someone to learn. Social climate and attitudes of teachers and others contribute to this problem. In the United States, girls have frequently viewed math and science as "boy subjects." Boys have tended to view arts and humanities as "girl subjects." These symbolic feelings may be conscious and/or unconscious. Even with the recent strides toward gender equity in professional fields, it is still relatively less common for girls to apply to engineering school or for boys to major in art history.

> A child's vantage point illustrated this defense in a humorous way: A 6-year-old boy's mother was a neurosurgeon and his father was a dermatologist. When asked what he wanted to be when he grew up, the boy responded, "a dermatologist." When asked why not a neurosurgeon, he said, "No. That's for girls."

Clinically, a variety of serious problems are associated with this defense. Some men consider anything about psychotherapy "feminine," and because of this gender symbolism (*sexualization*) they experience formidable resistance to treatment (Freud, 1937). Some women, although talkative with female friends, become quiet in mixed groups of men and women because they see speaking out as "something that egotistical, competitive men do"—as a woman in treatment once put it. In other words, such a woman may give up her "voice" if it has taken on masculine symbolism. Other facets of some women's inhibition of speaking up have also been described by Gilligan (1980).

The subject of inhibition of intellect has been of considerable interest to psychoanalysts for many decades. Baruch (1952) describes her analytic treatment of a supposedly learning disabled boy who, after treatment, evinced superior intellectual abilities and performance.

Sensorium. Inhibition of clear sensorium may also occur as a character defense in some people at times. One psychiatry resident would "zone out," as he described it, during the middle of heated, energetic class discussions regarding hostility. He remained relatively conscious. At other times, he was fine. He clarified for me that he had a "problem" with conflicts over hostility. In his case, the function of alertness had apparently become aggressivized, then defensively restricted.

Relationship to reality, or reality sense. *Inhibition of reality sense* (Frosch, 1964, 1966, 1970) occurred in Ms. T, 38, who explained to me that she and her husband had almost gotten killed when the United States invaded the Caribbean island of Grenada in the 1980s. (She also used *denial in deed*, described earlier.)

> Ms. T and her husband had ignored State Department warnings (which they felt were overblown and restrictive) not to sail to Grenada due to possible communist insurgent activity there. They sailed their sailboat to Grenada anyway, where they were quickly confronted by Cuban guerrillas. Although they escaped as the U.S. invasion began, Ms. T

said she was "amazed" because "there really were Cubans and they really had machine guns!" She said that although she had obtained the warnings, she "did not believe Reagan." (She thought Reagan viewed everything as a war.)

In retrospect, it seems that Ms. T had not only denied the reality by a deed of sailing to the island, she had also *projected* onto President Reagan her own aggressivized *sense of reality* (she was the one fighting—against the State Department), which, due to fears and guilt, she had *inhibited* in herself. She likewise shut off reality from the outside (State Department warnings) because of her inhibition in facing aggression, either external or internal. Her sense of reality was disinhibited when reality itself provided her with unmistakable data. (She could *test* reality, though a bit late!)

Reality testing. *Inhibition of reality testing* is common in neurotic people, who tend to make false assumptions about a person or situation. They consider checking out their impressions a process that is "too nosy" (i.e., too aggressive and impolite). In other words, the action of checking reality has taken on symbolism of destructive aggression (or at other times of sexual curiosity) and then been defensively shut off to relieve guilt. Inhibition of reality testing is quite different from the defect in reality testing seen in psychoses.

Tip.

> To test the difference between a defect in reality testing and inhibition of reality testing, you can interpret any abrogation of reality testing as a defense. You then wait to see if the person you are worried about comes up with an integrated understanding of the inhibition or repeats the misunderstanding of reality. (Also see Abend, 1982).

Discriminating between reality and fantasy (without testing). Inhibition of the function of discriminating between reality and fantasy may be found in certain teenage boys who emulate videos akin to Michael Jackson's (1987) "The Way You Make Me Feel."[3] The boys may begin to agree that the way to meet a sexy girl is to follow and corner her, which is the technique Jackson uses in the video. The video equates masculinity with not taking no for an answer and suggests that respecting a girl's defensiveness is sissified.

A teenage boy watching this video could easily develop the idea that masculinity means never accepting a "no" from a female. This fiction is actually perpetrated in the video by a father figure, who tells Michael to be "himself," meaning to aggressively assert his sexual interest regardless of the girl's response.

A vulnerable boy watching this may thereby *inhibit* his reality discrimination function, because discriminating between reality and fantasy has been irrationally equated with castration (unmanliness). In reality, he is liable to get arrested for "stalking."

Concentration. When concentration becomes symbolic of an act of submission to authority (aggressivized), children and some adults may unconsciously inhibit the function to preserve a sense of autonomy. That is, they unconsciously equate identity-diffusion with concentrating. Their distractibility may be due to *inhibition* of the concentration function to relieve self–object fusion anxiety. Distractibility can also be the manifestation of rebellious *aggression* as a defense, which may arise in children when their parents want them to do homework.

In oppositional, defiant children who also have problems concentrating, it can be difficult to judge if the ego function of concentration has been *inhibited* as a defense against conflicts over aggression. Alternately, the concentration problem may have come about due to a developmental delay such as ADHD (Spencer, 2002), and the child's oppositionality resulted from frustration with unempathic parents who expected too much from a child with limitations (Marcus, 1991).

Orientation. Orientation may take on the symbolism of recognizing ("owning") intense rage about an environmental situation, so the mind shuts off the orientation function to defend against the affect.

> For example, during one particular session, a 40-year-old woman was disoriented to the time and the date. When I discussed the protective nature of this, she began remembering how she was furious with her husband over the weekend because of plans he had made, without consulting her, for the next two weeks.

Secondary process. If the sense of time—part of secondary process thinking—becomes aggressivized (takes on hostile, restrictive symbolism), people's behavior may defensively inhibit time-oriented functioning; they can develop annoying traits of irresponsibility, unreliability, tardiness, and procrastination as defensive inhibitions. If the sense of time is sexualized (takes on a loving meaning), a person may consider tardiness for any reason (even a valid one) as evidence of not being cared about, or falsely equate punctuality with love.

Self-care. When cleanliness has become unconsciously equated with submission to authority, dirtiness may symbolize aggressive defiance—inhibition of the aggressivized self-care function.

Social skill. There are many individuals who have either transient or fixed deficits in social skills caused by inhibition of abilities that have taken on symbolic meaning. Frequently, using social skill means conforming, and to some people, conformity has the meaning of loss of identity (being destroyed). They may therefore develop, either consciously or unconsciously, a tendency toward asocial behavior that helps them feel "separate" (i.e., their *inhibition* of social skill defends against identity diffusion anxiety).

The movie *Finding Forrester* illustrates this defense in the protagonist. Forrester, a famous novelist, lives alone, wears his socks inside-out, and refuses to leave his apartment. He is quite aware of social realities but has inhibited his social skill as a defense against grief over a lost loved one. His social skills are somewhat disinhibited after his gratifying father–son style encounter with a lonely teenage boy causes Forrester to grieve. He then recovers some of his ego functioning and goes out in public before he dies.

Autoplastic adaptation—fitting into the environment (Lampl-de-Groot, 1966).

> A 23-year-old male medical student's two roommates complained of his hygiene and threatened to throw him out. He confessed he was not tidy. This turned out to mean he left dirty laundry on his bed (where he slept) for weeks at a time. Using his observing ego, he realized this was a continuing rebellion against his overly neat parents.

His failure to adapt was due to an inhibition of the autoplastic adaptational function. Adapting, to him, caused humiliation and anxiety over loss of identity. This symbolization of the adaptation function led him to defensively inhibit the function (and therefore not adapt to his living situation). At the same time, he expressed his anger at his parents (*displaced* onto roommates), and provoked his roommates to humiliate him (*masochistic provocation* of punishment to assuage guilt).

Work (movement from play to work). When working takes on symbolic meaning, the mind may inhibit the **play to work** developmental line (A. Freud, 1956) or cause a defensive regression to more direct pleasurable activities (play).

> A 15-year-old boy, whose father was a lawyer, was failing in school. The boy revealed that he was preoccupied with sex and wrestling. This was in contradistinction to his father, a workaholic, who had frequently tried to inculcate in his son the virtue of work. Because the boy had little contact with his father, he had unconsciously equated work with loss (of relationships).

The symbolism of work = loss led him to unconsciously turn off his work function and regress to pleasurable fantasy and activity. Interpretation of these dynamics helped him develop better perspective and move into better work habits.

Anticipation. The function of anticipating (extrapolating and planning) may take on symbolic meaning, and then become inhibited. In a rigidly structured household, a teenager may equate anticipation with constriction of fun, and develop a spontaneity = pleasure equation.

> A 28-year-old, single, bank vice-president complained that she could only enjoy sex with men if they were strangers she met at a bar and took home. This orientation, for her, conflicted with her wish to get married and have children.[4] Planned dates bored her, but she knew that more psychologically stable men would wish to plan a date with her. However, if she had to "plan" any social activity, it would no longer be what she considered "fun." She associated that her upbringing had been "stultifying—like mayonnaise!" Planning had unconsciously become associated with her hostility toward her parents.

Judgment. Inhibition of judgment occurs in extreme idealists (Blackman, 1991a). Essentially, such people unconsciously equate the use of critical judgment with hostile destructiveness. Therefore, when called upon to criticize someone or to judge the reality of perhaps dangerous qualities of another person, the idealist is unable. A "cockeyed optimist" will allow the convicted felony-rapist-murderer out on parole to give him "another chance" due to the idealistic notion that "everybody has a little good in them." Persistent inhibition of critical judgment leads to a character style of naivete.

Alloplastic adaptation. Aggressivization of alloplastic adaptation—getting the environment to go your way—can lead people unconsciously to equate successful maneuvering with evil activity. The adaptation function then comes into conflict with guilt, resulting in a defensive shut-off of social or political maneuvering. There is a differential diagnosis to be considered here between the successful maneuverer who is not a psychopath and the maneuverer who is. The psychopath uses deceit and misrepresentation in order to achieve success. The successful person who is not a psychopath engages in ethical yet aggressive social or competitive activity. Networking is different from lying. Getting a good deal on a new car is different from stealing the car.

Clinically, inhibition of alloplastic adaptation shows up in people who *do not position themselves for advancement.* Some of them may secondarily be envious of successful people and *project* their own unconscious, sexualized motives onto them. For example, "She slept her way into that job!"

Observing ego. When observing ego takes on a symbolic meaning, it can also be shut off by the mind.

> Ms. L explained that her father had frequently criticized her, during her childhood and adolescence, for thinking too much about herself.
>
> In the early phase of treatment, as in many of her personal relationships, she dutifully reported facts about her life but not her "inner world" of thought and affect. When I brought this to her attention, Ms. L reported that thinking or talking about herself made her feel guilty.

The guilt was due, in part, to her *identification* with her father's admonitions. She experienced self-observation as "nasty, selfish" and as a hostile rebellion against her father. She was consequently critical of her *aggressivized* observing ego and had defensively avoided using it.

Ego interests. Inhibition of ego interests (Kaywin, 1966; Loewenstein, 1972) can occur in circumstances where a previously enjoyable activity, such as tennis or music, is symbolically linked, for example, with painful memories of a lost loved one. The ego interest (activity) can then be shut off as a defense against mourning. The result of this defensive inhibition could be that people consciously or unconsciously avoid the tennis court or symphonies—with or without conscious knowledge of the inhibition of their interest.

Inhibition of developed skills can come about in adulthood when there is a "reinstinctualization" of ego interests. That is, the *sublimation (40)* that had resulted in a productive activity (ego interest) somehow weakens, and the ego interest then regains its symbolic meaning. Once the symbolism returns, it can draw the ego interest into conflict (often with the superego), causing the interest itself to be defensively abandoned.

Carson McCullers (1936) depicted this phenomenon in her short story, *Wunderkind,* which describes Frances, a 15-year-old girl who abandoned playing the piano because that pursuit had taken on symbolism and become conflicted. She no longer enjoyed her male teacher's overindulgence—he had helped pick out her junior high school graduation dress, and she slept at his house after her lessons. She felt she was losing in her sibling rivalry with a male student who was becoming famous. She felt her "passion" no longer could be expressed through her fingers on the piano, to please her teacher—she was instead noticing how his pants clung to his muscular legs. And she felt trapped by the hours of practice, which prevented her from socializing.

In other words, the previously *sublimated* meanings of playing the piano—symbolically winning her oedipal competition with her teacher's wife, outdoing the "brother"-student, and expressing "passion" through her fingers—had become too consciously associated with her piano skills. The ego interest she had developed (piano playing), in other words, became reinstinctualized, and that brought it into conflict with shame, guilt, and loss. She then defensively ran out of her piano teacher's house, away from him, and away from the resymbolized piano.

Cath, Kahn, and Cobb (1977) describe the development of a "disastrous slump" in the tennis game of a female patient who was usually a good player. In analysis, she pinpointed the beginning of this slump to the comment of a male tennis-aficionado friend that tennis was a "terrific way to let out your aggression." The patient's sister had drowned when the patient was a teenager, and her father had died from liver failure soon thereafter. She said, during a session, ". . . I don't want to hate anybody, on the tennis court or anywhere else."

Cath and his co-authors formulate, ". . . she still . . . [felt] guilty about them, believing that she somehow contributed to their deaths through her jealousy. As a result she . . . was extremely fearful of causing harm to others. . . . Thus, when someone harmlessly suggested that she was 'letting out her aggression' on the tennis court, she was unable to function" (pp. 114–115). That is, when her ego interest of playing tennis became reinstinctualized (took on the meaning of literally killing people, *displaced* from her conflicts about her father and sister), she felt guilty, and therefore instituted the defense of *inhibition* of the ego interest of tennis.

Self-preservation. Self-preservation may take on the symbolic meaning of killing someone else. This is not rare in schizophrenics but also can be present in those who experience "survivor guilt" (Niederland, 1981). Basically, the person feels guilty because surviving someone has taken on the unconscious symbolic meaning of having killed the deceased (see the example under ego interests, above). When guilt comes into conflict with the aggressivized ego function (self-preservation = homicide equation), not only may the self-preservation function be shut off, but the defense of *turning on the self* can make suicide attempts more likely (see chapter 8).

Executive function. The executive function, which steers sexual and aggressive urges, can become *sexualized* itself. In a situation like a college fraternity, there may be a group mentality (creating a social value system in that setting) that equates any steering of the sexual drive with being sissified or "wimpish." In other words, the idea of steering sexual satisfaction—utilizing selectivity, timing, caution, and mode of discharge—is consciously or unconsciously equated with femininity or lack of masculinity. Because of a late adolescent boy's shame over, in any way, appearing to be a wimp, he may shut off the executive function as a defense against the shame, and thereby become promiscuous. Promiscuity can become dangerous when also fueled by *counterphobic behavior* and inhibition of impulse control.

This defensive inhibition is not restricted to males. In the classic movie *The Last Picture Show* (Bogdanovich, 1971), Cybill Shepherd plays a high school senior who, because of a sexual selectivity = pariah equation, inhibits her executive function in order to fit in. She is thereby tragically coerced into emotionless sexual activity as a defense against ostracism (social anxiety) by a group of wealthy delinquent classmates.

49. Idealization (Kernberg, 1975; Kohut, 1971)

You think someone is the greatest, but it's not true.

People may idealize someone because of

a. *projection* of narcissism (Freud, 1914a), to relieve shame over inadequacy;
b. fusion of "grandiose self" images with those of "idealized parent imagos" (Kohut, 1971): people confuse another person with an overestimation of themselves, combined with glorified distortions of the other's value ("selfobject");
c. love, to avoid experiencing disappointments; and
d. *transference* (Freud, 1914b): they see the other person as possessing aspects of a parent they idealized as a child, thereby forgetting later disappointments with their parents.

50. Devaluation

You think someone is contemptible, but they're not. You think this to preserve your own self-esteem.

Although fairly overt in narcissistic people, devaluation can occur more subtly. It commonly makes a clinical appearance during treatment in those who complain that therapy is not helping them, in the face of evidence of considerable therapeutic activity (i.e., the patient's complaint is not based on reality).

Tip.

When someone complains "therapy is not helping," you need to consider whether you should continue treating the person. First try to interpret the person's *devaluation* as a defense versus anxiety over further relying on you, the therapist. If you're not successful with this interpretation, you may have reached "maximum therapeutic benefit" with that person, and referral to a different therapist may be in order for the person's benefit as well as yours. The combination of *devaluation* of you, *splitting* (that you're "all bad"), and *projective blaming* (it's all your fault), when accompanied by limitation in abstraction ability, is a configuration of defenses that can lead someone toward a spurious malpractice suit against you.

ADOLESCENCE AND LATER—SECOND GENITAL PHASE (13 TO 20 YEARS PLUS)

51. Humor (Zwerling, 1955; Vaillant, 1992)

You start kidding around so you won't have to think about how upset you are.

> Mr. OD, a 33-year-old, dyed-in-the-wool New Yorker transplanted to the South, had consulted me for depression and anxiety in relation to women. In his tenth session, as he took a chair in my office, he started smacking his lips loudly. He then suddenly asked in a quickly recognizable tone, "Eh . . . What's up, Doc?!"
>
> After I stopped laughing and we discussed his rather good impersonation of Bugs Bunny, he described his latest humiliating experience in his quest to find a girlfriend. We understood his joking with me was partially defensive, protecting him from depressive affect. He also turned the tables, asking me the questions (*identification with the aggressor before the fact*) before I explored his painful conflicts.

Humor is not always a defense mechanism. At times, you may purposely inject inappropriate meanings, exaggerations, condensed allusions, drive-related fantasies, sadistic symbols, and grammatical inversions for the purpose of producing pleasure.

When humor has become a preconscious automatism (an automatic defensive response in certain particular situations) characterized by getting "hyped up," talking fast, joking, and feeling invincible, all in order to relieve depressive affect, anger, and shame, we may refer to it as hypomania (Hartmann, 1939; Lewin, 1950; Almansi, 1961).

Tip.

> Don't always look at humor as a defense. Besides the pleasurable aspect of it, people in treatment may joke when they develop insight into themselves, associated with heightened observing ego and integrative capacities.

52. Concretization (Blos, 1979)

You stop using abstract thinking (which you are capable of using) and instead look for some concrete, physical cause as the explanation for your problems. For example, you blame a "chemical imbalance" or look for a virus so you won't think your problematic relationships make you upset.

> A 58-year-old woman was depressed due to the obvious deterioration of her 29-year marriage. When she asked me, "Don't you have a pill that could make all this go away?" I said, "Blaming everything on some chemical would be easier, wouldn't it?" She responded, "Yeah. OK. I guess I just have to talk about this horror show of a marriage I'm living in!"

In another case, Ms. PW, a 50-year-old depressed female mail carrier, evidenced inhibition of abstraction when she insisted that her "low mood" was a result of low estrogen and not brought on by her pleasureless marriage.

> Once Ms. PW had been given conjugated estrogens by her gyne-cologist to treat her depression, she developed headaches and became afraid she would get cancer. She complained to her family doctor, who prescribed analgesics and ran numerous tests (all negative). I was able to interpret these *concretizations* (inhibitions of abstraction) as ways of not facing her emotional conflicts.
>
> Ms. PW responded that she was embarrassed that she had once been hospitalized for depression. She felt frightened, as well, of relying on any doctor for emotional support. She then began to discuss the guilt and shame she felt about manipulating her husband's attention.
>
> Part of Ms. PW's history was that she had manipulated her hus-band into marrying her, when she was basically only interested in his money—for security, and to get away from her cloying mother.
>
> I interpreted that her *concretization* (inhibition of abstract think-ing in believing her depression resulted mainly from hormones) pro-tected her from guilt and secretly garnered her attention. Ms. PW was then able to understand the abstract concept that guilt over her wish to use and then leave her husband (self-criticism)—and not an imagined physical illness—was causing her depressive affect. Her conflicts had led her to seek concrete solutions that kept her sadistic/extractive wishes unconscious but allowed her the partial gratifications of distancing her-self from her husband while inviting male doctors to care for her and touch her during physical examinations.

Bass (1997) discovered that certain people, during intensive psycho-analytic treatment, rejected obvious interpretations by the analyst. These patients would, for example, concretely believe that the analyst was angry at them for being late and not see that they could be projecting. Bass explains: ". . . as the analyst was able to interpret the way in which . . . [Ms. MB] . . . felt it imperative to make him fit in with her perceptions, . . . [Ms. MB] . . . said, 'I want to change you. I want you to be more like me and stop being different' " (p. 667). Her concreteness was a defense used to relieve separation anxiety as it occurred in her *transference* to the analyst. In other words, when the analyst interpreted a projection, this meant to Ms. MB that the analyst thought differently from her. That perception caused her separation anxiety—a fear that she and the analyst were not one. Her *concrete* refusal to accept his interpretation was a defense against feeling anxious about that reality separation.

53. Disidentification (Greenson, 1968)

You endeavor not to be like someone, usually your mother or father.

> LZ, a 21-year-old woman, reluctantly complained that she was having second thoughts about marrying her fiancé. Her mother did not care for him, but Ms. LZ defended various transgressions of his as "minor" and stated that her mother was "obsessive-compulsive." I pointed out that she apparently did not want to be "picky" like her mother. She responded that she did not actually love her fiancé, but she hated the fact that her judgment agreed with her mother's. She concluded that her *disidentification* from her mother's apparent critical tendencies was one factor leading her toward marrying this particular man.

54. Group Formation (Freud, 1921)

You surround yourself with a group of people so you won't act on wishes for emotional closeness or sex. This is a sort of adaptive comfort-inducer for adolescents who are anxious about identity diffusion and sex, but is usually maladaptive in marriages.

> A young married couple consulted me because of fights. The wife objected to her husband's playing pool every night after work, leaving her alone with their 2-year-old child. The husband complained that his wife had lost sexual interest in him.
>
> Through other elements of my assessment, I determined that neither the husband nor the wife had much abstraction ability. He argued for his "rights" and felt his wife "controlled" him, though he was adamant that he was faithful to her and loved her and the child. She argued for her "rights" to not just have sex whenever he wanted it.
>
> Because of their limited ego functioning, I decided to utilize supportive technical approaches to their problem (see chapter 7). I told him that marriage involves giving up a certain amount of freedom (e.g., playing pool with buddies every night), at least if he wanted a reason-

able marriage to this particular wife. He responded to my pronounce-
ment (based on the object relations theory of mutual empathy) by revealing that he was afraid to handle the child by himself. It was, he felt,
"women's work." He had felt more comfortable (defended) in the company of a group of men.

I went further and modeled, by exposing limited personal information (both also supportive techniques), that I had found the in-
volvement with helping with childcare, when my son was a toddler,
quite gratifying, and that I thought it was hardly women's work (I also
argued with him—another supportive technique). He was surprised,
and said he would try it. I then added that I thought his wife would be
more receptive to his sexual advances if he were more helpful to her
(posthypnotic suggestion and an admonition directed toward the wife).
She quickly and enthusiastically agreed.

In social situations, many single adults who are looking for an intimate relationship can get irritated and disappointed by the typical "singles
club." One reason for their disappointment seems to be a clash between
two different philosophies of such a club. One philosophy is that the "club"
should be a meeting place where adults looking for a potential one-to-one
relationship can find each other; they could then leave for a more privaate
assessment of relationship possibilities. The opposing philosophy sees the
singles club as a reincarnation of adolescent-style, perpetual group activities that usually militate against one-to-one intimacies (i.e., a place for
"the gang" to hang out together)—using *group formation* as a defense
against one-to-one closeness.

55. Asceticism (A. Freud, 1936)

You avoid contact with humans to avoid painful loss or criticism.

> A 55-year-old retired Navy Captain had never been married. His sex
> life had consisted of one-night stands with women he met at bars in
> various ports—sometimes prostitutes. Without the structure of the Navy,
> he was depressed and lonely. When I explored why he did not at least
> attend happy hours at the officers' club in town, he complained about
> women not only wanting sexual intercourse but then wanting a "rela-
> tionship." He would get annoyed by their object-related wishes, and
> the women typically would become critical of him for not being more
> gentlemanly. He explained that his own mother had died before he was
> a year old and that he had been raised by a series of indifferent house-
> keepers while his father, a Navy Master Chief, was at sea or passed out
> drunk at home. At school, he had felt ridiculed by girls because he was
> not a good athlete.

In other words, his asceticism seemed to defend him against the anxiety, anger, and shame he experienced when relating to women as human beings.

56. Ipsisexual Object Choice

Your same-sex "buddy" relieves anxieties associated with heterosexual relationships. This is different from homosexual object choice, the complexity of which has an entire literature devoted to it.

This defensive operation can routinely be found in latency children and adolescents, who tend to congregate only with friends of the same gender to avoid heterosexually oriented anxieties. In certain adults, however, anxiety or depression (disappointment) about closeness with the opposite sex may lead to a preference to spend time with an ipsisexual friend. Some men, for example, ignore their families in favor of a fishing or drinking buddy. Analogously, some women are more emotionally intimate or spend more time with a female friend than with their husbands. (See also the case example under defense #54.)

ASSORTED

57. One Affect versus Another (Ackerman & Jahoda, 1948)

You focus on one emotional reaction to avoid experiencing another.

Parents who overreact to their teenager's staying out late by getting overly furious about the child's defiance of their rules are often not facing their fears about the child's safety and character development.

People who frequently get angry in order to avoid anxiety over closeness with a spouse are probably borderline, defending against self–object fusion anxiety.

58. Hyperabstraction

You ridiculously overuse abstract theories.

Although in schizophrenia we usually see deficiencies in abstraction ability, intelligent schizophrenics may engage in extreme abstraction, accompanied by *denial by words* and *reconstruction of reality*.

> A schizophrenic female college student called me "Bodhisattva." She explained that this was a term for a Hindu wise man. She did this because, she said, I seemed so wise that it fit. She could then weave that abstract idea of comparing me to a Hindu seer into an explication for the meaning of life.

I eventually learned from her that she was terrified that I would die, and that her supposed intellectual abstractions about me and the world actually protected her from any notion of my mortality. Her *hyperabstraction* defense was not terribly effective, unfortunately. She developed a delusion that she must die to preserve my life, and threatened suicide. I had to hospitalize her and transfer her to another therapist.

In people who are not psychotic, *hyperabstraction* can occur as a way of not associating to certain perceptions and memories. Renik (1978) reports regarding a woman he was treating, "Clarification of the perceptual experience is *avoided* by an *abstract formulation* such as: 'It was as if I were watching myself from a distance [or] . . . was split into two persons'" (p. 596). (Emphasis added.) In other words, she used *hyperabstraction* to aid her *denial* of certain unpleasant reality perceptions.

59. Reticence

You stop speaking to avoid being found out. In children, an entire syndrome, sometimes called "elective mutism," is described around this defensive operation (Kubie & Israel, 1955).

The "Silent Cal," chronically, automatically quiet and unresponsive as an adult, is probably shielding himself interpersonally from social anxieties (Slavson, 1969) such as fear of ostracism and humiliation. He is probably also unconsciously hiding from himself various symbolic meanings of self-exposure.

Used consciously, this defensive operation, as a special form of *suppression* operating conjointly with judgment, is nicely described by Turow (1977) in *One L*. In his first year at Harvard Law School, he was concerned about speaking out too much in class, because fellow students ridiculed as "gunners" those who volunteered answers too often. He therefore decided to speak out only during every other class.

Tip.

Although reticence can be interpreted or confronted as a defense, some people in treatment who suffer with object relations problems and/or depression may need you to speak more to them (without interpreting) to stimulate verbalization (Lorand, 1937; Zetzel, 1968; Kernberg, 1984).

60. Garrulousness

You're talking too much, but aren't circumstantial or tangential.

In people with so-called histrionic traits, their talkativeness protects them from many different anxieties. Those with borderline personality organization may talk to prevent the therapist (or anyone else) from invading their self-image with questions or ideas. The male "phallic-narcissistic character" (Rothstein, 1979), who unconsciously equates assertiveness with masculinity, may overtalk to avoid feeling emasculated (by the therapist symbolically "penetrating" him).

61. Avoidance

You stay away from situations because their symbolism generates conflictual affects.

Avoidance is usually a secondary defensive operation, after defenses such as *repression (25), symbolization (20),* and *displacement (19)* have already created a symptom (such as a phobia or an obsession). People aren't "afraid of anxiety," a teleological idea at best (C. Brenner, 1982a), but they may stay away from situations where they know, from experience, that anxiety-ridden, symbolic conflicts are generated.

Airplane phobias may be caused, in part, by defenses against guilt-ridden wishes to run away (sometimes romantically). When people then avoid airports, they actually avoid their conflicts over whatever running away means (the symbol of the airplanes), and they stay home, safe.

> An example from 1973: A beautiful young woman plopped herself down in a seat at a lunch table of single, male, second-year psychiatry residents in the hospital cafeteria. In a very playful, coquettish way, she said she had found out we were psychiatry residents and wanted to ask us a question: "What causes airplane phobias?" We all said very little in response to her question, since at that time we actually didn't know the answer. But we expressed curiosity about her question. She flirtatiously replied that she was supposed to go to Florida for the weekend but was experiencing fear of getting on the plane.
>
> One of my colleagues at the table plaintively asked her whom she was going to visit. She suddenly got up from the table, exclaiming, "I think this session has ended!"
>
> As she walked away, the other men chastised the questioner for "scaring her away." He pleaded abject innocence. We all surmised that she must have been going to visit some guy. Sour grapes.

What none of us realized at the time was that, aside from her conscious wish that we relieve her anxiety and free her to fly, this young woman may have unconsciously wished for us to save her, possibly from her ambivalence about something sexual. On the one hand, we could have cured her of her misgivings so that she could go and indulge. Or, we could have informed her that there was no cure, so that she had to *avoid* Florida, with whatever its attendant conflicts would be for her.

By asking whom she was visiting, my colleague touched on her possibly sexual conflicts (and exposed his competition with the imagined male Floridian). She then left the table to *avoid* the embarrassment regarding that subject and her guilt over the seductiveness on both sides in the lunchroom table encounter (i.e., she had become phobic about us, and apparently *avoided* whatever conflicts had been stirred up at the lunch table by walking away).

Sorry, no follow-up is available on whether she made it to Florida or if she did, what happened there. We never saw her again.

62. Passivity

You adopt a compliant or submissive attitude. If you do this on purpose, for a good reason, you are using judgment (ego function) to adapt "autoplastically." If, however, you automatically acquiesce in situations where activity is needed, your passivity is a maladaptive defense.

Pathological, defensive passivity usually wards off unconscious guilt over wishes to retaliate against, harm, or kill another human being. When an apparently yielding attitude simultaneously expresses resistance and anger, we might use the term "passive-aggressive" (one of the most commonly discussed compromise formations).

Normatively, the development of passivity is a milestone of the latency stage of development (ages 6 to 10 years), a fact that may attract many teachers to teaching third and fourth grade. However, if *passivity* and *reaction-formations (11)* (i.e., obedience) are too stringently enforced during latency, children may erupt at puberty into violent, antisocial behavior (Meers, 1975).

63. Grandiosity/Omnipotence (Freud, 1913; Kohut, 1971; Kernberg, 1975; Lachmann & Stolorow, 1976; Blackman, 1987)

You believe you are worth more than anyone else thinks you are. Thus, you don't have to face your limitations, which is an upsetting exercise.

There exists a group of insufferable, *omnipotent* human beings who have apparently suffered a developmental delay, probably because of overindulgent parents. Their childhood fantasies of specialness were either aggravated or insufficiently tempered by reality experience. Therefore, they think they are God's gift to earth and still are "special." They are, at best, difficult to treat; any mention of their narcissistic traits will predictably liberate intense rage and even suicidal thoughts (if the rage is turned on the self and then used as a hostile manipulation). Highly omnipotent adolescents, therefore, may only be treatable in a mental hospital setting.

A different group actually feels inferior and limited. But these self-centered individuals pump themselves up to avoid facing their limitations—and the depressive affect accompanying that reality. They operate more with *defensive grandiosity*. Grandiosity can be implicated in learning inhibitions in childhood and sometimes in adulthood, since the need to study confronts *grandiosity* as a defense—leading to the emergence into consciousness of anxiety or depression (Gillman, 1994).

> Mr. Q, a 23-year-old male graduate student with a study inhibition, had been protected by his mother during his childhood. She did not allow him to be physically abused by his father, although the father apparently did beat many of Mr. Q's siblings. Mr. Q developed, along with a host of other problems, a grandiose notion that he was "special" to her, which was aggravated when he was 5 years old. At that time, his mother left his father, taking Mr. Q in the car with her. She told him, at least the way he remembered it, that he would now be "her man."
>
> In one session, I had interpreted to him that he seemed to cling to a grandiose notion about himself in order not to face certain other very unpleasant memories and feelings about his childhood experiences. In the following session, Mr. Q said he was afraid he would fail an exam the next morning. He asked me what he should do. I asked if he had tried studying, which caused him to start laughing, almost uncontrollably. He said, "I hadn't thought of that!" as a joke, but admitted he had been avoiding studying because it "threatens my grandiosity!"

The more that grandiose defenses become connected with deficits in the relationship to reality or reality testing, the more the diagnosis shades toward psychosis (Frosch, 1964, 1966, 1983).

64. Passive to Active

Meaning 1. "You can't fire me; I quit!" Because you're afraid you'll be victimized, you cause your own victimization, to control its timing.

Without awareness of their defensive motivations, abused children will often try to get foster parents to behave in quasi-abusive ways toward them. In cases of sexual abuse, the child may become seductive in anticipation of a repeated hostile invasion (*transference [79]*). The constellation of defenses in an abused child also may include *seduction of the aggressor (39)*, *provocation (41)* (of sexuality, hostility, and punishment), *projective identification (4)*, *projective blaming (5)*, and *identification with aggressors and victims (35, 36)* (Blackman, 1991b).

Tip.

Foster parents have to handle children whose behavior almost invites the type of abuse that occurred before placement. The children's behavior and attitudes constitute an attempt to control the timing of anticipated physical, verbal, or sexual attack. It is sometimes useful to advise foster parents to explain this defense to the children. If you are the therapist, you can interpret this defense to the child in session.

It may be necessary to counsel the foster parents not to punish the children with hitting or isolation. Even "time out" (actually isolating children as a punishment) can make children who have been abused feel that the abuse situation is being repeated; they can then become more paranoid, provocative, and *actively seek further abuse (e.g., longer and longer time-outs) to control its timing.*

Meaning 2. You can't stand waiting because you associate it with *passivity*, with its attendant vulnerability to victimization. You therefore defensively take action—whether it's a good idea or not—to relieve the tension of waiting. This is a common defense in obsessive-compulsive individuals designed to relieve the endless doubting of their relationships and judgments (Kramer, 1983).

> After two years of a tumultuous relationship with a woman who periodically rejected him, a man walked in for his Monday session and announced to me that he had married her over the weekend. He couldn't stand his doubts any longer, so, he said, he "just did it. If I've made a mistake, you'll help me through the divorce."
>
> Some months later, I did.

65. Somatization (Kernberg, 1975; Deutsch, 1959)

You have conscious symbolic fears about your body and its functions, despite a lack of medical findings. You focus on your body to avoid depression, loneliness, and unfulfillment, the painful affects generated by (usually oral) deprivation.

The causes of somatization are not always simple. On the sicker side of the diagnostic spectrum, deficits in body image (Schilder, 1935), proprioception, reality sense, and integration (i.e., somatic delusions) cause complaints identical to the defense of *somatization*.

> A 55-year-old divorced businesswoman had developed pain in her abdomen. Two years previously, her serum lipase had been slightly elevated for a brief time, so a thorough abdominal workup was instituted, looking especially for pancreatic carcinoma. Nothing at all pathophysiological was found, the abnormal lipase was not reproducible, and no other abnormalities showed up.
>
> Nevertheless, after two years, she still complained of nausea, refused to eat, and therefore was cachectic looking. She had had an epigastric tube implanted for tube-feeding, and had been medicated with

antidepressants, analgesics, and antiemetics by different physicians; her current internist had continued those.

At a point where she had been rehospitalized for medical stabilization, I was consulted. On interview, she insisted that her pain was "real." Although I obtained a history of a traumatic rupture of a heterosexual relationship just prior to her pain beginning, she denied any emotional reaction to that and was certain her pain was unrelated.

She had also withdrawn from all relationships and, in response to my confrontation that her not eating would lead to her death, said, "I will go home and die, slowly. There is nothing to live for."

My impression was that she was regressed and had developed a somatic delusion regarding her stomach pain. I recommended that she be given antipsychotic medication and be psychiatrically hospitalized. Through persistent supportive techniques of argument and intellectualization (see chapter 6), I was able to help her accept both, although she did not give up her belief that her abdominal pain was caused by some as yet undiscovered physical malady.

On the less sick end of the spectrum etiologically, conversion symptoms defend symbolically against conflicts so well that people are often not worried about the affected body part. Charcot (Breuer & Freud, 1895) sarcastically referred to the lack of concern in people with conversions as *la belle indifférence.*

A 38-year-old married woman was in analysis for the treatment of panic attacks, airplane phobia, agoraphobia, and sexual inhibition, all of which had begun after her husband had broken his leg while horseback-riding. We had already understood that hiding in the house protected her from guilt about his accident: symbolically, her various angry wishes toward him (to hurt him) had come true. The situation was exacerbated by her many reactions to the untimely death of her beloved father in a horse-related accident when she was 12 years old.

About one year into her treatment, I took a week vacation. She asked where I was going. I attempted to explore why she wanted to know and to clarify what defenses and affects were at work. However, she only responded blandly that she was sorry to pry. She hoped that I, with my wife,[5] would have a good time.

Upon my return, she reported a fear of coming to my office. She was afraid she might find out I had died in a plane crash, and felt some "ridiculous" anger at me; she associated these feelings with the death of her father. When I connected the anger at me with her earlier fantasy that I would enjoy the vacation with my wife, she suddenly stiffened on the couch and clenched her hands as though grasping at something with the tips of her fingers. She reported this was involuntary.

I handled this acute conversion symptom analytically, by asking for associations. She said she didn't want to do anything wrong. She liked me as her analyst. She remembered with pain wanting to strangle her mother (with her hands). Suddenly, a torrent of crying burst from her as she recalled wishing her mother had died and not her father!

When her sobbing subsided, I interpreted part of the *transference*: she became paralyzed on my couch so she wouldn't hurt *me*. I would have to stay and take care of her, thereby not getting home to my wife. She cried more, and her hand spasticity disappeared. She then had a recollection, from about age 5, of wanting to sleep in bed with her father. When she found the bedroom door locked, she went to an older brother's room, thinking, "I hope my father dies. If I can't have him, that way no one (including mother) will!"

Her conversion—hand spasticity—occurred to punish her for her hostile wish toward her mother, to prevent her from acting on it, and to force her father to come to her. Actually, the overdetermination (multiple meanings) was much greater; those hidden meanings were discovered as the defensive elements of her physical spasticity were methodically analyzed over the next several sessions.

66. Normalization (Alpert & Bernstein, 1964)

Because it bothers you to admit you have an emotional disturbance, you convince yourself that nothing is really wrong with you, and that you are just experiencing one of the normal vicissitudes of life with which everyone suffers. For example, a 32-year-old married woman with a terrible temper said, "But it's normal to scream at your children, isn't it?" This defense is sort of the opposite of *exaggeration's (76)* variants of catastrophizing and pathologizing.

Normalization is extremely common in the parents of a child referred for evaluation of emotional problems. They tend to not want to see the pathological problems of their children, even if they had agreed evaluation was needed. Discussion of how normalization defends against their grief and self-blame can be of considerable importance in establishing a treatment alliance with the parents of a young child.

Tip.

> Don't get too exercised about adults who normalize during the consultation process. Look for the companion defenses of *minimization (75)*, *rationalization*, and *externalization*. Gently help the person utilize observing ego to notice the presence of these defenses. What's being warded off, don't forget, is likely to be embarrassingly *abnormal*.

67. Dramatization

You inject extra emotion into your behavior or speech to relieve conflict over not being noticed.

Tip.

> Try not to comment on the wish of dramatic people (to be noticed). It's usually more therapeutic to show them the defensive aspect of the *dramatization*—to guard against fear of not being noticed.

68. Impulsivity (Lustman, 1966)

A special form of *undoing (12)*, defensive impulsivity must be distinguished from a defect in impulse control (an ego strength—see appendix 2).

As a defense, a person acts on an urge in order to relieve tension or an unpleasant affect. For example, after her husband leaves her, a woman immediately goes out and has "casual sex" with a stranger to relieve her depression.

This defense is also illustrated in certain episodes of the T.V. show "Sex and the City," where a group of women toy with "casual sex" or "having sex like a man" in order to relieve their unhappiness, loneliness, sexual frustration, and self-esteem difficulties that are brought about by infelicitous encounters with narcissistic/psychopathic men.

69. Substance Abuse (Wurmser, 1974)

You use a concoction to quell intense, usually unpleasurable affects.

Most of the media focus on drug and alcohol abusers concerns ego weakness (in impulse control). However, not all substance abusers are weak. Some relieve terribly painful feelings with substances. Interpretation of the defensive use of substances can be helpful to drug abusers who have somewhat better ego functioning, particularly after they have first "dried out."

70. Clinging (Schilder, 1939)

Clutching onto people who reject you, a) to relieve depressive affect over losing them, b) a drop in self-esteem when they (symbiotic objects) are not in view, or c) anxiety over hostile impulses toward them.

71. Whining

Complaining because you don't want to see the shameful infantile quality of your unrequited wishes to be taken care of and pampered.

In fact, whiners may blame themselves for being unhappy but are less unhappy when they're whining than otherwise.

72. Pseudoindependence

Because you are embarrassed over oral wishes (to let others take care of you or to rely on their opinions), you become the Lone Ranger, not depending on anyone much (Kaplan, 1990, p. 19).

> Mr. K, a 61-year-old investment banker, had just had a heart attack. In spite of his cardiologist's orders to take it easy for a few days, the nurse found he was pacing in his hospital room, managing his investments on his cell phone, and sneaking cigarettes in the lobby (with his oxygen off).

Mr. K's *pseudoindependence* relieved his embarrassment over needing medical care, which he equated with shameful, infantile, oral gratification. Notice he was simultaneously using *grandiosity (63)* and *inhibition of reality sense (48)*.

73. Pathological Altruism (A. Freud, 1936)

A combination of *projection* and *identification with the victim (36)*. Helping the needy lets you ignore your own oral (dependency) urges, which are projected onto the recipients. You vicariously enjoy the gratification of being cared for; simultaneously, you punish yourself with deprivation, relieving guilt over your greediness.

Normal altruism derives from a combination of empathic attunement with the superego values of sharing and generosity. However, pathological altruism is a noxious, self-destructive defense that often coexists with *masochistic provocation (41)*, *reaction-formation (11)*, and *grandiosity (63)* in people who unwisely give away a large percentage of their life savings to bogus causes or organizations.

74. Gaslighting (Calef & Weinshel, 1981; Dorpat, 2000)

You create a mental disturbance in another person to rid yourself of feeling disturbed. The recipient graciously introjects the disruptions. Or you get someone else to believe he's stupid or going crazy. The classic movie, *Gaslight* (Cukor, 1944) suggested this term.

Tip.

> The victim of the gaslighter may be the person who consults you. This is a complicated situation if you have not met the gaslighter, who often refuses even a consultation, pinning all the problems on the "gaslightee." Be careful not to opine about the supposed perpetrator. You *can* interpret this defense by pointing out to people that the way they describe it, it sounds as though they feel more comfortable viewing themselves as "cracked" rather than feel critical of the person they describe as driving them crazy.

75. Minimization

You are conscious of a painful reality but give that reality little weight. You may be saying, "No big deal," a bit too often.

This can be a particularly difficult defense to interpret as pathological, especially when self-help books tend to suggest this defense be used *more* (*Don't Sweat the Small Stuff*, [Carlson, 2002], and the like).

Minimization is often seen along with *inhibition of critical judgment*, particularly in teenagers. Add a *counterphobic* mechanism, and the person is in trouble—not able to be critical, minimizing danger, and then prone to act in a dangerous way.

Tip.

> To interpret this defense when it *is* pathological, you might tell people that you realize some of their reactions may not, in fact, be "that big a deal." Nevertheless, either the frequency with which they say that phrase (or one like it) or the situation where they're using it make you think they're hiding other unpleasant thoughts thereby.

76. Exaggeration (Sperling, 1963)

You make too much of a deal over something, often so you and others won't think you're inadequate.

Catastrophizing. One variation of this defense has been called *catastrophizing*. This occurs in people who overreact to relatively minor events as though they are catastrophes.

> A third-grade girl brings home a C on a homework assignment. Her mother tells her she must do better, then punishes her by making her go to bed early and lectures her about the dangers of not getting into college with such bad grades.

Catastrophizing, as above, is usually a defense against anxiety that nothing will be done or that a bad situation will persist.

Pathologizing. A second subtype of exaggeration is *pathologizing*. This means that people judge as emotionally deranged something that is relatively normal.

> Ms. PQ worried because her only child, a 2-year-old girl, would sometimes hit her. Moreover, the girl was not yet potty-trained. When I explored the situation, I found that the daughter hit her mother when the mother was not paying attention to her.
> I explained to Ms. PQ that potty-training often was not completed at age 2, but could easily take until 3 or 4, especially with first children.
> Regarding the hitting, I advised that this was a common behavior in 2-year-olds. She should instruct her daughter not to hit but instead to tell her mother when she wanted something.

Ms. PQ was viewing the child's hitting and lack of potty-training as pathological. In the case of the potty-training, she was *pathologizing* to relieve her fear that the child would never be trained. In regard to the child's hitting, she was also *pathologizing* a normal response for a frustrated 2-year-old, as a way of avoiding facing the child's aggressive pursuit of her mother's time and attention.

Parents who overreact to their child's physical complaints, often when there isn't much wrong, can become overinvested in the child being sick. Due to multiple projections and symbiotic fantasies, such parents may develop a persistent obsession with their child's "need" for medical attention and special treatment; sometimes the children accommodate their disturbed parents' wishes by developing persistent psychosomatic or psychophysiological symptoms. Melitta Sperling (1957) coined the term "psychosomatic object-relationship" for the pathological tie between some mothers and their small children. More recently, pediatricians have dubbed the problem "Munchausen Syndrome by Proxy" (Mason, 2001).

77. Generalization (Loeb, 1982)

You see a person as just part of a group you don't like, so you don't have to hate that person so much (Blum, 1992).

> A married, middle-aged man realizes, through analytic treatment, that his "niceness" to his wife relieves his guilt over hostility toward her; and that, at the same time, he unconsciously expresses his hostility by "killing her with kindness." He then says, "But all women are a pain in the neck!"

In other words, his hostility is now directed at the group of "all women" (a change in defenses), so he still doesn't have to face his criticisms of his wife (C. Brenner, 1975).

78. Reconstruction of Reality (Freeman, 1962)

You change your opinion about what's going on, after denying the reality.

Neurotic people do this to relieve guilt or anxiety. Kanzer (1953) suggests that the therapist looks to reconstruct the current reality with such people, after essentially deconstructing their confusing descriptions. In other words, if someone has a distorted view of things, after getting clear that there are distortions, it may be necessary to figure what has been left out of the story and help the person fill it in.

More commonly, reality is painful, so schizoid or overtly psychotic people autistically create their own reality to aid the defense of withdrawal.

Note. In artistic people, including fiction writers, their creation of their own realities is often connected with a particular facility with regression in the service of the ego, which is not a defense. (I think of it as more of an ego strength.) So the capacity to write a fantasy novel like *The Golden Compass* (1996) does not make Philip Pullman, the author, psychotic. Rather, he demonstrates an ability to *formally regress (96)* (to utilize some primary process fantasy) to aid him in the intellectual pursuit of creative writing.[6]

79. Transference (Freud, 1914b; A. Freud, 1936; Loewenstein, 1957; Marcus, 1971, 1980; Blum, 1982)

First, you unconsciously shift memories of past situations and relationships (including urges, guilt feelings, and behavioral expectations) onto the image of a current person. Then you react to the current person with defenses you used in the past to handle the same or similar situations.

This two-part defense helps you forget the past occurrences (Freud, 1914b). At the same time, you try to master the unpleasurable memories by living through them again in displaced form and/or symbolically changing the outcome.

> Dr. G, a 40-year-old surgeon, consulted me because he was always late. This problem had caused him severe troubles at the hospital, especially with scheduling surgeries. He also had once been suspended from the medical staff for not finishing his charting on time.
>
> When I had made his initial consultation appointment for him over the phone, I had asked him to bring a check to cover the fee for that appointment, and he had agreed. When the initial consult came to

a close, I gave him a statement. He said that he had forgotten to bring his checkbook and asked if it would be "all right" for him to pay me next time. I thought this over for a moment and then said, "No."

We were both standing; Dr. G was looking me in the eye. With some irritation, he said, "Don't you think I'm good for it?" I responded that that was beside the point. He had made an agreement with me; now he wanted to break it, and he wanted me to let him get away with it. This seemed similar to how he was "late" in so many other situations, where he was upset that others weren't more lenient with him. I thought it was important that he pay the fee as agreed and then analyze why this made him angry. Dr. G said, "I saw an ATM machine down the block. You want me to go get cash and bring it back right now?" I responded that that would be fine, that he could leave the cash with my office manager, who would note the payment on his copy of the statement.

Dr. G proceeded to get the cash and pay the bill. Over the next six years of his analysis, we discovered that in that first session he had been repeating two of many problems he had had with his father. First, he wanted to express hostility toward me by breaking the agreement and getting me to let him "get away with it" as his father often had. Second, he provoked me to punish him for his disobedience, which his father had also done.[7]

These *transferences* protected him from recalling his anger at his father. Until we analyzed these behaviors, he had *idealized* his father. Analyzing the *transference* bases of his attempted misbehavior with me was quite helpful to him in understanding and eventually relieving his severe procrastination.

80. Dissociation

You not only forget a thought (*repression*), you are unaware of whole aspects of yourself, such as elements of identity, drive urges, guilt reactions, memories, and defenses.

Some therapists and analysts (I. Brenner, 1996, 2001) have reported finding "alters" (alternate personalities) in adults who have been sexually abused as children, theorizing that dissociation is a process where entire aspects of the personality are "split off" and become unconscious as a defense against inflamed affects from childhood.

Armstrong (1994) notes that the differential diagnosis of multiple personality disorder (mpd) includes schizophrenia: "Many of the symptoms of mpd . . . appear to mimic psychotic phenomena, such as hearing internal voices and experiencing 'made' feelings and actions" (Kluft, 1985) (p. 353).

Target (1998), contrarily, finds in her review that many studies suggest "recovered memories" are produced by therapist-induced confabulations. A related viewpoint (Frosch, 1983; Gardner, 1994) is that when people experience beliefs that they are inhabited by others who are responsible for their conflicting attitudes, those beliefs involve: *repression, isolation (of affect), compartmentalization, splitting, suppression, prevarication, transference, inhibition of observing ego*, added to *animism* and concrete thinking. This constellation of ego deficits and defenses is standard in many cases of schizophrenia, leading many authors to view multiple personality disorder as essentially a series of delusions (partly defensive) occurring in intelligent schizophrenics (Rosenbaum, 1980).

In a completely different vein, Whitmer (2001) has proposed an alternative definition of the concept of dissociation: ". . . In dissociation, the subject constructs his or her own experience through the meaning that another gives to the subject's own perceptions . . ." (p. 812).

Although he does not describe dissociation in terms of defensive activity, I think that the act of utilizing another to form concepts about the self-image is, at least in part, a defensive operation. Which affects are defended against may vary, but self-dissolution ("annihilation") anxiety is likely to be one.

Clinically, Whitmer's definition is applicable to many people in treatment who seem to turn over their view of themselves to a therapist, wife, mentor, boss, or the like.

81. Photophobia (Abraham, 1913)

You avoid the light to avoid, among other things, your intense, guilt-ridden wishes to look (scoptophilia), especially at forbidden, sexual situations.[8]

This defense is often a feature in agoraphobics. Others are overly "sensitive" to light, and may even ask you to turn down the light in your consulting room (a remarkable request considering that most therapists' offices are not extremely bright).

Tip.
When people ask you to turn down the light, you may be able to show them the displacement from their unconscious wish to "not see" too much in the session. What they don't want to see may then become conscious, along with the warded-off affects.

82. Apathy (Greenson, 1949)

You have no particular interest in engaging in activity.

Apathetic people are not necessarily lazy or negative. Their apparent lack of enthusiasm protects them from disappointment and/or anxiety over exposure of personal material. At the same time, they don't have to become aware of highly infantile, oral urges to be taken care of or to face their sadistic wishes to control the world (and not be controlled).

83. Intimidation of Others—Bullying (Knight, 1942; Blackman, 2003)

Very often, this behavior is designed to relieve the bully of guilt of of anxiety over loss of love. Knight found that the ". . . aggressive attitude provokes hostile responses which increase their anxiety and consequently the need for more aggressive behavior. Thus a vicious cycle is established . . ." (p. 443).

Intimidation is relatively uncommon in new patients; most people are in severe emotional difficulty when they first consult us and therefore usually are careful not to be offensive. However, certain people will begin consultations by "interviewing" us; that is, asking lots of questions about whether we feel we are able to treat them. They often subtly coerce the therapist into feeling guilty about unconscious (sometimes conscious) retaliatory fantasies the therapist begins to have in response to their subtle attack.

Tip.

> A person who consults you always has the right to know about your training, your general idea of diagnosis and prognosis, and most therapists answer those questions routinely. However, an excessive number of such questions can be a method of controlling the interaction as a defense against intense anxiety. You can usually bring this controlling feature to a person's attention, which puts the intimidation defense on the table for discussion and analysis.

84. Compensation for Deficiencies (Ackerman & Jahoda, 1948)

You develop a prejudicial hatred toward people who are not as deficient (especially in identity) as you are. You then participate in ostracizing and excluding them.

> A 31-year-old single man was still working on his bachelor's degree from college. He had had several "incarnations," for a while bartending, for a while trying carpentry, and had finally returned to school to major in sociology. He confided that he admired Hitler and Nazis because they knew what they wanted—perfection—and knew whom they hated—Jews. I was able to show him that, to the extent that he wished to identify with Nazis, he imagined he would better know who *he* was; this would relieve his depressing feeling that he had not been able to

"find himself." He agreed, then confessed to guilt about his interest in Nazism, which he knew was "strange" because he did not agree with their policies of world domination and genocide.

85. Psychogenic Tic (Aarons, 1958)

Your body suddenly twitches or jerks to discharge tension and avoid awareness of emotional conflict. Pseudoseizures represent a severe form of this defense.

Mahler (1944) differentiates psychogenic tic from neurologically based phenomena, and concludes that it ". . . may symbolize an aggressive gesture or *magic defensive motor action of the ego* against intolerable tension and conflict with the outside world" (emphasis added, p. 435).

Tip.

It's useful to keep in mind that this defensive operation may be implicated in children when some symptoms of Tourette's Syndrome are present, but the neurological evidence is lacking. It may then be possible to interpret the defensive warding off of aggressive or sexual fantasies through psychomotor discharge. Also, in adults, keep in mind that there may be a non-integration of psychomotor control with other elements of thinking, suggesting a possible psychotic predilection (Bender, 1944).

86. Introspection (Kohut, 1959; Fogel, 1995)

You look into yourself as a protection. In other words, you begin to utilize your observing ego to manage affect (similar to using intellect as a defense). Kohut (1959) points out, ". . . Introspection can . . . constitute an escape from reality" (p. 466).

In addition, certain people either have been brought up "overanalyzing" their thoughts and behavior as a means of controlling affects or have developed their observing ego to an exaggerated degree because of intense anxiety over loss of control.

Tip.

Fogel (1995) recommends: "Effective therapeutic work requires that [people in treatment who utilize this pathological defense] suffer 'traumatization'—experiences of dedifferentiation that undermine their considerable capacity to know what they feel and think" (p. 793). In other words, in such situations, allowing people in therapy to "run with it" is a mistake. They will make their own interpretations, and seem to know about their conflicts, but make no changes.

Not interfering with people's own "analysis" of certain compromise formations is often a good technique in late treatment, since the therapist's more passive stance helps foster people's autonomy and their ability to separate from the therapist. However, with the defensively introspective types, it's better to confront their introspection as pathological, along with their *distancing, intellectualization,* and/or *grandiosity,* when present.

87. Qualified Agreement (Abend, 1975)

You partly agree as a way of avoiding your rebellious anger.
Abend puts it this way:

> I have in mind those individuals who react not with doubt or disputation, but according to a formula that can be called the 'Yes, but' response, an analogue of negation. They appear to accept interpretations, especially those that are familiar because of previous analytic work. Characteristically, however, they add to their acceptance the belief—which they do not consciously regard as a contradiction—that certain factors in external reality have also played an important part in determining the behavior, thoughts, or feelings which are under analysis. (p. 631)

He adds, "these patients as a rule are quite unaware of the strength of their wish to disagree with interpretations" (p. 631).

88. Instinctualization of an Ego Weakness (Blackman, 1991a)

You get overwhelmed by emotions too easily because of weakness in affect-tolerance (see Appendix 2). However, you're so embarrassed about this ego weakness that you defensively believe it's feminine, not weak.

In heterosexual men who are so troubled by homosexual fantasies (Coates & Person, 1985) that they seek dynamic therapy, often the fantasies reflect a "feminine" symbolization as a defense against shame over weaknesses in impulse control and affect-tolerance. Conversely, "masculinity," to such men, can represent ego strength and/or violence.

This defense is also found in some women who excuse their ego weaknesses (in affect-tolerance or impulse control) by believing they are "just" feminine. Husbands who agree that their wives with such ego weaknesses are "just" the "weaker sex" or "more emotional" are probably using the defenses of *rationalization* and *instinctualization* regarding the disturbed women's deficiencies in functioning.

The equation of masculinity with violence and ego strength is sometimes seen in stereotypical "biker chicks," who are attempting to repair their own ego weaknesses by first *sexualizing* them and then attaching themselves to violent men whom they view as "strong."

89. Inauthenticity (Akhtar, 1994)

You fake it, perhaps habitually. This gives you a sense of connectedness to others at the same time you secretly keep emotional distance.

Although it is not uncommon for adolescents to "try on" various roles, to strategize socially ("and then what did you say?"), and to behave artificially (act "cool," for example), if any of these phenomena persist into adulthood, they tend to be pathological. Specifically, inauthenticity protects the person from anxiety over identity or from rejection due to exposure of actual reactions.

Tip.

> Inauthenticity should be confronted fairly early in treatment, since it prevents the honest flow of communication in sessions. My experience with defensive inauthenticity is that the falseness of people's emotional reactions can, at times, be brought to their attention with a bit of humor. A comment like, "I wonder if you *really* believe that?" may ease the way toward understanding the defense, especially if the response is along the lines of, "Well, maybe not, but I'm not used to being so honest!"

90. Hyper-Rationality (Spruiell, 1989)

You use reality testing and secondary process (logical, time-oriented thinking) to avoid affects.

Rationality is a complex of functions. Early in his career, Freud (1900a) coined the term "secondary process thinking" to refer to logical, time-oriented thought. Although there is mention of hyper-rationality in the analytic literature (Goldberg, 1976; Asch, 1982), it is not usually addressed specifically as a defense.

Tip.

> Essentially, if almost everything people in treatment tell you makes sense, you can question why emotional, nonrational material is missing. You might point out that they are utilizing an avoidance maneuver, such as, "Just the facts, Ma'am." Or you might refer to the mechanism as a kind of "stiffness." Either way, be prepared for an outpouring of emotion once you touch on this—and it may be rage directed at you for disturbing their sense of control—an anal feature discussed by Rosegrant (1995).

91. Vagueness (Paniagua, 1999)

You only allude to what you're thinking, so nobody can really tell the details, which stay hidden.

> A middle-aged woman complained in session that she had "a terrible weekend." Her husband was irascible. Their conversations were "useless." Then they had a "distant peace." When I pointed out that she seemed to be sidestepping any details, she began crying, and said the details were "too painful." She then gradually revealed some of what went on.

Tip.

> Vagueness is extremely common in the initial consultation, although it occurs later as well. You can bring vagueness to people's attention by noting to them that they're giving you the "headlines" without the full story, which suggests to you that they're having some trouble getting into the details.

92. Hyper-aestheticism (Paniagua, 1999)

You get preoccupied with beauty and/or truth, thereby avoiding unpleasant realities, your own aggression, or objectionable affects.

This is a particular problem in highly cultured people, who may go on about the beauty of certain ideas, expositions, and the like, taking up time from the understanding of their personal problems. However, anyone may get into commenting on the decor of your office or the glorious weather to guard against "unpretty" thoughts.

Tip.

> A fairly facile entré into this defense is to address exactly the issue of the prettiness of what someone is describing, perhaps as "a bit prettier than some other thoughts and feelings you've mentioned lately."

93. Glibness

You speak readily, but you don't mean a lot of it.

> A single, 35-year-old woman in treatment reported a dream in which a man (who looks like me, her analyst) asks her to marry him. She then went on at some length about her dependency, citing various theories about her loneliness, including *identification* with her mother's reclusiveness. Although these understandings were correct, deriving

from previous work in treatment, and not *inauthentic*, they did not seem to be heartfelt.

I pointed out to her that she seemed to be going over previous understandings about dependency, sort of like she was performing on an exam, but I wasn't sure, at this point, whether she meant a lot of what she was saying. I noted that she somehow had not directly addressed the material in the dream about her fantasies of marriage to me. She responded, "You're right! I don't want to go there!"

94. Physical Violence (Glasser, 1992)

You "nullify the object" that you have unpleasurable feelings toward, by neutralizing the person's effects on you.

Physical violence has a long and controversial history—pacifists versus doughboys (WWI), isolationists versus war-readiers (WWII), hawks versus doves (Vietnam). However, in the consulting room, we generally see problems in personal relationships, where physical violence is a particularly noxious defensive operation. Although seen a bit more commonly in men, women who beat their children also utilize this defense.

Glasser's (1992) contribution to our understanding of violence is that it is not simply a discharge of hateful destructiveness nor just a defensive mechanism for self-preservation. In certain situations, people can use physical violence as a defense against allowing anyone to even have an effect on them. The idea of obliterating the emotional connection between the self and other usually has determinants from object-relations pathology (i.e., holding onto other people and at the same time attempting to destroy the impact of their emotional life on the self).

Tip.

> Look for this defense in people in the throes of divorce. They are likely to wish to obliterate the irritating effects of the estranged spouse and may displace this attitude onto their children. So, in an otherwise kind mother who suddenly smacks her son in the face for "making a mess with his dinner," you can try to interpret that at that moment she must have unconsciously wished to stop the child from causing her any emotional disruption and that "making a mess" is what she feels her husband did—make a mess of the marriage.

95. Identification with the Injured Object (Kitayama, 1991)

You are sure you're wounded, and function that way, but it's not true. The false belief is protecting you.

A 40-year-old man was not finishing his work. He then would confess this shortcoming to his wife, who tried to help him. When I pointed out to him that he seemed to thrive on presenting himself as injured and lacking in capacity, he agreed. He called himself a "wounded bird." He then thought how he was like a chick, which, as a 3- or 4-year-old boy, he had tried to save. It had fallen into a well and was chirping. He thought it was hurt. Also, he had almost fallen into the well himself, as his mother did not watch him closely.

His identification with the wounded chick shielded him (defense) from awareness of shame over his intense longing for a mother figure to tend to him. At the same time, he unconsciously *displaced* his wish for maternal succor onto his wife.

96. Formal Regression (Freud, 1900a; Blum, 1994b)

You stop using logical, time-oriented thought (secondary process thinking) and instead think in a symbolic, condensed fashion (primary process). The shift from secondary to primary process protects you from coming to painful conclusions.

This defense is routinely found in marital arguments, where one or both of the parties agree that they are "arguing over nothing."

Example 1. A husband complained that his wife "brings up things from 10 years ago that I don't even remember!" In other words, he was baffled by her *condensation* of current-day difficulties with ancient irritations that came up as an apparent defense against the intensity of her current frustrations.

Example 2. A homemaker complained that her husband "picks arguments with the children irrationally." Actually, she felt guilty that she, herself, was not working, and she allayed her own criticism of her children's laziness by joking about their "good life"—in not being pressured to do their homework the way she had been in her youth.

In addition, she had been frustrated with her husband's long work hours. She complained about his work schedule, but she knew he had only limited control over it. She therefore felt "irrational" herself, for being irritated with him.

Aside from *projecting* onto (seeing in) her husband both her own critical attitude toward the children and her own feeling of "irrationality," she had also defensively *regressed*. She *condensed* her children with herself, so that she was angry at her husband for criticizing the children for not working, as she was also critical of herself for not working.

97. Hypervigilance

You keep an eye out all the time, even when it's entirely unnecessary.

This defense protects people from anxiety-laden thoughts of being surprised by aggression, sexuality, or affects from others. Hypervigilance often shows up after a drive urge is first *projected*: people's own sexuality or aggression is seen in others; then they become hypervigilant to protect themselves from their own projected (forbidden) thoughts.

98. Temporal Displacement to the Future (Akhtar, 1996)

You keep imagining how good something would be "if only . . ." or "some-day. . . ." These fantasies shield you from grieving over the unattainable and from experiencing pleasure (forbidden) in your present life.

Tip.

> Akhtar (1996) recommends several steps in treating those who utilize this defense, including the following: rupture the person's excessive hope, analyze the effects of such rupture, facilitate the resultant mourning, and reconstruct the early scenarios underlying the need for excessive hope.

99. Fatigue

You feel tired, but there's no logical reason for this. Tiredness protects you from knowing about some nastiness within yourself.

Fatigue is an extremely common complaint heard in general medical practices. Each decade brings with it some new potential "medical" explanation for the phenomenon. Most recently, "chronic fatigue syndrome" was attributed to the supposed Epstein-Barr virus. The decade before, hypoglycemia (in the face of a normal glucose tolerance test) was popular. Once the usual medical entities that can cause fatigue (including cancer, thyroid disease, adrenal disease, infections, diabetes, rheumatoid arthritis and other "collagen" diseases) have been ruled out, the diagnostic effort usually turns to the emotional sphere.

Enter fatigue as a defensive operation—especially common in those who feel guilty about a wish to demand that others take care of them. The tiredness forces others to do so, but the fatigued people themselves are unaware of their conflicts about dependency. Simultaneously, the principle of multiple function applies: the tiredness also punishes them so that they are prevented from enjoying the oral (dependency) gratification.

100. Frankness (Feder, 1974)

You are apparently candid and forthcoming. But your penchant for "the truth" shields you and others from "the whole truth and nothing but the truth" about your aggressive hostility.

Frankness can become a part of obnoxious verbal confrontation, a preconscious automatism—that is, an automatic reaction, consisting of several defenses, that is triggered in certain situations of conflict (Hartmann, 1939). The obnoxiously frank person may ream people out for their mistakes. Those people may have erred, but the frank person overdoes it to keep other affects under wraps.

There are definitely times when it is healthy for human beings to get "in their face" with people who may be attempting to manipulate them. In fact, people who have trouble standing up for themselves frequently consult us for treatment. However, frankness, whether disarming or obnoxious, can also be quite maladaptive when used automatically and repeatedly.

Obnoxiousness often appears in people who fear being victimized. The fear of victimization may be due to identifications with victimized parents or siblings, or to transference expectations based on their own experiences with parents, siblings, or others. The obnoxiousness is designed to insure that the victimization does not occur again. People who use this mechanism tend to lose jobs, alienate friends and lovers, and suffer thereby.

Tip.

> As with many defenses, there is a difficulty in interpreting this one as a maladaptive mechanism. Complainers can easily feel that "reality" demands they maintain their frankness or obnoxiousness. Alternately, they may express pride in their supposed forthrightness.
>
> The subtlety of therapeutic intervention lies in communicating to people that you do not view honesty or self-protective aggression as pathological, but that the style they are using is counterproductive and shields them from irrational fears. Along the way, you may also have to interpret their transference fantasy that you are trying to stop their self-protective aggression or are attempting to get them to "behave."

101. Turning Self-Criticism onto the Object

You are feeling guilty and self-critical, but instead criticize something or somebody else.

> Mr. UV, a 33-year-old man hospitalized for suicidal ideation, complained that his wife was overweight. He said he kept telling her she was "turn-

ing into a fat pig" and that she ate too much. I opined that she no doubt had a reason for overeating. Mr. UV asked, "What? I can't figure it out." I responded, "It's probably because you're cruel to her." He said, "That's what she says. Why is it cruel?" I answered, "The point is that you are sadistic, and are criticizing her, but would rather argue about it." Mr. UV said, "I'm sorry. I don't mean to argue. I'm usually that hard on myself. I'm my own worst enemy."

The following day, when I saw Mr. UV for session, he said he had thought about my confrontation of his sadism and agreed with me. He then asked, "Why didn't I see that myself?" I responded, "Because you're also self-centered." Mr. UV laughed and said, "Oh. Thanks. Any other compliments?" I clarified that he was now criticizing me, as he had done to himself—for being cruel and sadistic. He understood and said, "Sometimes when I thought of ending it all, I felt like I 'deserved it', but I couldn't figure out why."

Later, I had a conjoint session with Mr. and Mrs. UV (who was only 10 to 15 pounds overweight), and she openly confirmed that she knew the reason she ate too much was that she had a hard time putting up with his "constant criticisms."

4

Defenses Used
in the Diagnosis
of Psychopathology

The literature on using defenses in psychological diagnosis begins with Freud's (1894) early work, later modified by Anna Freud's (1936) seminal monograph. Vaillant (1992) differentiates defensive operations by their level of "maturity," meaning the psychosexual level at which they originated, and then suggests that the use of more mature defenses indicates healthier mental functioning. Willick (1985), contrarily, demonstrates that diagnostic distinctions in adults based on the level of maturity of their defenses is less useful than ego function assessment in differentiating psychotic from nonpsychotic states.

In general, with the exception of several particularly noxious defenses (especially *denial, projection, reconstruction of reality,* as well as *regressions in reality testing, in integration, and in containment of primary process*), diagnosis and treatment selection first require the assessment of the state of autonomous ego functioning (Hartmann, 1939; Knight, 1986; Busch, 1997). Determination of psychotic versus borderline versus neurotic ("higher") levels of functioning (Kernberg, 1975; Abend et al., 1983; Goldstein, 1997) depends considerably on the intactness of the ego functions of:

- integration/organization (Bleuler, 1969)
- abstraction
- reality testing and relationship to reality (Frosch, 1964)
- self-preservation
- secondary versus primary process thinking
- perception
- memory

- psychomotor control
- judgment
- anticipation (Bellak & Meyers, 1975)
- speech
- forms of intelligence (Hartmann, 1939)
- adaptational abilities
- self-care
- concentration and attention
- executive function (steering sexual and aggressive urges) (Hartmann, 1955)
- moving from play to work (ability to work and not play)

MORE ABOUT AUTONOMOUS EGO FUNCTIONS

Some people have mental disorders caused by the effects on the brain of metabolic, endocrine, vascular, neoplastic, toxic, infectious, or hereditary (syndrome) disturbances. Usually, these "organic" etiologies lead to deficiencies in one or more basic mental functions, such as

- Sleep–wake cycle: for example, disturbed diurnal sleep pattern in hyperthyroid disease
- Perception (using the five senses): for example, loss of smell in olfactory nerve tumors
- Sensorium (the alertness of someone who is awake): for example, drowsiness in marijuana intoxication
- Memory (recall of perceptions of people, places, and things): for example, forgetting one's children in Alzheimer's Disease
- Orientation (knowledge of person, place, time, and situation): for example, loss of location sense with Alzheimer's Disease, or with high fevers
- Motor control (control of movement): for example, seizures in epilepsy
- Speech: for example, loss of articulate speech after left middle cerebral artery stroke.

Each of the highlighted functions noted above is an autonomous ego function (Hartmann, 1939, 1981). These functions of the mind are not designed primarily to manage emotion, but are basic mental operations that develop over a long period of time. However, autonomous ego functions and their development *are affected by* organic illnesses *and* by emotions and defenses (see chapter 3, defenses #47 & #48).

Psychotic illnesses may result from hereditary or inborn weaknesses in certain ego functions. In many cases of schizophrenia (see appendix 1), disturbed thinking seems to be caused by an inability to organize and integrate thoughts, to use abstraction ability to understand the world, and to keep bizarre, dreamlike thoughts out of consciousness (containment of primary process fantasy). For example, a young man believed that hospital nurses were working for the FBI, were taking money from pimps, and were out to steal his money. He could not prevent these fantasies from becoming conscious, and could not use reality testing (to check out their reality) or secondary process (logical) thought. Although he was using *projection* (he was the one feeling greedy and sexually pressured), *transference* (his father had worked for the FBI), and *displacement* onto the hospital staff, none of those defenses was useful in differentiating his psychosis from a non-psychotic state. The defective ego functioning was key to the diagnosis.

Psychosis may also result when acutely inflamed emotions melt down several ego functions simultaneously, although meltdown of functions does not have to reach a psychotic level. For example, a student had difficulty concentrating after her grandmother died. Although not psychotic, her concentration, an autonomous ego function, was temporarily overwhelmed by intense depressive affect (grief). If her autonomous ego functions of integration and reality testing had been melted down as well, she might have believed that her visual and auditory memories of her father were "real" (breakdown in relation to reality), and that he was present and talking to her (breakdown in reality testing).

Unfortunately, it is not uncommon to find ego meltdown in girls who have been sexually abused by rape. If the abuse is chronic, their resulting intense rage, fear, pain, and depressive affect can erode the development of certain autonomous ego functions, such as concentration, relationship to reality, abstraction, integration, intellect (Blackman, 1991b), and later, executive function (steering pressure from aggressive and sexual wishes).

So, in psychotic illnesses, whether due to organic brain pathology, emotional trauma, or chronic weakness, we generally find damage to autonomous ego functions. The neuronal mechanisms (Edelman, 1992) involved in these deficiencies in thinking are essentially not known. (There are some interesting statistical correlations with the metabolism of dopamine and other neurotransmitters in the central nervous system.) Nevertheless, many analytic researchers (Bellak, Hurvich, & Gediman, 1973; Willick, 1993) consider the fundamental mental problems in psychoses to be deficiencies and not defensive operations. (For opposing views, see Lidz et al., 1957; Arlow & Brenner, 1964; Boyer, 1971; Waugaman, 1996.)

Other autonomous ego functions that may be disrupted in psychosis include: memory, self-care—hygiene (A. Freud, 1956), social skill (Slavson, 1969), autoplastic adaptation—fitting in to the environment (Knight,

1986), movement from play to work (A. Freud, 1956), anticipation and judgment (Hoch & Polatin, 1949), alloplastic adaptation—managing the environment (Hartmann, 1939), observing ego—self-reflection (Kohut, 1959), ego interests—hobbies and avocations (Hartmann, 1955), and self-preservation.

When autonomous ego functions are damaged or deficient, upsurges of affects and wishes can lead to defensive activity. The same full range of (101 plus) defenses may occur in psychoses and in nonpsychotic conditions. *Projection* and *projective blaming* are often used by schizophrenics ("You're crazy, Doc, not me!"), but can also be employed by normal people on occasion (leading to marital disputes), and by phobics. (The bridge phobia results from projection onto the bridge of unacceptable anger and guilt, for example, leading the bridge phobic to fear the death penalty upon crossing the bridge.) *Intellectualization* may be used by normal college students to guard against social anxiety or by schizophrenics to mask unrealistic beliefs. *The key finding in psychotic people is a severe breakdown in reality testing and other ego functions, not primarily the use of specific defenses.*

In addition, the ego strengths that must be considered in diagnosing and treating anyone include affect-tolerance, impulse control (of eating, sexual, and aggressive urges), pain and frustration tolerance, containment of primary process (condensed, symbolic) thinking (Hoch & Polatin, 1949), development of adequate sublimatory channels (Kernberg, 1975), using fantasy as trial action (Hartmann, 1955), and utilizing mentation rather than somatic channels for affect discharge (Schur, 1955). (See appendices 2 and 3.)

As a rule, the more that autonomous ego functions and ego strengths are disturbed, the more the person shades into the psychotic range (Bellak, 1989). Further, the more that the capacities for self and object constancy (Mahler, Pine, & Bergman, 1975; Settlage, 1977; Kramer, 1979, 1992) are weakened, the more therapists must worry that they are dealing with a person with borderline or psychotic illness (see appendix 3).

Moreover, the superego needs close attention. Superego abnormalities can occur in people who have adequate, weak, or defective autonomous ego functions and ego strengths. In other words, severe liars, cheats, and criminals can be "high functioning," borderline psychotic, or overtly psychotic.

Although assessment of defensive operations is a key activity for dynamic therapists, it is critical to formulate diagnostic distinctions among those people who possess enough ego, superego, and object relations capacities to be treated with analytic techniques (see chapters 5 and 6). Specifically, if someone has sufficient abstraction ability, integrative functioning, reality testing, and observing ego, some ego strength (see appendix 2), some capacity for empathy, trust and closeness, and sufficient integrity, the therapist can use analytic interpretive techniques (see chapter 5) to relieve or modify pathological (maladaptive) defense constellations.

In addition, one tried and true way of determining whether people's abstraction and integration are sufficient for an insight-directed therapy approach is to offer a "trial interpretation" of defense and affect. You'll then see if people can understand and/or use the intervention therapeutically.

MORE ABOUT OBJECT RELATIONS AND DEFENSES

In order for people to be treated through confrontation and interpretation of their defenses, they must have some ability to maintain a set of functions and capacities in close relationships.

The disturbance in self–object differentiation present in borderline and psychotic people usually is manifest clinically in aberrations in their capacities for empathy, trust, closeness, stability, and/or warmth. A handy mnemonic device for keeping these capacities in mind during evaluation is **Warm-ETHICS:** **W**armth, **E**mpathy, **T**rust, **H**olding environment, **I**dentity, **C**loseness, and **S**tability problems in interpersonal relationships. The more limited people are in these areas, the more disturbed they tend to be and the less treatable they will be with interpretive approaches.

Warm-ETHICS

Although many people have relationship problems that involve disturbances in warmth, empathy, trust, holding environment, identity, closeness, stability, and ethics, they rarely mention these as presenting problems to the therapist. Instead, they usually complain of suffering with symptoms such as inhibitions, obsessions and compulsions, phobias, anxiety, depression, and unresolvable "relationship problems." The therapist also may discern their character problems, such as bullying, "wallflower" shyness, passive-aggressiveness, womanizing (the Don Juan), battleaxe-style criticism and hostility, dependency, and narcissism.

In addition to people's chief complaints and their discernible symptoms, we also need to be looking, during assessment, for deficits in:

1. Empathy: Do they not attune themselves to others' feelings? And does this deficiency impinge on their sense of ethics; that is, their integrity in relationships? (Damage to the superego can occur when there is a long-standing deficiency in empathy and closeness.)

2. Trust: How damaged is their trusting capacity?
3. Holding environment: Do they not view their immediate world as relatively reliable?
4. Integrated identity
5. Tolerance for emotional closeness in relationships
6. Stability in relationships
7. Human warmth

When we see disturbances in any of these areas, we should not just formulate about defense mechanisms, guilt, and conflict. We also need to look for defects and defenses involved in intrapsychic conflicts causing the clinical manifestations of object relations trouble: **Warm-ETHICS.**

Warmth. Warmth can be faked. But most people experience pleasure in making human contact. Pleasurable interactions, accompanied by smiling, are common, routine experiences. However, people with object relations disturbance may manifest a coldness or a lack of responsiveness to warm human contact. They seem to have difficulty mobilizing themselves toward warm connections, and may be suffering with a deficiency caused by perpetuation of what Mahler and her group (1975) call "low-keyedness." Because such people also may be using *isolation of affect* and rigid rules, they are often confused diagnostically with warm, neurotic obsessive-compulsives.

Cold people usually have endured an early disturbance in excitement due to relative unresponsiveness from their mothers or fathers. That history has caused them to become withdrawn, unenthusiastic, and apathetic. This fundamental developmental damage, which seems to have its origins during the rapprochement subphase (16–25 months of age), can continue or become exacerbated through adolescence and into adulthood.

Deficiency in warmth must be differentiated from *empathic inhibition* (Easser, 1974). *Inhibition*, or defensive relinquishing of an extant capacity for warmth and attunement (see below), occurs as a resolution of intrapsychic conflict—such as a shield against an expectation of disillusionment *transferred* from prior disappointing relationships.

Empathy. Empathy is a complex subject. Perhaps the best definition has been proffered by Buie (1981). He points out that one way empathy can develop involves our having had the same experience as others, where their report stimulates parallel affects in us. For example, a woman who is pregnant describes her feelings about pregnancy to a female therapist. The female therapist, who also has been pregnant, will immediately have certain knowledge of affective reactions based on her own experience. The downside of this type of empathic attunement is that it may become distorted by *projections* from the therapist. In other words, if the therapist has had a similar experience, the therapist may project onto people in treatment, and thereby misjudge the reality of their reactions. In other words, the therapist's having had a similar experience could actually interfere with the development of empathy.

If you have not had the same experience as the person you are treating, Buie is not pessimistic about the capacity for empathy to develop. He clarifies that "creative imagination" can be used by the therapist to conceptualize the experiences of people in treatment. A female therapist can thereby empathize with an impotent man's anxiety over sexual performance. Similarly, a male therapist can imagine what a pregnant woman may be feeling.

Buie also makes the important point that psychoanalysts and dynamic therapists are in a position to attune themselves to other human beings through knowledge of the psychodynamics of that other human being. In other words, as a man you are treating is getting angry at you, you think to yourself, "This guy always gets angry when he is depressed about something." General knowledge of his dynamics would lead you to interpret to him that although he is expressing anger at you, your awareness of what has been going on in his life makes you feel that the *anger* is a defense, protecting him from exposing embarrassing feelings of depression and inadequacy.

Lastly, Buie gives credence to Freud's observation that there is a way people can intuitively pick up things from each other without conscious awareness. Buie calls this "resonance." For example, as someone is speaking with you, you find yourself getting nervous. As you review your own thoughts, you cannot find any particular conflict in yourself that is creating your nervousness. However, the person who is talking to you, you notice, seems flat, guarded, and bland. This could lead you to formulate that the person is using *isolation of affect* and possibly *suppression* as defenses, at the same time that you are picking up, through resonance, the affect that they are trying to keep from their own awareness.

Marcus (1980), in his seminal paper on countertransference, defines countertransference in a way that helps clinicians distinguish their own disruptive reactions from empathic reactions that facilitate therapy. Marcus notes a tendency, still common today, to use the term countertransference to refer to all reactions of the therapist to the person in treatment. In contrast, his three-part definition allows the therapist to determine if an intervention has been favorable or unfavorable for the treatment.

First, countertransference has its roots in the unconscious or preconscious (thoughts available through a shift of attention) of the therapist. Second, countertransference has specificity to the patient's *transference* or other material.[1] Third, to be called countertransference, the therapist's reaction also defensively interrupts or disrupts the therapeutic process.

Ms. C, a 28-year-old woman in treatment with a female therapist, related an incident from the prior evening where she became angry at her husband because he insisted on "popping" a Viagra before having intercourse. When Ms. C expressed anger at her husband, he stormed out of the room and drove to a male friend's house to smoke a joint.

The female therapist said to Ms. C, "You were pretty rough on him," thinking Ms. C would respond with insight into how she defensively *attacked her husband* to relieve her own anxieties about sex. The therapist felt "tuned in" in confronting Ms. C's defensive hostility.

However, Ms. C actually responded, "I'm rough on him?! How about me? Do you know he's been taking Viagra since we were on our honeymoon? He's only 33 years old! I don't think you get it; I don't think he loves me; I think he's trying to prove something. Why are you saying I'm rough on him, when I've been trying to be more assertive now for two years?"

Ms. C's expostulations indicated that the therapist's intervention—about Ms. C being "rough" on her husband—had been a countertransference reaction, where the therapist had momentarily *identified* with Ms. C's husband (what Racker [1953] termed a "complementary identification" with the patient's introjects of others).

From the standpoint of technique, since the countertransference reaction had disrupted the therapeutic process, I recommended that the therapist admit to Ms. C the momentary lapse in empathy but not go into any detail about its possible causes. In the next session, the therapist did so. Ms. C thanked the therapist, and then had further thoughts and reactions about the therapist's "imperfection," which reminded her of the way her father always blamed her, during adolescence, for any social problems she had with boys. These latter associations indicated that Ms. C had also *transferred* onto the therapist a considerable amount of anger that she had been harboring toward her father for his "insensitivity."[2]

Closeness, Stability, Identity. Closeness and stability in relationships both tend to hinge on the stability of identity (or self-image). Where there has been damage to the self-image in early childhood or in adolescence (Blos, 1962), closeness in adult relationships can cause self–object fusion anxiety. This anxiety is often relieved by the creation of *distance*, by moving away from the love object physically or emotionally, or by picking a fight (*hostility* as a defense). Akhtar (1992a) has delineated "tethers, orbits, and invisible fences" as different patterns of distancing found in different individuals. Weiss (1987) found that married men who "needed" another woman in their lives were living out patterns that defended against persistent anxieties over self–object fusion. Goldberger (1988) found the same dynamics in women who felt a compelling "need" for two male lovers in their lives simultaneously.

The use of Warm-ETHICS correlates with other areas of assessment of object relations. The interpersonalists have suggested through the years that there are essentially three levels of interpersonal functioning when it comes to relationships. The lowest level is "narcissistic" (actually, autistic). At this primitive level, people do not see other humans as separate at all, but misperceive human reactions in terms of their own fantasies and desires. These "narcissistic" people live in a sort of dream world, constantly making mistakes due to their poor reality testing and judgment. A woman suffering with such autistic functioning was portrayed in Helen Reddy's (1973) hit song, "Delta Dawn."[3]

A somewhat higher level of interpersonal functioning is described as "need-satisfying." People at this level (sometimes also called "narcissistic") have a generally callous attitude toward those with whom they form relationships. Such people use others for sex, money, or personal advancement, but seem to have very little interest in closeness and little concern about other persons' feelings or functioning.

Finally, the healthiest interpersonal functioning involves "mutual empathy." At this level, people attune to each other, particularly in regard to moods, desires, and sensitivity. They try to understand and help each other. One of these levels does not exclude others from operating to some extent. The healthier the human being is, the more mutual empathy is present.

Developmentally, Mahler and her group (1968, 1975) define four stages of the intrapsychic foundations of relationships. In the "autistic" phase (0 to 2 months of age), there is very little distinction made by the child in its perceptions and memories of experiences of the self with others ("objects"). The "symbiotic" phase (3 to 6 months of age) ushers in the "separation-individuation" phase (7 to 36 months), where a desire for enmeshment or fusion alternates with anxiety about fusion. When anxiety about merger of the self with the object image arises, defensive *distancing* maneuvers are instituted. When there is too much distance, lonely feelings of devastation arise in connection with being separate, and the child uses other defense mechanisms to reinstate closeness and/or fusion: *crying*, *whining*, and *clinging*.

The separation-individuation phase goes on from about 7 or 8 months of age until 3 or 4 years of age. Through four subphases of separation-individuation, the child hopefully develops fairly stable and reliable images of the self and of other people (self and object constancy). After age 3, average-expectable children can be separated for longer periods of time from their mothers without severe separation anxiety developing. Before age 3, it is not known exactly how much daily time the mother figure must spend in interaction with a child for the child to successfully achieve self and object constancy (McDevitt, 1976).[4] The most that can be said is that the risk of difficulty increases as the complexity of child-rearing arrangements involves more separations from important mother figures; parents should be watchful while the child is traversing the various subphases and make adjustments as they are able.

Parents also know, as Erikson (1950, 1968) and Blos (1962) describe, that conflicts about separateness, intactness, and identity persist and normally need to be re-resolved throughout adolescence, generally coming to some closure by the time of majority.

OBJECT RELATIONS AND CHARACTER DEFENSES IN PERSONALITY DISORDERS

In adults, some personality disturbances may be based on separation-individuation conflicts (Marcus, 1971; Hamilton, 1990). To understand these particular types of conflicts requires, first, understanding the unresolved separation-individuation dynamics from early childhood and their recapitulation in adolescence. Second, personality elements based on structural theory should be integrated: the conflicts involving drive wishes, affects, and defenses that contribute to personality disturbance coalesce with the separation-individuation problems (Pine, 1990).

Some personality disturbances involve guilt over separation, and *reunion* as a self–object fusion defense against that guilt. This pattern is seen in people who allow invasive parents to control them, even as adults, to relieve guilt over hurting the parents by appearing too "separate." In the movie *Best Friends* (Jewison, 1982), Burt Reynolds and Goldie Hawn depict this problem in a humorous way. In addition, some types of *emotional distancing* occur to defend against self–object fusion affects—where the distancing simultaneously punishes the person, to relieve guilt. All of these features contribute to the compromise formations that result in pathological personality traits.

To illustrate, let's take a quick look at common personality problems.

First, there's the "wallflower," a person suffering with *social inhibition*. We usually think of wallflowers in terms of defense mechanisms like *avoidance* and *inhibition of speech*. But separation-individuation dynamics may also be causing her to be a "moon" (see below), utilizing a *distancing* defense to avoid closeness with other people.

There's the "bully" (Knight, 1942). Usually we think about him in terms of the aggressive drive and the defensive use of *projective identification*: the bully tries to stimulate fear in other people so that he will not feel frightened himself. But he may also be unconsciously craving attunement and convinced no one will ever feel it, so he stimulates fear, pain, and hopelessness in others; this relieves his own sense of self-dissolution and depressing separateness by making him feel that the other person has emotions identical to his (intimidation, rage, and fear).

The "Casper Milquetoast" is the shivering, retiring man, afraid of his own shadow, using the defense mechanisms of *passivity* and *asceticism* (withdrawal) to guard against guilt over aggression. However, he also may be *avoiding* any object contact that causes self–object fusion anxiety.

The "Don Juan" (Ferenczi, 1922; Alexander, 1930) is the womanizer. We usually conceptualize him using theory about a sexual drive and maybe some deficits in the superego. But he also may be a "comet" (see below), who enjoys the rush of intense, *sexualized* closeness but then must escape to defend against self–object fusion depressive affect (feeling of nothingness) (Wolf, 1994).

The "gold digger"[5] (Bergmann, 1995) is the woman who is after money. We believe she is narcissistic, especially when it comes to the oral drive (the wish for money). She uses sexuality to that end (*sexualization* as a defense) and feels little guilt due to superego *lacunae*. To complicate matters, she may also *avoid* warmth and closeness by defensively (callously) focusing on oral gratification (*oral libidinal regression*). To guard against identity diffusion anxiety, she uses quid pro quo sexuality to *avoid* closeness.[6]

The "battleaxe"—the aggressive, hostile woman—usually leads us to theorize about drives, especially the discharge of aggression. But she may also be defending against severe separation anxiety. The *hostility* prevents her from getting close, yet she keeps people tethered to her through verbally hostile control. Her husband will stay distant, maybe out fishing or drinking with the boys, before he goes home to "the cold shoulder and the hot lip," but she remains married to him.

The "nerd," the social misfit, suffers with the defense of *inhibition* of adaptation, conflicts over expressing aggression, and deficient social capacities (as ego functions). The nerd may not be able to abstract, understand situations, or function socially with other people. But his asocial behavior can also be defending against his self-image dissolving, through dangerous conformity into some group.

"Practical jokers" have been described by Arlow (1971) as having a "character perversion." Most often males, they suffer with massive castration anxiety but defensively create fear by shocking other people. Pulling the practical joke scares others and expresses hostile aggression toward them. However, the joker, by inducing anxiety about the safety of the environment (Winnicott, 1969), can also be creating in others (*projective identification* or *gaslighting*) the instability he feels in his own sense of well-being (Sandler, 1990).

In addition, there's the "wild man" or "wild woman," who has a "wild hair." We usually think of these people as possessing deficits in impulse control, judgment, and executive function. But they can also be "comets" (see below) who crave the intensity of the moment at the same time they defensively maintain their sense of freedom. The opera *Carmen* concerns a wild woman with a freedom fetish (Blackman, 2000; see appendix 5).

The various manuals of the American Psychiatric Association purportedly describe different personality disturbances without referring to any theory of causation. Analytic theories of causation, however, can be used to explain them:

- Dependent personality involves orality and *libidinal regression.*
- The passive-aggressive personality is based on the respective defense mechanisms.
- Borderline personality and narcissistic personality disturbances, which cause problems in relationships, involve difficulties with *distance* and closeness based on disturbed self and object differentiation.
- The schizoid personality diagnosis is based on the defense mechanism of *distancing* from close relationships (*asceticism*).
- Avoidant personalities stay away from situations of emotional turmoil (conflict) as a defense.
- And the histrionic personality uses emotionality defensively.

In examining causation of these personality disturbances, conflict theorists point toward conflicts over guilt, orality, anality, sexuality, and aggression, all managed by defenses. Object relations theorists emphasize the various defenses and wishes regarding closeness, distance, stability, and warmth.

Akhtar (1992a) has furnished us with the useful concept of "optimal distance." In order to understand the clinical utility of this concept, object relations theory points to suboptimal, defensive distancing in certain types of adult psychopathology. Conflicts over closeness are not pathological for 2-year-olds during rapprochement; they are struggling to form distinct, stable self and object images. Nor is unease with closeness considered pathological for 13-year-olds, during their adolescent recrudescence of rapprochement; they are struggling to establish their identity. But some adults, instead of finding gratification in human closeness and wanting to repeat it based on the pleasure principle (Schur, 1966), experience severe anxiety in relation to closeness and then institute a series of distancing defenses.

To fully understand object relations difficulties, C. Brenner's (1982b) reformulation of the concept of compromise-formation is also necessary. Brenner explicates Waelder's (1936) idea that "multiple function" is present in every psychic act and in every psychic symptom: multiple causation. That is, several memories, lots of superego conflict and lots of drive conflict, as well as several defenses, are responsible for producing any particular symptom or thought.

To integrate object relations theory and defense theory, consider the following: *In adult psychopathology, compromise formations can simultaneously involve closeness and optimal distance in a variety of different ways that are conflicting with each other.* In other words, some people set up distant relationships, but yearn for closeness. Elements of both wish and defense also enter into the way they set up those relationships. So the concepts of defense and of compromise formation are critical to the understanding of object relations problems.

Some people in therapy complain that they're depressed and lonely. A "supportive" therapist (see chapter 7) says, "Why don't you engage in some activities and meet some people?" They reply, "I can't do that. I'm too nervous that somebody would get to know me." The therapist counters, "Well, if people don't get to know you, then you're going to be alone." They agree, melancholically, "Yeah. That's why I'm depressed."

If people request antidepressant medication, and you respond by prescribing it, you (symbolically) give them a bit of closeness: they put your medicine in their bodies. At the same time, they may then want to see you three weeks later—and not get too close. Such people experience some closeness, symbolically, when they put your medicine in their mouth, and keep distance by not seeing you too frequently. That's a common compromise-formation in those who complain of depression but who also harbor persistent conflicts about separation-individuation in adulthood.

Other pathological compromise-formations that can persist into adulthood (Kramer, 1979) include "tethers," "orbits," "invisible fences" (Akhtar, 1992a), "moons," "comets," and "Runaway Bunnies" (Blackman, 2001).

People who construct psychic tethers, in relation to a therapist or others, defensively keep distance but don't relinquish an emotional tie. Kramer (1992) describes a latency-age boy she treated who, before each of her vacations, would make a chain. He told her, "I'm going to use this chain magically. When I pull on it, you will hear me and you will magically come running to my side when I pull. But if I don't pull it, I won't need you."

Some of the adults Akhtar treated used the word "tether" in explaining their relationships to certain other people (1992a). If such adults get too emotionally close to another human being, they react as though their self-image were going to dissolve. They then defensively create distance by *avoiding* the person, by picking arguments, or by not being available emotionally. "Gone fishin'" captures one variant of the behavior that avoids but holds on by a tether.

Second, Akhtar describes "invisible fences" that people may erect to establish or maintain *defensive distance*. You may notice as you're just beginning to get some detailed, intimate information, some people suddenly say something like, "I can't get into that; I have a wall up and you're never going to get through it."

> Once, after I had commented to a woman I was treating that I could see that something had upset her, she returned for her next session angry and said, "I feel like I'm never going to talk to you again. I'm a *porcupine* and I'm taking my porcupine stance and if you get close to me, I will prick you."

In spite of the fairly obvious phallic symbolism in her associations (the painful "prick"), in this particular case, her use of pseudophallic imagery was a way of instituting *defensive distance*. She was anxious about the closeness she had experienced when she felt I had some empathic attunement to her. There is another lesson in this: *sexualization* can be used as a defense against anxiety resulting from problems with self and object constancy.

Third, Akhtar references Volkan's term, "orbits," in his explanation that optimal distance ". . . is best viewed as a psychic position that permits intimacy without loss of autonomy and separateness without painful aloneness" (Akhtar, 1992a, p. 30). The "satellite state" (Volkan & Corney, 1968), on which Akhtar relies, was described as "captive bodies orbiting within a gravitational field of an intense though ambivalent dependency. Their distancing attempts, that is, travels, jogging, assertiveness, reassured them against the dread of [self–object] fusion, while their imaginary tethers provided them 'distant contact' (Mahler, Pine, & Bergman, 1975, p. 67) with the analyst, who remained available . . . " (Akhtar, 1992, p. 39). In other words, some people form satellite-style relationships both to defend against closeness with the loved object and to hold onto the object.

Escoll (1992) reports a fantasy (actually a compromise formation) from the therapy of a different child, about orbits: being in a spaceship to establish distance from earth and home base, yet maintaining connection by staying in orbit. Adults with such compromise formations tend to want a "home base" somewhere, very much like in latency-age games where the idea is to attack the opponent and then go "home." In the child's game, "Sorry," a player can move "Home" after knocking another player back to "Start." If you're lucky in "Sorry," you'll slide backward, and quickly wind up "Home" before your opponents (siblings?). In baseball, the object is to get away from home but then to return to home as quickly as possible (a "home run" is fastest) to obtain a score.

Contamination of adult secondary process thinking by defenses designed to reduce separation anxiety (and fear of loss of the object's image) occurred in a man I treated who, before any business trip, had to leave his office and drive by his house to make sure the house had not burned down. When he would return, the first thing he did was drive home to see the house again. He wished to see the house in order to concretely recreate its image in his mind. These patterns relieved his anxiety about object inconstancy (Blum, 1981).

Technically, Kramer and Akhtar caution the therapist to be concerned about people who at the start of therapy say they want to be "finished" in 2 years, or even in 6 sessions. Setting a limit often represents the establishment of an escape route—a defense against anxiety about how much closeness they can tolerate.

Some patients refuse to recline on the couch (for analysis) as a defense against anxiety over losing the image of the therapist, due to their problems with object constancy. Reclining on the couch tends to engender fantasies about the analyst. For these analysands, not seeing the analyst creates a fantasy that the analyst is "really not there" emotionally. Some patients with borderline personality organization can actually regress severely—into transient psychotic states—using the couch. It's usually better to have them sit up so that they can see the therapist and thereby maintain a more integrated image of the therapist and of themselves.[7]

I describe "moons" and "comets" in chapter 3 (defense #46). Moons are people who maintain a relatively fixed emotional distance from another person. They orbit around that other person without getting too close and without falling out of orbit. When there is a threat of either losing the mother planet (separation anxiety) or getting too close to the mother planet (self–object fusion or annihilation anxiety), they will institute a variety of defensive operations, including disappearing (e.g., to the tool shed) or becoming obsessed with web-browsing on their computers.

Comets warm up for a while and can enjoy emotionally close relationships. However, after some period of time, they will also develop self–object fusion anxiety (or depressive affect, as in marriages where one spouse feels he or she has lost elements of personal identity) and then institute defenses (such as taking a solo vacation or losing interest in sexual activity).

"Runaway Bunny" is a term I have taken from Margaret Wise Brown's (1942) remarkably popular children's book. A recent review describes the book:

> *The Runaway Bunny* begins with a young bunny who decides to run away: "If you run away," said his mother, "I will run after you. For you are my little bunny." And so begins a delightful, imaginary game of chase. No matter how many forms the little bunny takes—a fish in a stream, a crocus in a hidden garden, a rock on a mountain—his steadfast, adoring, protective mother finds a way of retrieving him. . . . (Everything Preschool, 2002)

In adulthood, people who function like the runaway bunny are, unfortunately, quite disturbed. They are constantly running away emotionally from people who care about them who, in turn, chase the runaway bunny and catch him (or her). The running away is a defense against self–object fusion anxiety, and the reunion is a defense against separation anxiety (an unpleasurable sensation plus the thought that the object image will disintegrate). The pattern of running away and being received home again is very common in certain alcoholics and philanderers.

To sum up, we can conceptualize character problems as constellations of defenses that guard against both structural and separation-individuation conflicts (Dorpat, 1976). Both sets of conflicts seem to contribute to the compromise formations that make up character pathology.

DEFENSES AND SYMPTOM COMPLEXES

As far as symptom complexes are concerned, diagnosis also rests largely on assessment of the primary modes of defense the individual is using. Table 4.1 and the discussion that follows describe typical defense constellations found in different syndromes.

In examining these symptomatic clusters of defenses, first keep in mind that literally any defense constellations may be present throughout the full range of people, from relatively normal to psychotic. As we have seen, the determination of psychotic versus nonpsychotic functioning rests largely on an assessment of the person's autonomous ego functions, ego strengths, and object relations development. That said, certain constellations of defenses are typically found in specific syndromes. The particular grouping of defenses actually plays a significant role in defining psychological problems (psychopathology).

To begin with, "neurotic" symptoms are essentially caused by unconscious defenses guarding against affects generated by mental conflicts.

Anxiety Syndromes ("Hysteria" Variations)

In panic/phobic disorders, we find *symbolization, condensation, displacement, projection, masochistic provocation, one affect versus another, transference,* and *avoidance.*

> Some years ago, I participated, along with several colleagues, in a phobia symposium for the general public. As an introduction to my psychoanalytic presentation, Dr. P, the general psychiatrist-moderator, presented his own case of Donna, a young married woman with a phobia of telephones. She would not touch one, nor would she enter a

TABLE 4.1. Defense Constellations

DEFENSE CONSTELLATIONS CHARACTERISTIC OF NEUROSIS (DSM III-R: 301.8)
General—Found in all Neuroses

19. displacement	27. libidinal regression
20. symbolization	32. identification with a fantasy
21. condensation	79. transference
25. repression	

Additional Specific Defense Constellations
Obsessional Type (*ICD 9 CM* 300.3, *DSM-IV* 300.4)

11. reaction-formation, perfectionism, hyperpunctuality	17. compartmentalization
	42. rationalization
12. undoing and rituals	43. rumination
13. isolation	45. intellectualization
14. externalization	

Depressive Type (*ICD 9 CM* 300.4, *DSM-IV* 311.0)

15. turning on the self	62. passivity
37. identification with the lost object	53. disidentification
38. identification with the introject	11. reaction-formation

Masochistic Type (*ICD 9 CM* 302.8)

35. identification with the aggressor	62. passivity
36. identification with the victim	64. passive to active
39. seduction of the aggressor	95. identification with injured object
41. provocation	100. frankness
	83. intimidation of others

Anxiety (Hysterical) Type (*ICD 9 CM* 300.1)
Histrionic Subtype (*DSM-IV* 301.5)

46. socialization	67. dramatization
22. "illusion" formation	68. impulsivity
39. seduction of the aggressor	76. exaggeration
64. passive to active	77. generalization
32. identification with own fantasy	92. hyperaestheticism
47. instinctualization: especially erotization	93. glibness

Inhibited Subtype (*DSM-IV* 300.11)

59. reticence	48. inhibition of erotized ego function: conversion
62. passivity	49. idealization
65. somatization	56. ipsisexual object choice
73. pathological altruism	91. vagueness

Phobic Subtype (*ICD 9 CM* 300.2, *DSM-IV* 300.21)

1. projection	62. passivity
61. avoidance	57. one affect versus another ("panic")
44. counterphobic behavior	

(Continued)

TABLE 4.1. Continued

DEFENSE CONSTELLATIONS CHARACTERISTIC OF BORDERLINE
(All Defenses Applicable to Neurosis, Plus)

General for Most Borderlines (*DSM-IV* 301.83)

28. ego regression	30. topographic regression

Additional Specific Defense Constellations

Paranoid Type (*DSM-IV* 301.0)

2. introjection	65. somatization
1. projection	14. externalization
3. projective identification	16. negativism
4. projective blaming	18. hostile aggression
5. denial in deed	74. gaslighting
8. splitting	76. exaggeration
	97. hypervigilance

Narcissistic Type (*DSM-IV* 301.81)

34. identification with ideal image or object	63. grandiosity/omnipotence
49. idealization	60. garrulousness
50. devaluation	67. dramatization
52. concretization	46. socialization
53. disidentification	89. inauthenticity
	100. frankness

Schizoid Type (*DSM-IV* 301.2)

55. asceticism	61. avoidance
59. reticence	62. passivity
40. sublimation (without people)	72. pseudoindependence

Impulse-Ridden Type (*DSM-IV* 312.39)

57. one affect versus another	70. clinging
64. passive to active	71. whining
68. impulsivity	35. identification with the aggressor
69. substance abuse	

Antisocial (Psychopathic) Type (*DSM-IV* 301.7)

5. projective blaming	42. rationalization
10. deanimation	46. socialization
16. negativism	33. identification with parents' conscious or
23. prevarication	unconscious fantasies
35. identification with aggressor	76. exaggeration

DEFENSE CONSTELLATIONS CHARACTERISTIC OF PSYCHOSIS (*DSM-IV* 298.9)
(All the Above, Plus)

6. denial: per se, in word, deed, fantasy	55. asceticism
7. dedifferentiation	58. hyperabstraction
8. splitting	78. reconstruction of reality
9. animism	80. dissociation
10. deanimation	94. physical violence
3. hallucination	

---

room where a phone was present. He explained that he saw her for a session once every two weeks, and prescribed desensitization exercises to help her get closer to the phone and an antidepressant medication. These are still common techniques used to treat phobias.

After a year of these non-dynamic treatments, Donna described an "amazing" epiphany. She reported that she had been thinking about phones and about her troubled marriage. She remembered that just before she developed the phone phobia, an old boyfriend of hers had called to invite her out. She had put him off and he was to call back. She had even considered calling him back but never did.

Donna confided to Dr. P that she thought she had been avoiding the phone because the urge to see the old boyfriend was "too tempting" (i.e., it was too guilt-inducing, too appealing to her wishes and so too anxiety-laden). Her phobia had disappeared after she realized this. Donna had already stopped her antidepressant and now discontinued her sessions with Dr. P, apparently cured of the phobia.

An important differential point in diagnosis and treatment is that the neurotic defense of *oral regression* is also a compromise formation (see chapter 1). That is, although *oral regression* avoids anxiety generated by conflict among sexual, hostile and guilty wishes, elements of those conflicts are simultaneously expressed by the regressive symbolism. Patients may also choose reality situations for gratification that unconsciously provoke punishment to alleviate guilt.

Donna's phone phobia, for example, *symbolically avoided* her sexual wishes toward the boyfriend, thereby shielding her from her guilt. She simultaneously obtained less guilt-ridden oral gratification from her male psychiatrist, through his listening attentively and "giving" her medicine to put in her mouth. However, the therapy relationship not only reinforced her regressive (oral) defense, but Dr. P's attentiveness and medication also provided oral and symbolically sexual gratification. Donna no doubt felt guilty about those symbolic gratifications with Dr. P. In addition, her guilt was probably magnified as she got closer to the phone through desensitization exercises, since *symbolically* she came closer to a sexual rendezvous with her old boyfriend that would angrily cuckold her husband.

As her conflicts escalated (guilt over sexual wishes toward the boyfriend, hostile-aggressive wishes toward her husband, and guilt over symbolic gratifications from Dr. P), her increased anxiety seems to have stimulated her integrative function and her observing ego. She was insightful enough to make her own interpretation. Moreover, that insight, being itself a compromise formation (C. Brenner, 1982a), also defensively caused her to *avoid* returning for treatment. Dr. P, in a *displaced, symbolic* way, had been gratifying her wish for an extramarital sexual contact that would hurt her husband, and thus inflaming her guilt. She, therefore, now became phobic of Dr. P, and *avoided* him.

Conversion symptoms can be added to the anxiety syndrome, some-times along with ingratiating/seductive attitudes ("histrionic"—actually *seduction of the aggressor*).

> Mrs. GN, a 37-year-old woman married to a family practitioner, pre-sented complaints of airplane phobia, panic attacks near airports, and an inability to enjoy sexual intercourse. She did not become sexually excited.
> Part of the analysis of her sexual dysfunction (a conversion symp-tom) revealed that it was a result of conflict: not responding prevented her from becoming aware of anger toward her husband for being "more attentive to his patients than to me and the children." He had not even been present at the birth of their children because he refused to switch call with colleagues. Simultaneously, Mrs. GN's sexual inhibition ex-pressed her hostile rejection of him, and punished her for such hostility (no pleasure in sex). That conflict was kept unconscious through *re-pression* of her actual thoughts abetted by *identification with the aggres-sor* (husband).

Depressions

Depression can be viewed as involving depressive affect along with typical constellations of defenses. What distinguishes various levels of depressive illness is the degree of deficiency in ego functions (more severe = "psy-chotic depression" or "major depression with psychotic symptoms"), the degree of limitation of ego strength (depressive affect eroding affect toler-ance, leading to meltdown of memory and sleep-wake cycle, e.g.), and the degree of damage to object relations (depressive affect associated with withdrawal from important loved people ["objects"]).

Depressive affect can be generated by a variety of situations. Again, recall that depressive affect is composed of an unpleasurable sensation plus a thought that something terrible has already happened that cannot be fixed. Perhaps the most common dynamics contributing to the pessimistic beliefs characteristic of depressive affect are (1) unresolved grief due to *minimization* and *suppression* and (2) *turning on the self of anger and criti-cism* as defensive against guilt over rage (Blatt, 1992).

In unresolved grief, the person *suppresses* the thoughts of a lost loved one and/or *isolates* the unpleasurable sensations. *Identification with the lost object* causes the person to begin acting something like the lost object (using phrases, telling stories, becoming critical, embracing a cause, or engaging in other special behavior). If there had been any anger toward the lost person, guilt may occur, causing that anger to be *turned on the self.* This also results in depressive affect.

Cory, a 30-year-old depressed man, came from a highly disturbed family where he had been physically abused. Nevertheless, he had had a warm relationship with an older brother, Todd, who protected him. Todd had even "loaned" him an old girlfriend to initiate Cory into sexual activity.

When Cory was about 22, Todd was killed in a motorcycle accident. Cory related to me with some shame that he had had sexual intercourse with his brother's widow after the funeral. When I pointed out to Cory that this behavior made him something like his brother, and magically kept his brother "alive" (interpretation of *identification with the lost object* as a defense against grief), Cory began sobbing uncontrollably. After a few minutes, he explained that he had "shut off all feelings" after his brother had died (*suppression* and *isolation of affect*) and that he had "never grieved" over Todd. He added that his sister-in-law no doubt represented some aspect of Todd and that he preserved his tie to Todd by the sex with her (*sexualization* as a defense against the depressive affect associated with Todd's loss).

Even though his sister-in-law had been interested and cooperated with the sexual activity, Cory felt considerable guilt over the sex with her. We figured out that sex with Todd's widow represented *displaced* anger Cory felt at Todd for dying, leaving him alone. Part of Cory's guilt resulted from that anger, which he felt "Todd didn't deserve," and the guilt caused Cory's anger to be *turned on the self,* resulting in depression as well.

Another common cause of depressive thought content is the failure to meet goals. The failure may occur because the goals are unrealistic or because the person's defenses prevent reaching a realistic goal. In either case, there is disappointment that accompanies the thought of irreparability.

Ryan, a bright, 18-year-old college student had always "had it easy" in high school. But he began attending a competitive college, where the work was not easy, even for him. His *grandiose* attitude that he could get good grades without studying was punctured. He now began to feel depressed, which led him to begin drinking with buddies and lying to seduce young women. When I pointed out that the alcohol abuse and cad behavior seemed to be reinforcing his feeling that he could get away with anything (confrontation of *alcohol, sexual activity,* and *grandiosity* as defenses), Ryan became sad and said that he hated to think of his father's death when he was 16; in fact, he felt his father would be ashamed of him, now, a failure. He knew his father would have expected more of him (*identification* with father's ideals creating the boy's ideals).

Ryan's goal of graduating from college, which appeared realistically commensurate with his intellectual abilities, had been impeded by his defenses of *grandiosity, sexual activity,* and *alcohol abuse.* His resultant failure to meet his ideals (based on *identifications* with his father) caused him to feel depressed.

Borderline Personality

People with borderline personality often present with complaints that involve defenses as described in the "neurotic" examples above. The diagnosis of borderline personality, however, besides being based on weakness in ego strengths (especially in impulse control, affect tolerance, and containment of primary process fantasy), often includes the finding of certain prototypical defenses. Note that the same defenses can also be used by psychotic individuals. In psychotics, by definition, ego functions and object relations are more damaged.

The defenses characteristic of borderline personality organization include: *grandiosity, devaluation* (of others), *hostility* (to create distance), *primitive idealizations, massive denial, projection, projective identification,* and *splitting* (Kernberg, 1975).

> John,[8] a 40-year-old homosexual attorney,[9] was depressed about a recent breakup with his partner of a few months. He therefore "walked the streets" in a bad area of town, bought ecstasy, and picked up a homeless man. John proceeded to engage in mutual, unprotected anal intercourse with this man, after first doing ecstasy with him and drinking. When they were done with the sex, the man beat John up and stole his wallet and car keys. John had to walk several miles to his home. He didn't call the police because of the potential for humiliation professionally and personally.
>
> In session the following day, John referred to the homeless man as a "worthless piece of shit." John initially seemed oblivious to his own problematic behaviors of drug abuse, unprotected intercourse, and getting beaten up.
>
> The understanding of this incident required many sessions. What became clear was that John had *denied* the obvious reality dangers of contracting AIDS and being killed. He was *grandiose* to buy ecstasy on the street and not think he'd get caught and lose his license to practice law. He *devalued* the homeless man by seeing him as worthless. By "buying" the man with ecstasy, John simultaneously could see the man as "needy" instead of John (*projection, devaluation*).
>
> It turned out, on further exploration, that John had also induced some of the man's hunger by flaunting a $50 bill during their initial meeting (*projective identification*). I later learned that another apparent reason the homeless man beat John up was that John had spanked him, without his permission, during anal sex. We could then see that John discharged *hostility* as a defense against various other affects, in-

cluding depression over losing his partner, separation-depressive affect (loss of self associated with losing the partner–object), and self–object fusion anxiety with the homeless man. Further, John *masochistically provoked punishment* to relieve guilt.

John's borderline personality organization included narcissistic, impulsive, sadomasochistic, self-destructive, and paranoid elements. However, his intact observing ego, integrative functioning, as well as some capacity for mutual empathy with me, made it possible to interpret the above defenses and compromise formations, which eventually led to a cessation of his self-destructive behavior.

Psychosis

Although psychotic people are usually understood in terms of defects in ego functions (especially integration, abstraction, relationship to reality, and reality testing—see appendix 1) and deficiencies in object relations (damaged capacities for Warm-ETHICS caused by tendencies toward self–object fusion), certain prototypical defenses can also be delineated.

In the following example, the person in treatment demonstrated the use of *ego regression, formal regression, reconstruction of reality, dedifferentiation, deanimation,* and *dissociation.*

> Tim, a 29-year-old graduate student, had still not finished his Ph.D. in English literature and felt that "depression" was interfering. He had been a graduate student for about 8 years and was supported by his mother, a successful accountant. He had not had any relationships with anyone since finishing his coursework 5 years previously. During college, he had had sex once or twice at fraternity parties but had never had a girlfriend. His comments about these problems included the notion that "women are all just after money" (*deanimation*). In other words, he tended to see the problem as "women," and not as his awkwardness and inhibition (some *reconstruction of a painful reality*).
>
> He slept a lot (*topographic regression*). At other times, he listened to classical music in his one-room apartment. He spent hours imagining scenes where he was in the television (*dedifferentiation*), play-acting a part (*dissociation*)—such as conducting the New York Philharmonic while photographing Phyllis Schlafly being raped by Democrats and a variety of animals (*ego regression* in containing primary process thinking). When he stopped these imaginary journeys, he found it hard to "come back to the real world."

Don't forget that any of the syndromes defined by defenses in the neurotic and borderline categories may also coexist with psychosis. This complication makes diagnosis in the mental health disciplines more difficult than in any other health field. And then there's the matter of attempting to alter the pathological patterns of defense, once you spot them.

Treatment based on psychoanalytic principles generally involves two goals: (1) relief of the presenting symptoms and (2) strengthening of other mental functions: ego functions, ego strengths, and object relations. There are essentially two broad areas of technique that can be used to accomplish those aims: interpretive and supportive. The balance between supportive versus interpretive interventions depends on the diagnosis of the person in treatment and on the state of mind of that person during any given session. The following chapters address the problems involved in selecting the proper treatment and then successfully utilizing both interpretive and supportive techniques.

5

Interpretive Techniques

Psychoanalytic treatments (Compton, 1975; Gray, 1994; Blackman, 1994; Dorpat, 2000) require that you first decipher how people keep themselves from experiencing emotions. Secondly, you bring to their attention their maladaptive defenses. In other words, dynamic psychotherapy and psychoanalysis are treatments where *what the therapist says,* and *when,* are the components of technique. Analytic therapists often refer to the different kinds of things they say to people during treatment as "interventions."

ANALYTIC ("INTERPRETIVE") INTERVENTIONS

Instructions and Establishment of the Treatment Alliance

Instructions can be given in the second session, or whenever you have completed the initial evaluation and decided to go ahead with treatment. Some people beginning treatment may not know what to do. For them, especially in once-a-week psychotherapy, some description of the process may be facilitative. Typical instructions might include telling people to talk about, as best as possible, their thoughts and feelings regarding the chief complaint. They also can recount all their thoughts and feelings about important relationships in their lives, past and present. They should bring in any dreams and daydreams they can recall. Importantly, they should certainly report positive and negative reactions to what the therapist has said, and about treatment. Fantasies about the therapist may be useful, in addition to any stray thoughts they may have while sitting in your office.

Some people are self-starters and begin associating and relating to you immediately. Often they don't need any instructions. In treatments where the therapist sees people more frequently, such as 3 to 5 times a week (as in psychoanalysis), instructions can be a bit less inclusive, since resistances become an issue more quickly and free association, as a goal, allows the analyst to examine the analysand's contiguity of thought as well as the thought content.

The notion of an alliance between you and the people you treat comprises two sets of concepts. Instructions about the "frame" need to be given, usually in the second session, and surround the following aspects of the therapeutic relationship:

The working alliance (Greenson, 1965). Persons in treatment must

- come to the sessions you set up for them;
- pay the agreed-upon fee in the manner you request;
- talk; and
- acknowledge that they are seeing you for specific problems, and that your role is to tell them things that hopefully will help them understand themselves better.

The therapeutic alliance (Stone, 1961; Zetzel, 1956). Persons in treatment must

- develop, through interactions with you, mutual empathy and
- respond favorably to initial defense interpretations relating to resistance.

If any of the above are breached, attention should be paid to understanding the breach—and its defensive meanings—*before* entering into an understanding of the dynamics of the person's pathology.

Exploration

You ask people questions, hoping to find defenses to interpret. For example, you might say something like, "You said your wife walked out of the house and went to her sister's. What had happened between the two of you before she walked out?" Although such an intervention ignores the person's defenses of *vagueness* and *suppression,* you are looking for more noxious defenses, such as *hostility, provocation of punishment,* and *gaslighting.*

Kanzer (1953) recommends the therapist ask questions, at times, to "reconstruct the present" life of people in treatment, especially if they are regressed. Dorpat (2000), on the other hand, points out that too much exploration can make the therapist into a sort of Grand Inquisitor, setting up unconscious sadomasochistic dynamics—where people in therapy feel they must comply by answering questions, or else. Gray (1994) suggests that too much exploration bypasses people's resistances, such as *vagueness, suppression, passivity,* and *reticence,* which might be useful to confront and understand in early sessions.

Exploration is a useful technique, but watch out for getting provoked into asking too many questions, and certainly try to monitor the reactions of the person you are treating—not only to your questions, but also to being asked to begin with. The old idea of "expressive-emotive" or "exploratory" psychotherapy turns out to be a bit problematic.

Confrontation

You see people you are treating using an unconscious defense and bring it to their conscious attention. For example, you might say to a person who's leaving out a lot of details, "You seem to be experiencing some block in relating what you're thinking and feeling today." By definition, when you confront people in treatment, you don't try to explain *why* they are using certain defenses.

Clarification

You summarize a pattern of defense, as in this example of clarifying the defense of *minimization:* "So you convince yourself 'it's no big deal' with your husband, your mother, and your boss." Or, after a woman has described how she copes with 17 problems her children cause her, you comment on her *suppression*, "So you try very hard not to get angry with them, and to roll with the punches."

Sometimes a clarification can be used to avoid questioning people. A statement à la *Columbo*, the modest TV detective of the 1970s (Peter Falk), can be quite effective in eliciting information without invading the patient's autonomy. Something like, "I don't quite understand what's happening" or "This sounds very confusing" invites people to explain themselves, if they choose to.

Dynamic Interpretation

You explain to people what defenses they weren't seeing. Then you show them which affects were being warded off. If you have the data, you can also discuss what conflicts generated the affects. To interpret *reaction-formation* and *turning on the self* as defenses against guilt over destructive anger, you might comment, "You seem to hate yourself when you're angry at your son; so you then become '*too nice*,' which makes you feel better; however, the anger then gets *turned on yourself*, which causes you to feel depressed."

A further detail is that you have a choice of interpreting intrapsychic conflict and defense at a particular psychosexual level or between psychosexual levels. At the *same level*, some examples would be as follows:

Oral level. "You are quite embarrassed about your wish for me to help you. I think the embarrassment causes you to want to *avoid* sessions. You'd rather handle your problems on your own, in some ways."

Anal (separation-individuation) level. "When you stay *silent*, you stubbornly protect yourself from exposing embarrassing material; at the same time you wish that I could read your mind."

First genital/latency level. "It appears that you don't want to be a prick, which would make you feel guilty. Instead, you *bend over backward* to be nice, all the while hating it, and when you do speak up and "stick it out," you do it in such a way that you *induce others to punish you* (to relieve guilt)."

In some situations, interpretation of *libidinal regression* (or *progression*) may be preferable. That is, you interpret conflict *between psychosexual levels*:

> A 29-year-old obsessive-compulsive man gets into an argument with you about appointment times. You show him how his penchant for *power struggles* (*anal level*) keeps him from experiencing shame over depending on you (*oral level*) and simultaneously shields him from having to think about his problems with premature ejaculation (*mature genital level*).

Transference Interpretation

You figure out that people are using the same defenses with you that they used with their parents. Only with you, the defenses are entirely unnecessary.

> A man has explained that his father never seemed to pay attention to him; he therefore ignored his father. When he then mumbles while talking to you, you comment: "When you *don't speak clearly,* I think you are guarding against a fear that I am uninterested in what you say, as though I were your father. If I ask you to repeat something, this relieves your fear, but if I don't, you can be convinced that I am like him, and I don't care."

Genetic Interpretation

You show people how conflicts from their pasts are being displaced onto current-day situations:

"I think you allow your husband to visit his mother for over two hours during dinnertime every day because you are trying very hard not to be critical and controlling in the way that you hated in your mother when you were young" (*disidentification* from mother as a defense versus guilt).

or:

"You seem to avoid women because you are still protecting yourself from humiliation, as though you are still in high school and the girls will make fun of you for being overweight."

Dream Interpretation

You explain how the symbolism in a dream explains certain conflicts, involving defenses, that people had been unaware of. It's useful to refer to people's thoughts ("associations") about various symbolic elements in the dream—either in the same, previous, or following sessions—in order to do this accurately.

> Mr. NN, a 35-year-old married engineer, suffered with premature ejaculation. He dreamed: "I am in court being tried for something. Someone tells me the jury is stacked against me. I walk out. Then, I'm sitting alone, sucking on my own penis, and my penis is like three feet long."
>
> He associated to how he felt a little guilty that he had avoided dinner with his wife and two children the previous night because he wanted to watch a football game. He thought of never relying on anyone. I could then interpret the *symbolism* of his defensive *avoidance* of closeness with his wife: he would rather suck on himself, only he preferred to see himself as "macho" (three-foot penis) than admit that he was avoiding guilt over wishes to rely on his wife in an infantile way. He then remembered that he had asked her to make him some hot milk before he went to bed.

Another example of dream interpretation:

> Ms. L, an inhibited 29-year-old woman, dreamed: "There are men chasing me. I'm afraid and running. There's some sexual connotation. I run down this street that looks like the one I grew up on, and I run into Ms. Smith's house and lock the door. Then I wake up." Ms. L associated the men to "men in general" who "usually have one thing on their minds." Ms. Smith's house was "always so comfortable and welcoming."
>
> Ms. L also thought one of the men in the dream looked like Chuck, a really "cute guy" she had liked in high school; but she had never revealed her interest to him. I interpreted to Ms. L that the dream seemed to indicate that she defensively *hid* in the company of women,

whom she viewed as safe. Part of her fear seemed to be caused by her *projection* onto men of her own sexual desires ("cute" Chuck), which she viewed as dangerous; she therefore hid from men's sexuality and her own. She responded, "Right. I didn't want Chuck to know how I felt. I would've felt humiliated."

Resistance Interpretation

A 35-year-old man was 25 minutes late for his first appointment and said he had lost the sheet where he had jotted down directions to my office. I said in response: "So you almost didn't have to meet with me today." He laughed, remembered intense dislike of a former therapist, and theorized that perhaps he had been anticipating disliking me as well.

Resistance interpretation is also covered in the next section on detecting defenses. In short, you will often attempt to demonstrate to people that their lateness, missing sessions, difficulty talking, forgetting to pay the bill, or vagueness can symbolically indicate a reluctance, of which they have remained relatively unaware, to pursue treatment.

Linking Interpretation

You verbally link different ideas someone has brought up in a session, because you think there is a connection.

> For example, you suspect *passivity, turning passive to active,* and *masochistic provocation* are the defenses at work, so you say, "You began the session by complaining about how your husband tries to order you around as though you were one of his army recruits. Now you are asking me to tell you what to talk about. Perhaps there is some way you feel you must take orders from me, too?"

Reconstruction

This seldom-used analytic technique involves speculating about what probably happened to people earlier in their lives that led to their current troubles. This technique can be of some help in situations where someone cannot remember what happened, either recently or many years ago.

Reconstructions are bound to be at least somewhat inaccurate. For this reason, it's dangerous to become preoccupied with reconstructing a history of childhood sexual abuse when the person in treatment has no recollection of abuse. Overzealous reconstruction could cause a person in treatment to develop False Memory Syndrome (Blum, 1996) to please the therapist (a form of *gaslighting*, where the therapist gets people to believe they have a certain disorder).

In other words, if the therapist attempts to reconstruct a history of childhood sexual abuse without the person in treatment actually remembering it, the patient can *introject* the therapist's belief as a defense against anxiety or guilt over disagreeing with the therapist. The person can also use *passivity* (go along with the therapist's suggestion), *reaction-formation* (be too nice when actually feeling rebellious and angry), and *dedifferentiation* (give up aspects of identity to become more like the therapist, as a guard against separation anxiety). These are the same defenses that make people vulnerable to gurus and cults. It is much safer to deal with the effects of people's being sexually abused when they have a clear memory of it to begin with.

On the other hand, judicious reconstruction of other situations may stimulate useful memories of persistent conflicts and defensive operations, which can lead to therapeutic insight.

> Mr. CX, a 40-year-old man, would verbally attack his superiors at work, leading them to retaliate by ostracizing him and limiting his advancement. I made a linking interpretation of this self-destructive behavior with his previously-reported memories of his father punishing him, throughout his school-age years, by whipping him with a belt. Mr. CX first objected to the term "whipping," preferring "beating" or "spanking." Moreover, although he clearly remembered many whippings, he recalled no emotional reactions to them.
>
> I reconstructed that he probably had experienced anger at his father regarding the beatings, but had *suppressed* it and become stoic. At the same time, he seemed to be *displacing* his anger onto his current superiors, who *symbolically* represented father figures; he enacted a *transference* to them, where he criticized them and then was punished anew. Mr. CX responded by recalling other times his father had "manipulated" him as a young adult, when he remembered getting mad but tried to please his father anyway. We also figured out that he had *identified with the aggressor* and was "beating" his superiors as his father had beat him (another defense against feeling the anger at his father).

DETECTING DEFENSES

Essentially, there are two methods of determining the presence of defense: *deductive* and *inductive*.

Deductive Techniques

You can deduce defensive activity from certain objective observations. As in Table 5.1, when someone *stops* the flow of information, *shifts* material suddenly, *misses sessions*, makes *complaints* about things that may relate to

TABLE 5.1. Finding Defenses Deductively

CONFLICTS ——————>——————>——————>	—— conflicts about to erupt ——>	The ACTIVITY
LIBIDINAL DRIVE (oral, anal, genital) ⟺		STOPS talking
AGGRESSIVE DRIVE (destroy, revenge) ⟺		SHIFTS material
SUPEREGO (guilt, shame) ⟺	**INTRAPSYCHIC** ↑ CONFLICT → **AFFECT** sensation + thought (anxiety) (depression) (rage) ↑ → **DEFENSE** (keeps thoughts or sensations out of consciousness) ↑ →	MISSES sessions DISPLACES complaints Uses SYMBOLS YWTAQ (You want to ask a question)
REALITY ⟺		
OBJECT RELATIONS TROUBLE (clinging, distance) ⟺		
↕ *genetic interpretation*	↕ *confrontation* (defense only)	↕ *dynamic interpretation* (defense+affect)

120

you (Langs, 1973), speaks too *symbolically* ("Life is like a box of chocolates
. . ."), or otherwise relates in ways that make **Y**ou **W**ant **T**o **A**sk a **Q**uestion (YWTAQ), the person probably is using defenses. Table 5.1 illustrates how defenses guard against affects generated by intrapsychic conflict among wishes (drives), guilt (superego), reality, and relationships.

Gray (1994) stresses that interruptions in a person's flow of verbalizations indicate defenses that can be gently confronted as the person is talking. Moreover, the points of interruption often occur just as a person is almost aware of powerful feelings and urges.

Many people present prominent resistances to treatment at the beginning. Others wish to quit treatment prematurely. In either case, you may find yourself having to make an intervention regarding the defenses contributing to the resistance. The scenarios that follow demonstrate some of the typical themes of resistance and *the sort of idea* (not the exact words) you will want to get across to the person in treatment in response.

Concretization and intellectualization.

> Person in Treatment: discusses various theories regarding using medication for a "chemical imbalance"—to *not* reveal painful, embarrassing emotions or experiences. For example, "I read an article that says all depression is caused by a chemical imbalance. Some say it's a vitamin E deficiency."

> Response: "I think it's more comfortable for you to believe that—and to discuss these theories with me—than to think of what kind of conflicts you are experiencing in your (serious relationship/work)."

Normalization and generalization.

> Person in Treatment: makes assertions that the presenting problems are usual, not out of the ordinary, and "doesn't everyone?" For example, "All husbands feel this way, don't they?"

> Response: "It seems to me that you don't want to think you have a serious problem; must be quite embarrassing to you to have to consult me."

Rationalization and minimizing, sometimes causing pessimism.

> Person in Treatment: "It's no big deal. I'm used to the abuse. My husband had a bad childhood; he can't help it. There's really nothing I can do about it."

Response: "On the one hand you sound like his defense attorney —making lots of excuses for him; on the other hand, you seem to have adopted the notion that you are completely helpless, like a small child. In both cases, there's a way that you discuss this trouble in your marriage where you will not allow anything I say to be meaningful to you—apparently you already think I'm going to try to talk you into something you won't agree with."

Projection and externalization.
Person in Treatment: "You probably think I'm an idiot. . . ."

Response: "I think that's your conscience talking: you must be quite self-critical, and now you expect me to be just like your harsh, judgmental conscience."

Reticence and passivity, sometimes causing compliance.
Person in Treatment: "I have nothing to talk about [pause]. What would you like me to tell you?"

Response: "Why don't we start by thinking a bit about how you immediately put yourself in a position to please me."

Socialization and humor.
Person in Treatment: "I really like your office. My decorator would be envious!"

Response: "Thanks, you have good taste, too. I guess you'd like to think that the rest of what I have to offer you will demonstrate as much competence, but you're not yet sure."

Inductive Techniques

Aside from deducing the presence of unconscious defenses using objective criteria, four of your own reactions can tip you off that people in treatment with you have pathological defenses at work. It's best not to share these emotional responses with people. Rather, you want to reflect on your reactions to formulate the defenses that the patient may have at work. Obviously, using inductive reasoning requires objective confirmation of your theories, such as "floating" an interpretation of defense with people, to see if they agree.

The **4-point rule for inductive determination of the presence of a defense** can be remembered by the acronym **WEBS**—What, Empathy break, **B**ull, and **S**houlds.

WHAT?!" reactions. When you want to say to someone in treatment with you, "What?! Why on earth did you do that?"

> A therapist reported on her treatment of Ms. I, a 26-year-old, depressed, divorced woman. Ms. I had allowed an exboyfriend to visit after he had telephoned in an intoxicated state. Upon his arrival at her apartment, Ms. I lectured the exboyfriend about his drinking. He then physically threatened her as he walked out the door. The therapist actually said to Ms. I, "I'm perplexed! Why did you do that?" Ms. I responded that she didn't know, but it was OK, and no big deal, and it turned out all right.
>
> In supervision, I pointed out to the therapist that, in relation to the inebriated boyfriend, Ms. I seemed to be using *reaction-formation* (being overly nice to a boyfriend she hated), *provocation of punishment* (inviting him over and then lecturing him to get him to threaten her, to relieve her guilt over wanting to kill him), *minimization* (his danger-ousness was "no big deal"), and *projective identification* (inducing anger, criticism, and confusion in the therapist)—all of which had stimulated the therapists "What!?!" reaction.
>
> Technique-wise, I advised the therapist to reflect on the "What?!" reaction internally, to formulate about Ms. I's defenses, and then to interpret the defenses and conflicts. Asking Ms. I to explain her own unconscious affects and defenses only made Ms. I self-conscious, leading her to *minimize*.

Empathic nonattunement. This occurs when the person in your office is expressing a particular affect or attitude, but you find yourself not sensing it. Your apparent callousness might signal a countertransference interference. But another likely possibility is that your block in empathic attunement indicates the person is using a defense.

> Ms. H, a 35-year-old married woman, was crying profusely in session. She complained that the man with whom she had been having an extra-marital affair for 5 years refused to see her after she suggested cutting back on their sexual activity. Moreover, when she then confessed the affair to her husband, he berated her and then refused to talk to her for several hours.
>
> As Ms. H cried and complained about feeling victimized by both men, I felt a little irritated and critical. Since I noticed I was not expe-riencing the sadness about which Ms. H was complaining, I suspected that she was probably using defenses. I used my private—critical—reaction to formulate that she might be using *provocation of punish-ment* as a defense.
>
> I then pointed out to her that in both cases she seemed to manage so that first she tortured the man and then wound up punished by him. She responded, with a sudden laugh, "You mean I'm creating this whole

damn drama!?" She went on to associate to how she had felt tortured, at 19, by her first serious boyfriend dropping her after she accidentally became pregnant by him. She explained, bitterly, how he had not even shown up for, or contributed to, her abortion. Since then, she realized, she felt guilty that she was "taking it out on" (*displacement*) other men and staying in control herself (*identification with the aggressor*).

Bull. Someone is free associating in session about things that either seem meaningless or that have been analyzed at length already. You might comment, "You've spent a good bit of time telling me about the traffic on your trip last weekend; my impression is that you're trying to tell me everything, but that you're somehow avoiding getting to other, more upsetting things."

> A man I was treating studied his psychopathology on the Internet. He began one session by stating that he probably had Seasonal Affective Disorder, since he thought he got sad in the Fall. When I attempted to interpret this *intellectualization* as guarding against his guilt about cheating on his wife, he admitted, "I was just shooting the breeze. I thought that'd get a rise out of you!"

Renik (1978) points out that an overly strong focus on "non-threatening . . . material abets and fortifies the defensive operation of withdrawal of attention from disturbing . . . thoughts" (p. 590).

Shoulds. People in treatment tell you horrible situations they're in. They explain this using *isolation of affect* and perhaps *whining* a bit. You feel a desire to tell them what they *should* do. This is a time to interpret their defenses, particularly *passivity*.

> In the movie "Analyze This" (Ramis, 1998), Billy Crystal plays a therapist who, in an early scene, is treating a passive, sad, whining woman. He imagines jumping out of his chair and screaming at her something like, "Why don't you stop complaining and get a life!? Why don't you *do* something?!" However, all he does in the session is sigh and tell her he'll see her the following week.
>
> Actually, Crystal's imaginary response indicated a type of empathic reaction with the woman he was treating. What he did not do, though, was the necessary second step: utilizing his "should" reaction (about what his patient should do) to formulate her defenses of *passivity* and *isolation of affect*. His internal reaction, in a skilled therapist's hands, would have tipped him off that his patient should have been having the same reaction but was instead warding off the affects necessary to take effective action to solve her problems. The proper intervention should have been a confrontation of her *passivity, apathy,* and *isolation of affect*.

ORDER OF INTERPRETATION

Defense constellations should usually be pointed out, along with the affect being avoided, in the following order:

1. Defenses That Threaten the Person's Life

Defenses that can threaten the person's life include *turning anger against the self, inhibition* of judgment or self-preservation, severe *denial* and *rationalization* about a dangerous reality, and *masochistic provocation* of severe punishment.

> Mr. B, a 32-year-old accountant, was referred to me by his estranged wife's therapist due to threats to kill himself. He was certain his wife was "misguided" in her insistence on divorcing him after 11 years. They had two children, who he felt should bring her to her senses, but he was frustrated with the situation. He expressed no anger at her for insisting he move out of the house a couple of months earlier.
>
> Complicating the situation was his perception that his wife was kind to him. She never absolutely said they would never get back together. Mr. B told me that he frequently babysat for his own children in the home he and his wife had previously shared. He continued to pay the house mortgage and the rent on his own apartment, and complained about the expense of this arrangement.
>
> In fact, he related in his first session with me that he became suicidal after a recent babysitting experience. He had stayed in their old house for the weekend while his wife visited an out-of-town boyfriend with whom she claimed to have a platonic relationship.
>
> When she returned on Sunday evening, she made Mr. B go back to his apartment against his wishes. He said he had thought that her allowing him to babysit in their old house meant that she was holding out hope to him about the marriage; he became suicidal when, later Sunday night, she apparently unplugged her phone so he could not contact her to continue to persuade her of the "error of her ways."
>
> I interpreted to him that he was not allowing himself to understand what was a rather obvious reality: that his wife was probably done with him but was using him as a free babysitter. I felt he used *denial* (in words and in fantasy) to ward off his intense grief over the demise of the marriage and his anger at her.
>
> Mr. B's response was to begin crying. He blurted out, "Why does she have to do this? Why can't she grow up and do the right thing?!" Upon recognizing that he was, indeed, angry at her, he immediately made excuses for her, saying she was "under a lot of stress at work," for example.
>
> During the following sessions, I made further interpretations regarding his recurrent defenses of *denial, rationalization, turning on*

the self, and *reconstruction of reality.* As he understood these defenses, his acute suicidal plans abated, although he was still unhappy. He stayed in treatment for several months without a suicide attempt or a need for hospitalization.

When his company changed insurance carriers, Mr. B could no longer afford to see me, and he therefore changed therapists. Six years later, I received a request for information from a different therapist; he had not attempted suicide in the interim.

Another example of defenses that threaten a person's life was reported by Dr. H, a fourth-year psychiatry resident with training in dynamic psychiatry:

He was called to see Mr. CC, a 27-year-old single man, who presented to the Emergency Room with suicidal ideation. When at first hearing the history, Dr. H suspected Mr. CC would be a "routine admit" for major depression. But a dynamic approach turned out to be more therapeutic than Dr. H had envisioned.

Mr. CC had developed suicidal ideation after his girlfriend came home to their apartment at 4:00 a.m. drunk, admitting she had had sex with another man. He was trying to be "understanding" because one year prior, he had cheated on her with another woman. He now felt he had "no right" to be angry—signaling to the resident on call that Mr. CC felt guilty. The resident then interpreted that Mr. CC seemed "overly understanding" (*reaction-formation*) to relieve guilt, and simultaneously was *turning murderous rage onto himself.*

Mr. CC cried, described severe anger at his girlfriend, but stated he felt he had caused the problem. When she berated him for his affair one year previously, he admitted he had dared her to "return the favor" if that would get her anger "out of her system." The resident, recognizing the *masochistic provocation,* interpreted that Mr. CC *brought punishment on himself* to further relieve guilt. Mr. CC then recalled lifetime guilt because of adolescent sex play with an older sister.

He no longer felt suicidal, as he had developed a beginning understanding of his conflicts. Instead, he requested follow-up outpatient treatment from the resident, which was provided the next day.

2. Defenses That Interfere With the Collection of Crucial Information

These can include *projection* of hostility (causing mistrust of the therapist), *suppression, reticence, vagueness, devaluation, displacement,* and *negative transference.*

In a teaching session with residents in the room (Blackman, 1997), Ms. BB, a 22-year-old married, female nursing assistant presented a chief complaint of memory loss regarding a recent incident where she had been suspected when diazepam (Valium) was missing from her ward in the hospital. She said she would work a whole day and then remember nothing about that day. In response to my exploration, she denied using alcohol or drugs.

She complained of "problems I have. They are not just problems; they upset me. I wonder whether I'm all right. Sometimes I think I'm OK." She gave minimal information.

Having already discussed resistances in our seminar, Dr. M (one of the residents) was prepared to use analytic technique. At my request, rather than probe for details, he confronted her with her defenses of *suppression* and *vagueness*. Ms. BB responded, laughing (defensive), that there was so much to tell she did not know where to start. She seemed embarrassed, although she did not say so; Dr. M interpreted Ms. BB's embarrassment as one of the motives for her defenses.

Ms. BB agreed and then confessed that at least once, when she arrived home, she found a bottle of diazepam in her pocket; she had no idea how that happened. She voluntarily related her current "amnesia" to a shoplifting incident in late adolescence, which she also claimed not to remember. She blandly described herself as "two different people."

Noticing that none of the residents seemed incredulous, I stopped the interview to discuss differential diagnosis. From my forensic psychiatry experiences, I suspected Ms. BB was *lying* because (1) she had recently committed a criminal act (stealing diazepam), (2) she was cagey about what she told us, and (3) she had a history of criminal activity (at least one incident from adolescence) from which she was apparently absolved after claiming amnesia.

Although I could see it would be difficult to diplomatically discuss the differential diagnosis—which included (hysterical) amnesia, psychotic *regression* (with memory meltdown) and *prevarication* (to avoid criminal prosecution)—I decided it would be in the residents' best interest to somehow get at the diagnosis, if I could do so without insulting the patient.

First, I asked the residents to discuss their formulations. They seemed preoccupied with *repression* as the only cause of the supposed amnestic states. I quietly pointed out that the differential diagnosis included *ego regression in integration* and *prevarication* (since the history suggested superego pathology). I explained that hysterical amnesia would usually require a hypercritical superego conflicting with sexual and/or aggressive drive derivatives in the presence of relatively intact autonomous ego functions.

At my request, Dr. M then confronted Ms. BB's *avoidance* by pointing out that he could see she was having difficulty saying what was bothering her. She said it was embarrassing because "people will think I am crazy." She said this with a little laugh, so that her use of the word "crazy" appeared to be a *dramatization* (histrionic defense). To myself, I wondered if she were *projecting* onto other people her own sense of impending ego fragmentation.

To facilitate the retrieval of more material, I suggested Dr. M clarify with the patient that her *vagueness* seemed to be automatic. He went overboard, and said to her, "I realize that you are not purposely trying to not tell us things, and that you are not lying to us, but some of the things you are thinking that you are not telling us could be helpful to us in making a diagnosis." (After the patient left, we discussed how he had been pushing Ms. BB and exculpating her in a way that might not have been appropriate since there was a possibility she was lying. However, the result of his reassurance turned out to be fruitful, despite the inaccuracy.)[1]

Ms. BB responded, "It's not really me, it's the things that happen to me." With some gentle exploration from me, she admitted that the things that happened to her included experiences where furniture, utensils, and cups and saucers would "go flying across the room." She justified these perceptions, insisting that there was "no reason for this," that she was not "imagining it," and that she was not "drunk or sleeping." Further, she would "see people" who would talk to her, although it was hard for her to tell what they were saying. I clarified with her that she did not feel her experiences emanated from conflict inside her. Rather, she felt they were "real," and not part of her thinking. The clarification of her concreteness and dereistic thinking gave evidence to all of us that she was psychotic.

To further substantiate the diagnosis, I then explored with her, myself, whether she experienced blocking. She admitted she often had to ask people what she had been talking about because she could not follow her own thoughts.

With these data suggesting psychotic illness, I alerted the residents that I was going to show them some different techniques. I had formulated to myself that the patient was *intellectualizing* and *rationalizing* about her symptoms, and was more regressed than she wanted to admit (due to shame). She seemed to be defensively *deceiving* us about the extent of her "amnesia," which I thought might be periods of integrative regression (thought disorganization). I therefore addressed Ms. BB's apparent *prevarication* by telling her that I did not think she had entirely forgotten whole days of activity. I also suggested (supportive technique) to her that if she thought very hard, she would probably remember something about the lost days.

She responded that she did not recall anything. I then argued (supportive technique) that, in my experience, people did not usually forget things 100 percent. I wondered if she may have had so much difficulty with her thinking during those days that it was hard to remember exactly what she was thinking. I suspected she might remember feeling disorganized and frantic. She replied that her mind was often "on fire," and that she had "too many thoughts." She would not sleep for two or three nights in a row. She volunteered that she would "take Benadryl to go to sleep."

I led her, by highballing (supportive technique to reduce her superego reaction), and asked her: "Do you take 10 or 15 at a time?" I expected she might then admit to taking a few at a time. But she surprised all of us. She laughed nervously and said no, she actually took 25 or 30 diphenhydramine capsules (25 mg each) at a time, because otherwise she would "never sleep at all." The residents and I agreed that neuroleptic medication seemed preferable. She was agreeable to that plan.

After the patient left, I presented my formulation that Ms. BB probably stole the diazepam in states of frantic desperation caused by her integrative deficit, her break in reality testing, and her failure to contain primary process. Once she had been caught, she probably feared she would be punished for the theft, and therefore lied. Dr. A then mentioned that although Ms. BB had been suspected of stealing the diazepam, no formal charges had been pressed due to her "amnesia."

Further discussion centered around her chief complaint of amnesia, which had originally not been questioned. It appeared that because of her embarrassment over her psychotic thinking and symptoms, she had consciously *suppressed* data and had *intellectualized* by implying she had multiple personality disorder. Her defenses of *isolation of affect, conscious withholding, prevarication* and *intellectualization,* if unaddressed, could have led this psychotic patient to have been erroneously diagnosed with multiple personality disorder (Gardner, 1994).

We could now avoid attempting to relieve her symptoms with dynamic interventions. She lacked the ego functions (integration and abstraction) for that approach, and instead needed medication and supportive interventions.

3. Defenses Causing Resistance to Treatment

The following defenses can cause resistance:

- *Repression* and *avoidance* are prominent when people forget all the material from a previous session or come 15 minutes late to the following appointment.
- *Suppression* of important material such as suicidal ideation (content and situation), and sexual conflict details, including fantasies.
- *Transference-resistance* and *projections,* causing mistrust and devaluation, identification with the abandoner, and externalization of superego (often manifested as a fear of punishment or disapproval from therapist).

An example of a person with resistance based on negative transference feelings displaced from prior therapists was Mr. F, a 52-year-old man who complained of "depression." He requested "Prozac or one of its clones." I interpreted, "That way you could try to relieve the unpleasant feelings without having to tell me about your marital problems." Mr. F responded, "I've had talking therapy before. The other therapists just sat there and listened. It's probably my fault, but it didn't help." I responded, "Perhaps you expected me to be as frustrating, so you'd rather run the show, take some medicine, and not have to trust me either." Mr. F said: "I never thought of that. Maybe. I hate to think of all the money I squandered on useless hand-holding!"

4. Defenses That Contribute to the Person's Overall Psychopathology

These include *inhibition of speech, identification with the aggressor, passivity, repression, reaction-formation, avoidance* (of situations), and *symbolization* and *condensation*.

DEFENSES IN NEUROSIS

Ms. D, a 43-year-old, twice-divorced woman, consulted me for treatment of moderate agoraphobia and depression after being laid off from her job as a librarian. She was let go ostensibly because of a reduction in force; however, she felt a "younger woman," who had been competitive with her, had angled with the (male) head librarian to take over her position. Ms. D was now receiving unemployment insurance; she wanted to go back to work, but when she left the house, she frequently had severe panic attacks.

During a session some months into treatment, she admitted she had not felt like coming to see me. When I commented that perhaps she might be *avoiding* mentioning any negative feelings toward me or the treatment (resistance interpretation), she asked, "Why did you focus on sex the last time?" I clarified that she was the one who, in the prior session, had mentioned that she was lonely but was not going to "stand on a street corner." I had connected her joke, at that time, with avoiding sexual matters, which she had already told me were conflictual to her. But now she seemed to want to pin the responsibility for mentioning sex on me (*projection* and *projective blaming*).

She agreed with my confrontation of her distorted recollection, and added, "Better to blame you than to have to talk about it!" And she chuckled. She then asked if she could have a cup of coffee. I interpreted that she might feel better with just coffee and a chat, safer than sexual material (*libidinal regression* as a defense). She responded, laughing again, "The coffee and cigarette are usually after sex!" We again discussed that it would be handy to blame me for this last joke, too.

Ms. D called to cancel her next session because of a severe headache. When she appeared for the following session, she could not recall anything about the session that preceded her three-day headache. I first interpreted to her that forgetting (*repression*) was, I thought, connected to the headache. She asked that I remind her what she had forgotten. I mentioned the discussion of avoiding talking about sex, her wish for coffee and joking about it, and wanting to blame me. She responded, "Oh, now I remember. That was terrible—I shouldn't joke that way!" I then interpreted that she seemed highly self-critical, and that perhaps the headache had punished her *and* kept her away from her session and her thoughts about sexual matters.

She agreed, confessing something she had "never told anyone": she had had a third marriage to a man of a different race, which she had broken up, though he was devoted to her. She wondered if she had tortured him to express anger left over at her first husband, who she complained had tortured her emotionally. I linked possible reactions she may have had toward her recent male ex-boss. She exploded with rage: "He needs to have an operation and you know where! That sonofabitch!"

Through the examination of her resistances to treatment, we were on the way to connecting her agoraphobia, depression, and conversion symptoms with her conflicts regarding her ex-boss, her ex-husbands, and eventually her father—all having led her to hide from the workplace, where she would re-experience guilt, rage, and temptation.

DEFENSES IN BORDERLINE PERSONALITY ORGANIZATION

When people who consult us show evidence of problems in the Warm-ETHICS arena (see chapter 4) as well as ego weaknesses (in impulse control, affect-tolerance, containing primary process), there is a rule of thumb that may be helpful. That is, interpret *distancing* defenses first, putting off until later any interventions regarding defenses related to conflicts involving wishes versus guilt.

> A 37-year-old married man is aggrieved due to his philandering. He complains that he can't stop because his mistress engages in specific, stimulating activities with him; his wife refuses to cooperate with his fantasies and requests that he engage in foreplay that he does not enjoy.

Your first interventions should probably address how he creates *distance* from his wife by having a mistress. He also *avoids* emotional closeness with his mistress by engaging her only in fantasy activity. In other words, control of how emotionally close he gets to others should be elucidated before other elements of his conflicts. (For greater elaboration on this type of pathology, see Marcus, 1971.)

The reason for this order of intervention is that the *separation/distancing* activity guards against anxiety over mistrust. If the conflicts surrounding mistrust are not elucidated first, so that the man can understand his tendency to run away from intimate exposure of emotional material, when you start talking to him about other dynamics symbolically involved in his behavior, he will start feeling anxious about trusting you and likely quit treatment before you are able to help him.

DEFENSES IN CONSULTATIONS AND SHORT-TERM THERAPY

Work with defenses is important in short-term therapy, long-term therapy (like psychoanalysis), and even during certain consultations (Blackman, 1994). It is a common misconception that confrontation and interpretation of unconscious defense is only useful in long-term psychotherapy (once-a-week for over a year) or psychoanalysis (3 to 5 sessions a week for over a year). There are times when a dynamic interpretation during consultation can be useful or even quite therapeutic.

> Mrs. Jones, a 30-year-old married woman, was brought for consultation to a resident class (6 residents) by Drs. F and G because of diagnostic and treatment concerns. She was being considered for ECT because of intractability of her depression. She had not responded to antidepressant medications or to the "insight group" wherein Drs. F and G had been treating her for the past four months.
>
> When I said to Mrs. Jones that I understood she was unhappy that her current treatments had not been helpful, she laughed and agreed. [I made an empathic, clarifying comment—a supportive technique aimed at establishing an alliance.] I then asked her to tell me about her problems [instructions—dynamic technique].
>
> She proceeded to tell me that she had been depressed since she was a small child and had problems relating to her mother. After she talked about this for a few minutes, I confronted [interpretive technique] her defense of *temporal regression* by pointing out to her that I understood there had been many things that could have produced her unhappiness, but I thought she was steering clear of discussing what had been going on for the past four months.
>
> She was somewhat surprised by this confrontation and said that she couldn't think of anything special that had been going on lately; there was "no trigger." She then returned to her theory that her problems started when she was four years old, when her parents had separated. [I felt she was still using *temporal regression*, now abetted by *intellectualization, avoidance,* and some hostile-rebellious *transference.* But I did not have enough data. I therefore used a different technique— exploration—to obtain more information.]

I asked her if she was working. She said no; she had stopped four months ago (!). She had been working as a receptionist, although she had a bachelor's degree in math from Stanford. When I clarified [interpretive technique] that it sounded as though she had not really found herself [self-image disturbance leading to identity diffusion], she immediately agreed that was a major part of her problems. She did not know what she wanted to do, what kind of work she might enjoy. When I asked her what she imagined she might enjoy [more exploration], she responded that since she was a little girl she had wanted to be a hairdresser; she then began laughing and said her mother was appalled by this. When she told her aunt she wanted to be a flight attendant, her aunt got angry and told her she should be a pysicist! Mrs. Jones volunteered, "The only thing I ever wanted was to get married and to have a family. . . . " We agreed this was an unresolved problem regarding her identity.

I then drew her attention to how we had gotten away from what had been happening just before she came for treatment four months earlier. [I confronted her defenses of *avoidance, intellectualization, temporal regression*.] In particular, I noticed she had not mentioned her marriage. She then admitted she was a bit embarrassed [the affect being defended against] about some of her marital problems.

She explained that she had met her husband when she was in college and he was at in law school. When she said rather blandly that she had not been able to get pregnant, I pointed out that she seemed to talk about this rather matter-of-factly and that I suspected she had stronger feelings about the frustrations than she cared to experience [dynamic interpretation of isolation of affect]. She responded by acknowledging frustration about the pregnancy issue, but then stated, using *intellectualization* and *rationalization*, that she wasn't sure that she really wanted children "all that much," anyway.

She then revealed that she had actually gotten pregnant, but this was not discovered until about *four months ago*. After multiple medical visits for gastrointestinal-type pain, she finally saw a senior obstetrician, who correctly diagnosed an ectopic pregnancy in the fallopian tube. I explored what had been done to treat the ectopic, but she veered away from the question, instead sighing about how difficult it had been to finally get to the right doctor. She became preoccupied with the vagaries of the diagnostic process, again appearing as an intellectual person who had already "coped" with that adversity.

I therefore interpreted that much of her preoccupation with the details of the diagnostic process seemed to shield her from experiencing grief about losing the baby. She responded by tearing up and said she had not let herself feel much about the loss. [Instead, it appeared she had *rationalized* that she was ambivalent about child-bearing: she had wished all her life to have a family but was not sure now. She seemed to project blame onto other physicians who had missed the diagnosis.]

Mrs. Jones then volunteered that she had "accidentally on purpose" gotten pregnant in a prior relationship before meeting her husband. [The appearance of new information, as well as affect discharge, are two indicators of a correct interpretation.] She had immediately obtained an abortion, and at the time this caused her to feel "relieved." She did not connect her current depressive feelings with any of that disruptive history. [It seemed to me that she was using *compartmentalization* as a defense to manage her inflamed conflicts about these situations.] She stated she had "never told" anyone about the prior abortion—she meant no previous therapist.

She interjected, as a correction, that she had recently confessed the prior abortion to her husband, who was not angry and was not going to "abandon" her as she had feared he might.

In relation, she explained that pregnancy had been an "issue" in her family. Her mother told her that she had not wanted to become pregnant with Mrs. Jones when she did.

Completing the mental status assessment, Mrs. Jones was an articulate, modestly dressed woman, who showed none of the disturbances in any autonomous ego functions that could have suggested psychosis (see chapter 4). There was no evidence of distancing defenses typical of narcissistic or borderline patients, who have problems with emotional closeness. Rather, she was overly nice [*reaction-formation*], *suppressed* grief, and seemed to be suffering with as yet unclarified conflicts involving guilt over sexual and aggressive urges.

Since she had responded well, in this consultation session, to interpretations of her defenses of *avoidance* of grief and of *isolation of affect, temporal regression,* and *intellectualization,* I asked her if she would be interested in pursuing individual therapy with Dr. F intensively, rather than ECT and the group. She was agreeable and hopeful, she said for the first time in months.

After Mrs. Jones left the room, the residents expressed shock at how complicated her life was. They had not known of the prior abortion or the tubal pregnancy. Nor had they been aware of the conflicts Mrs. Jones was having regarding work versus homemaker roles.

Another case was even more dramatic, in that it led to a relief of the presenting symptom after the initial evaluation session.

I was consulted by an obstetrician to see Ms. F, a 26-year-old, married woman in her third trimester of pregnancy, hospitalized on an obstetrics unit. She had hyperemesis gravidarum (severe vomiting associated with pregnancy), which was not responding well to antiemetic drugs.

During consultation, I was able to find out that Ms. F had not really wanted this pregnancy and had even considered having an abortion during her first trimester. However, her husband had pressured her into keeping the pregnancy, although it was her fourth and they had severe financial problems. The findings of her ambivalence toward the pregnancy (Freud, 1893; Blum, 1979) and her having an unsupportive husband (Kaplan & Blackman, 1969) suggested to me that she was defending against anger.

She said, "You have to understand my husband. He comes from a large family and always wanted at least four children." Over the next half hour, I discussed with her that she seemed to have a tremendous amount of conflict about this pregnancy and that part of what she was doing was making a number of excuses (*rationalization*) about her husband's rather controlling attitude. She was also being, perhaps, a bit too considerate of his feelings (*reaction-formation*). I thought she was trying hard to avoid being critical of him (*inhibition* of the aggressivized ego function of critical judgment), since that would have made her feel bad about herself (guilt) for disappointing him and for her own (hostile-destructive) wish to abort the fetus.

She responded with intense sobbing, which went on for a while. When she calmed down, she almost spit out: "I could kill him. He just thinks of himself. He never helps with the other kids! I must be out of my mind to go through with this! But I do love the baby and don't want to hurt it!"

I then interpreted that I felt her love for the baby was part of the conflict that made her feel guilty. I opined that it was possible that some of her throwing up symbolized (a) *punishing herself* for her hostility toward the baby and her husband, and (b) wishing to expel the baby. She thought this was interesting, and discussed further with me the considerable ambivalence she had about her marriage and this pregnancy.

When I returned to see her the next day, she reported she had stopped vomiting for the prior 24 hours, although her antiemetic medication had been stopped the day before. She, herself, thought discussing things had been helpful. She did not vomit any further while she was in the hospital and was discharged a few days later with antiemetic medication p.r.n.

6

Differential Diagnosis and Treatment Selection

The process of elucidating disruptive defenses, as described in chapter 5, can be extraordinarily therapeutic to suffering people, but only under the following conditions:

1. They cannot be psychotic.
2. They cannot be felonious criminals (rapists, murderers, armed robbers, grand larcenists, heinous child abusers).
3. They must possess the following capacities:

Autonomous Ego Functions
- relatively intact integrative functioning (can organize thought, stay coherent)
- relatively functional abstraction ability (can read between the lines, appreciate symbolism)
- relatively intact reality testing (can understand that fantasy is different from reality)
- some self-observation ability

Superego
- some sense of guilt or shame

Ego Strength
- some ability to keep bizarre thoughts out of consciousness (contain primary process)
- some ability to avoid intoxicating substances, and some impulse control in general

Object Relations
- fair facility to develop trust in and empathy for another human being

In other words, after assessing multiple mental operations for diagnostic purposes, it is also important to determine a person's treatability with a psychodynamic approach. People who have psychotic and near-psychotic conditions, who have physical illnesses of the brain, or who otherwise manifest severe damage to ego functions and object relations, generally can't be treated dynamically.

Unconscious dynamics (the relationships among drives, affects, superego, and defenses) are so fascinating that many therapists (and most books on psychotherapy) focus on making dynamic interventions without first assessing ego functions and object relations capacities. The result is that some people with subtle ego deficits, treated with analytic therapy directed at defense and affect, do not get better. On the other hand, people with intact ego functions, who are highly treatable with insight-directed therapy, may wind up being treated with medications and/or support (see chapter 7) and similarly may not fare as well as they could.

Of all the autonomous ego functions, the most critical for assessing treatability with any form of insight-directed psychotherapy are:

1. **A**bstraction ability.
2. **O**bserving ego.
3. Sufficient **R**eality **T**esting.
4. **I**ntegration.
5. **C**oncentration
6. Clear **S**ensorium (alertness).[1]

People's integrative function must be operating reasonably for them to undergo insight-directed treatment. If integration is deficient, treatment will be quite ineffective even if the therapist points out previously unconscious defenses (such as *projection* or *identification*) or previously unconscious motivations (such as competitive aggression or symbolic sexualization). In order to experience improvement in their current relationships and symptoms, people have to be able to put together (integrate) the new understandings about themselves. In schizophrenic or severe borderline cases, where the integrative function is flawed, the discovery of previously unconscious contents and mechanisms usually cannot be integrated and does not usually have a therapeutic effect. In fact, defense interpretations may be overwhelming, and disrupt the ego functioning of people with schizophrenia or psychotic bipolar illness (Loeb & Loeb, 1987).

The presence of abstraction ability is also mandatory for insight-directed psychotherapy. This is not the same as intellect. In fact, some intelligent people may not possess much abstraction ability. To utilize a psychodynamic treatment approach, people must be able to understand abstract concepts and to be affected by them. For example, a person must be able to understand that anger at a boss may be unwittingly *displaced* onto a spouse.

Abstraction may be more or less deficient regardless of someone's diagnosis. In some situations, where people have mildly deficient abstraction ability, the amount of interpretive work has to be curtailed, although it need not necessarily be eliminated. However, with such people, linkages between unconscious or conscious defenses and affects must be made succinctly by the therapist, or integrated change will not occur. Contrarily, in people with excellent abstraction ability, overexplanation or overinterpretation by the therapist can be sensed by them as an insult; with such people, simply pointing out a defense is often sufficient to bring about insight.

If people have no capacity to observe their own mental contents and processes (observing ego), psychodynamic treatment is relatively contraindicated. Unless the therapist can help them develop this function, psychodynamic treatment is doomed to failure.

Therefore, for the person suffering with a bridge phobia, for example, a preliminary defense confrontation in the first interview might be something on the order of, "Have you ever considered the possibility that your avoidance of bridges has symbolic meaning?" People who immediately agree, realizing that it may be *symbolic*, but cannot figure out what the symbols mean, are well on their way to successful treatment with insight-directed therapy. However, those who immediately are concrete, say they do not "buy in" to that idea, and concretely *intellectualize* about the cause of the phobia generally have a more clouded prognosis with insight therapy. They may need psychotropic medication if the concreteness cannot be ameliorated through confronting it as a defense (see chapter 3, defenses #48 and #52).

You can test the operation of integration, abstraction, and observing ego during an initial interview by asking, for example, "What kind of person was your mother when you were an adolescent, and how does that compare with how she is now?" You then observe people's capacity to use integration and observing ego—to discuss, in an abstract way, characteristics of their parents and to contrast these with current characteristics. (Many people can more easily describe the features of others' thinking than their own).

Those people who say they have never thought of who their parents are, or that they can't conceptualize what is asked of them, have a guarded prognosis with insight-directed therapy. A better response, as far as prognosis goes, might include something like, "Funny you should ask that, but when I was 13, my mother was very liberal. She allowed me to go and come as I pleased; she seemed to have a relaxed attitude toward my developing sexual interests. But when I got to be 18 or 19, she seemed overly concerned for some reason, and I think maybe this was due to the fact that she and my father were having problems. I don't know, but since I have had children, she has seemed withdrawn and critical for some strange reason, so it's hard for me to be around her these days." The prognosis here is better due to the active presence of observing ego, abstraction, and integration.

It is my impression, through years of teaching, that many mental health practitioners and trainees do not accurately assess these three functions—integration, abstraction, and observing ego—in people they are beginning to treat, especially if those people are intelligent or socially skillful (different ego functions). Therapists may then take people into insight-directed therapy who are not suited for it. This is unfortunate for the person in treatment. In addition, the inevitable treatment failure can produce a demoralizing effect on therapists, who may *generalize,* feel that dynamic treatment is ineffective, and doubt their capacity to do it.

Phenomenological diagnosis is also utilized to determine treatability with insight-directed treatment. In general, schizophrenia is a contraindication to insight-directed treatment, since most schizophrenics have deficits in integration and abstraction ability. Some schizophrenics and other psychotics, however, may have relatively intact observing ego, recognize when they are getting sick, and be able to cooperate with their therapist in outpatient supportive therapy.

People with deficits in orientation and sensorium also cannot be treated with insight-directed work. Usually, if they are transiently intoxicated, some other approach will be necessary for that session. Those who are chronically intoxicated require detoxification before attention is paid to their defense mechanisms, although confrontation of *denial* of the seriousness of their addiction may precede their amenability to detox.

Deficits in self-care, where hygiene and general body maintenance are neglected, are suggestive of a latent schizophrenic illness. Exceptions to this rule would be adolescent or adult cases where people *symbolically* are rebelling against conformity by not taking care of themselves. Much caution should be exercised before attempting to treat such people with insight-directed therapy, and those persons who possess integration and abstraction ability need to be carefully differentiated from those who do not. Where people's teeth are rotting, their skin is scaly and unwashed, or their clothing is unwashed, the deficits tend to make analytic treatment contraindicated.

A particularly difficult area of assessment surrounds the self-preservation function. Chapter 8 is dedicated entirely to the problem of suicide assessment. Briefly, those persons who have a history of repetitive, relatively serious suicide attempts, or whose behavior reflects a lack of concern for their own well-being, often fall into some type of psychotic category (due to severe defects in several basic ego functions), but may be underdiagnosed as "really bad borderline."[2] Sometimes, if suicidal people have enough integrative functioning, abstraction ability, and observing ego, interpretation of *turning of anger against the self* (and of other defenses) may be useful in deterring further suicidal activity. However, without sufficient abstraction and integrative capacities, interpretation of dynamics is ineffective, the risk of suicide is chronic and severe, and there is a guarded prognosis with any type of treatment. When people have a deficiency in the self-preservation function, hospitalization and other supportive approaches, including psychotropic medication, are indicated (see chapter 7).

Deficits in judgment are common, but on their own do not preclude insight-directed therapy. Many neurotic and immature people have difficulties with judgment, as do many treatable borderline cases. However, severe lapses in judgment about the environment and serious deficits in reality testing are relative contraindications to insight-directed treatment.

Problems with adaptation need not necessarily pose contraindications to insight-directed therapy, since many neurotic (phobic, obsessional, panicky) and immature people possess sufficient ego functioning to understand, eventually, their difficulties with adapting (often due to defensive *inhibition* of judgment—see defense #48).

In the case of intellect, those aspects that have to do with understanding problems and posing questions are very important to the issue of treatability. Well-developed intellect can be an asset in therapeutic work. On the other hand, we know that high academic capacity may be present in the face of severe deficits in integration and in abstraction. Paranoid schizophrenia has often been called the psychosis of the intelligent.

Speech and language are generally necessary for successful insight-directed therapy, although some people who have organic deficits in speech can be treated with insight.

> Ms. ST, a 65-year-old depressed woman, had just suffered a left middle cerebral artery occlusion that left her with an expressive, but not a receptive, aphasia; that is, she could understand language but not speak accurately.[3] The modification I used in treating her was that periodically I guessed certain words and let her choose from them, like a multiple choice test. This managed the dysnomia (inability to say the names of ideas, people, and things) that had resulted from her stroke. Ms. ST was able to choose the right word when I mentioned it, although if left to her own devices, she could not produce it.
>
> She was able to come to understand that her depression after the stroke was largely based on defensive *turning blame onto herself* because she could no longer live up to her (ego) ideal. This ideal was based on an identification with her mother's values.

Ms. ST's mother had been a teacher who had sent Ms. ST for elocution lessons as a child. Ms. ST had learned to value speech, and had prided herself on her vocabulary and her articulateness as a teacher and administrator. Her depression after the stroke was caused not only by her grief over her loss of her speech capacity, but by her guilt and shame that she was not living up to her lifelong ideal of articulateness that was based on identifications with her mother.

The explication and understanding of these dynamics greatly relieved Ms. ST's depression. She was able to significantly modify her expectations of herself based on the reality of her situation, rather than on her mother's values, with which she had defensively *identified*.

7

Supportive Therapy Techniques

Finding defenses is extremely important, regardless of the therapeutic approach. What you should do once you detect defenses, however, varies. If people also present severe deficiencies in abstraction, integration, or basic trust, it's usually best to use supportive techniques in treating them (Stewart & Levine, 1967; Blackman, 1994). This chapter concerns supportive techniques based on analytic theories, some involving defenses.

REPAIRING EGO FUNCTIONS

When you have determined that one or more autonomous ego functions is deficient, try to supply at least some aspect of them to the person for incorporation. Following are some general rules of thumb for techniques you can use when attempting to treat people with deficits in ego functions.

Integrative Function

Damage results in tangentiality, circumstantiality, blocking, inability to conceptualize, and other disorganization such as verbigeration, loose associations, and flight of ideas.

- Prescribe antipsychotic medications (lower doses in borderlines).
- Stop the patients' disorganized verbalizations by interrupting them.
- Organize the sessions to focus on certain problems.

Abstraction

Damage results in concreteness of thought.

- Explain the meanings of relationships, events, and other things the person in treatment does not see: read between the lines.
- Argue and persuade regarding meanings of people's actions and reasons for laws, traditions, and customs.

Reality-Testing

- Reinterpret reality for people based on your understanding of their reports of events.
- Prescribe antipsychotic medication or refer for prescription.
- Offer hypotheses for the actions of others.
- Give analogies to easily understandable world events.
- Nullify false conclusions.

Speech

- Correct the person's misuse of phrases.
- Advise and model language the person can use in different difficult situations.

Self-Preservation

- Confront self-destructive tendencies (e.g., point out that anorexia is self-destructive) (Wilson, Hogan, & Mintz, 1992).
- Advise better ways of solving problems.
- Use intellectualized "interpretations" of dynamics.
- Hospitalize and/or prescribe antidepressant medication.

Adaptation

Remember, adaptation can be alloplastic (maneuvering the environment) or autoplastic (fitting in to the environment).

- Advise and exhort regarding more adaptive behavior.
- Practice by discussing plans for action.
- Offer rationalizations to reduce shame.

Judgment and Anticipation

- Offer your own judgment regarding situations.

Play to Work

- Assess the person's capacity to work.
- Advise based on the person's reality capacity and model for superego change (e.g., I would . . .).

Example

> Ms. XK, a 40-year-old female high school teacher, enjoyed teaching Latin, but was depressed in her personal life. She was lonely and had no friends. She had always lived alone.
>
> She admired and became sexually attracted to a 15-year-old female student in one of her classes. Ms. XK wondered if she should ask the girl out for dinner one night, *rationalizing* that the girl probably had been out on dates already.
>
> I felt there was damage to Ms. XK's reality-testing function and to her ability to contain primary process fantasy. She was unable to use fantasy as trial action to anticipate consequences, and her abstraction ability was limited. I therefore advised her that I did not think she should do what she was imagining doing. I explained (my version of reality, which I felt was better than hers) that it was against most high school rules for teachers to date students, even of the same gender, and this one was under the age of consent, as well, which made Ms. XK's plan illegal.
>
> I further argued that if the girl ever reported Ms. XK for even asking her out, I anticipated that Ms. XK would lose her job, which she liked and needed (judgment, anticipation, and self-preservation). She reluctantly agreed to not pursue the girl to whom she was attracted (executive function and impulse control).

STRENGTHENING FOR EGO WEAKNESSES

Find the limitations in ego strength (including affect-tolerance, impulse control, and containing primary process thinking—see appendix 2) and suggest, persuade, argue, model, or express understanding. Rules of thumb for these techniques include:

- Verbally express genuine empathic reactions.
- Offer choices for clarification.
- Educate regarding the world, children, and so forth.

Example

> A 21-year-old gay alcoholic college student, who had been dry for a few weeks, called me at home at dinnertime because he was having

trouble studying. He complained of "drifting off" and was afraid he would go to the park for unprotected sex again, to relieve tension (and risk AIDS, thereby).

Considering his weaknesses in affect-tolerance and impulse control, I first expressed understanding that he was feeling overwhelmed. He thanked me, but then asked if I had any ideas that could help him. I responded by advising him to go to the college library, to find a quiet place to study, but also to give himself breaks where he could talk to his friends for distraction and emotional support. He appreciated this idea, followed up on it, and avoided the park.

In situations where there appears to be damage to an ego strength or to an ego function, another technique directly involving defensive operations is recommending new defenses.

RECOMMENDING NEW DEFENSES

Typically, we think of recommending the following:

- Suppression
- Isolation of affect
- Intellectualization
- Rationalization
- Humor
- Minimization (not denial)
- Identification with the therapist
- Generalization
- Verbalization to repel projective attacks
- Avoidance
- Displacement into social or political issues

Example:

A depressed, mildly suicidal, 47-year-old schizophrenic English professor, who never made friends, had worked in colleges in several small towns in the deep south of the United States throughout his life. He had always "despised rednecks" because of their "lack of culture" and their "uncouthness," though he, himself, had been raised in the deep south on a farm.

During a year of once-a-week supportive psychotherapy, I offered him *rationalizations, intellectualizations, disidentification from his parents,* and *modeling after me,* as well as some other defenses.

During treatment, I suggested that perhaps, eventually, he should move to a larger city (advice). I said to him that I thought he would be more comfortable around more educated and cultured people (*rationalization* and *joining*), and that I felt he needed to be less like his parents (exhortation to *disidentify*). I added that I, myself, had enjoyed living in larger cities (modeling for him to *identify with*] because the opera, symphony, and professional sporting events are generally superior (advising *sublimations* and *condescension*).

He thought this was a good idea and applied for a teaching assignment in a small college in a large city, which he obtained. He later wrote me that he felt he had more "space" where he was, and he didn't have to put up with "the *hoi polloi*" (*rationalization* and *condescension*). Moreover, he could attend cultural events he enjoyed without having to worry about "someone wanting a relationship."

REPAIRING OBJECT-RELATIONS DAMAGE

In people who use a variety of distancing defenses, the following can be used, though they are the most dangerous techniques and backfire the most frequently. I should probably put a sign on them that says, as some extreme sports warn, "Don't Try This at Home!" They are techniques only to be used by experienced therapists, or by therapists under supervision.

- Clarify distancing defenses.
- Explain the fantasies of self and object dissolution that are defended against.
- Exhort the person to be more or less open emotionally with other people.
- Offer sublimated, limited warmth in interaction in the session, alternating with silence (*distance*).
- Carefully reveal "public domain" type of information about yourself—that which could be obtained easily in your community (e.g., your views, values, preferences, adaptational strategies, or hobbies).

Revealing personal information is by far the most dangerous of object-related techniques, since it can easily be taken by people in treatment as a seduction. Think three times before any self-disclosure, and then watch carefully to see their responses. *Do not reveal* personal elements of sexuality or your own personal difficulties. *Do not under any circumstances ever touch a person in treatment.* (Shaking hands upon first meeting people in the waiting room and at the close of the final session is customary.)

The therapeutic reason for possibly revealing anything personal is that it may strengthen the patient's capacity for object ties, and therefore increase ego strength (Alpert, 1959). Selective self-revelation is often considered safer in the treatment of children. However, a side effect in the treatment of adolescents and adults is that the offer of personal closeness can cause them to become suicidal—actually due to your enhancement of closeness with them. The borderline group of individuals—where self-disclosure is often recommended (Renik, 1999)—can develop self–object fusion anxiety due to pleasurable interactions with the therapist; they will then tend to defend against the anxiety by *getting angry* toward the therapist. But because the therapist has been "nice" to them, they can feel guilty, and then turn that hostility on themselves (Harley & Sabot, 1980 p. 178), resulting in a suicide attempt.

There are other complications of supportive techniques. One is that the people with whom you are working may begin to see you as omniscient. Another is that you may not understand people's situations exactly, and therefore can mistakenly project onto them based on your own history and experience. Your advice and modeling may therefore be inaccurate or even destructive.

In comparison, when people who *can* use abstraction and integration (who should be in insight-directed treatment) ask you how you would handle a situation, you should interpret their question as a manifestation of *transference* to you as a parent, where they wish to *identify* with you. You then show them how, if you enacted such a wish with them, they would not have to face unpleasant feelings about their parents.

8

Defenses in the Assessment of Suicidal Propensities

Assessing suicidal people is difficult, fraught with pitfalls, and potentially dangerous to both the suicidal person (who might commit suicide) and to the therapist doing the evaluation (who may be sued if the person commits suicide after evaluation).

There is an extensive literature on suicidology, which I will not attempt to review here. (For a good bibliography, see Cutter, 2002.) Rather, I would like to present a summary of much of the common psychological knowledge about what factors heighten the risk of people actually killing themselves after you've evaluated them. Then we can *add*, for precision, the use of defense theory and technique.

DEMOGRAPHIC HIGH RISK CRITERIA

Age: teen or elderly

Race: Caucasian more than African backgrounds (U.S. Public Health Service, 1999)

Prior suicide attempt: 40% of suicides made a prior attempt (Jacobs, Brewer, & Klein-Benheim, 1999)

Family history of suicide attempts

Prior or concomitant thoughts or attempts at homicide

Gender: 3:1 women attempters; 3:1 men succeeders

Availability of weapon or means

Drug and alcohol use, abuse, and withdrawal (Sederer & Rothschild, 1997): 220/100,000 = 20 times the suicide rate in the general population (11/100,000) (U.S. Public Health Service, 1999)

Person communicates suicidal plans: 70% of suicides (Jacobs et al., 1999)

Prisoners: three times the general population = 33/100,000 (Sederer & Rothschild, 1997)

HIGH RISK CRITERIA BASED ON DIAGNOSIS

Schizophrenia (high risk, always): 10–15% or 10,000 to 15,000/ 100,000 (Sederer & Rothschild, 1997)

Major depressions, especially connected with object loss (Blatt et al., 1984a, 1984b)

Severe impulsivity (impulse-ridden personality) (Jacobs, 1999)

Borderline personality: 45% when coupled with depression and substance abuse (Davis, Gunderson, & Myers, 1999)

Masochistic personality or symptoms

Inability to contract for safety (controversial)

Hopelessness, helplessness (Rochlin, 1965; Beck & Steer, 1988; Cassem, 1988): bad feelings about the future, loss of motivation and expectations

SHNEIDMAN'S (1999) HIGH RISK CRITERIA

Lethality—deadliness of attempt
Perturbation—state of mental disruption
Inimicality—self-destructive patterns of behavior or action

Lethality

In people who have attempted suicide, you must consider how close they came to succeeding. If they have not attempted suicide but are thinking about it, then the lethality of their fantasies also becomes a factor. For example, if someone is thinking about taking an overdose of alprazolam (Xanax), the danger is not extreme because it is difficult to kill oneself with this drug. In contrast, a person who is contemplating jumping off a bridge or driving into a concrete embankment is likely to pose more danger.

Perturbation

In addition, how churned up the person is may have some bearing on the dangerousness question. This is usually a reflection of the state of ego strength (affect-tolerance, impulse control, and containment of fantasy).

Inimicality

Finally, if people's characters are such that they are their own worst enemies (that is, they engage in behavior on a regular basis that is inimical to themselves), they are more likely to actually try something.

"Occult" suicide attempts are those that occur in the face of rationalizations, where the "reality" seems to be something besides a suicide attempt. The most common occult attempts are one-car auto accidents.

LITMAN AND TABACHNICK'S (1967) HIGH RISK CRITERIA

Some suicidal types are not typical and don't necessarily present the standard criteria. For example, there are the suicide-prone versus the accident-prone.

Suicide-Prone

- "loser, dependent, passive, immobilized, constricted" (p. 252)
- "helpless, hopeless, exhausted . . . confused" (See also Weiss & Hufford, 1999.)
- loss of symbiotic love object leading to "fantasies . . . around escape, withdrawal, punishment, revenge, rebirth, and reunion" (p. 253)

Accident-Prone

- "winner, impulsive, quick and decisive, independent, adventurous"
- "rebellious and defiant of authority"
- hates "being boxed in or losing autonomy" (p. 253)
- counterphobic tendency to prove invulnerability

DURKHEIM'S HIGH RISK CRITERIA

(1897, excerpted in Jones, 1986)

Altruisme—to save face or another person
Egoisme—withdrawal from loved ones
Anomie—loss of social restraint (major life catastrophe); loss of reputation/humiliation

Altruistic

Altruistic suicides are relatively rare in western civilization today. *Hari-kiri* was, of course, practiced in Japan for centuries when shame was unbearable. Clinically, you may encounter this type of suicidal ideation in people who believe that because of financial reverses, they are worth more to their loved ones dead than alive due to life insurance benefits.

Egoistic

Egoistic suicidal ideation may occur when the separation from a loved one brings with it the belief of permanent loss followed by permanent aloneness.

Anomic

Anomic features occur in those situations where, for example, someone has lost a child. The degree of that catastrophe may precipitate suicidal ideation in vulnerable individuals. Catastrophic loss of reputation can also bring on a suicide attempt. This seems to have occurred in the case of Admiral Michael Boorda (Holliman, 1996), who apparently took his own life after he was publicly embarrassed by *Newsweek* about having improperly worn some combat medals.

MENNINGER'S HIGH RISK CRITERIA (1933)

Suicidal thoughts involve conflicts over wishes to die, kill, or be killed. All three of these factors have symbolic significance and are overdetermined by a variety of conflicts in each individual. Guilt, nonsatisfaction of a wish to kill due to impracticability, and ambivalence toward the hated object can all contribute to suicidal preoccupations. These are tied in to Freud's (1917) concept of persistent, unrelieved mourning being due to hostility turned toward an internalized representation of a lost, but ambivalently hated loved one.

JACOBS'S HIGH RISK CRITERIA (DAVIS ET AL., 1999)

1st Components

Impulsivity
Antisocial features (including dishonesty)
Interpersonal aloofness

Malignant narcissism
Self-mutilating tendencies
Psychosis with bizarre suicide attempts
Focus on impulsivity and hopelessness

2nd Component

Substance abuse

3rd Component

"Suicide Perspective" as determined by the psychodynamic formulation

4th Components

Borderline Personality: associated with increased likelihood of completed suicide with concomitant

1. Intolerable psychological pain
2. Hopelessness/helplessness
3. Ambivalence
4. Thought constriction
5. "Egression": tendency toward action

AKHTAR'S HIGH RISK CRITERIA—"THE 7 D'S" (2001)

Disorganized thinking
Disorganized social life
Dishonesty (Dorpat & Boswell, 1964)
Disease (physical)
Drug or alcohol abuse
Damage to self-regard
Dislike of the patient

Disorganized Thinking

Disorganized thinking occurs in psychotic and near-psychotic states. Therefore, if a suicidal person's thinking seems disorganized, that would throw him or her into the diagnostic group of at least borderline psychosis, which makes a suicide attempt more likely.

Disorganized Social Life

Disorganization of social life may involve complications in extramarital affairs, conflicts between homosexual and heterosexual lovers, or other features of a deadly soap opera. These difficulties should not be taken lightly.

Dishonesty

When people in the emergency room of a hospital do not seem to be coming clean with you, a good rule of thumb is to hospitalize them. Determining dishonesty can be difficult, but some intuition as well as catching them in obvious contradictions may give you a clue.

> A 43-year-old man had a one-car accident and was brought to the ER. He at first told the admitting physician that he had fallen asleep at the wheel. He later told a mental health nurse that he actually had had a suicidal impulse while arguing with his estranged wife on a cell phone, but assured the nurse that he was no longer suicidal. He was discharged from the ER and then killed himself within hours.

Disease

Physical diseases, especially serious ones like cancer, can cause enormous damage to a person's self-worth, as well as untargetable anger. Therefore, diseases make suicide more likely.

Drug or Alcohol Abuse

Drugs and alcohol disinhibit judgment and interfere with impulse control; the weakness may be sudden, as in acute intoxication, or slowly developing, as in binge alcoholics. Not only that, but many drug abusers are dishonest. So if you can detect any history of drug abuse, the risk is much higher. If the evaluee is dishonest as well, the risk takes several leaps upward.

Moreover, most drug abusers have deficits in self-care (Gabbard, 1994) and impulse control (Treece & Khantzian, 1986).

Damage to Self-Regard

Damage to self-regard may be generalized. The more the person feels worthless, hateful, useless, stupid, and the like, the more suicide is a likelihood. Beware of the person who just attempted suicide who says, "I was stupid . . . ," even if that expression is used as a reason for assuring you that there is no further risk. The complaint about stupidity may not reflect renewed ego strength but, rather, even more self-hatred and self-devaluation.

Dislike of the Patient

One of Akhtar's most interesting points is the increased suicidal risk when you, the therapist, in some way start to dislike the person you are assessing. You may notice you'd like the interview to end already. You may have a hard time concentrating, or you may consciously become aware of irritation—sometimes while discussing the case with a colleague. The main reason for disliking suicidal people is probably their defensive use of *projective identification,* whereby in subtle ways they induce in you their considerable hostility and self-hatred. Since they may turn their hostility *against the self,* and you may *identify* with their criticism of themselves (and become critical of them), both affects make people you dislike a higher suicide risk.

HIGH RISK CRITERIA FROM EGO PSYCHOLOGY AND OBJECT RELATIONS THEORY

Paralogical Explanations of Complicated Life Situations

> A 23-year-old Navy woman was medically evacuated by helicopter from her ship after she attempted suicide. On evaluation, she explained that she felt no reason to live, because everyone was mean.
>
> She had been engaged to a man on shore duty. Some time after her ship deployed, she got drunk and had sex with a male sailor, which, to her surprise, left her pregnant. She asked the male sailor to marry her, which he refused to do. She then called her fiancé, and told him they needed to get married at once because she was pregnant due to sex with a male sailor on the ship. Her fiancé broke up with her. She then slashed her wrists.
>
> When this case was presented to me, I advised lengthy hospitalization for suicidal propensities due to her severe paralogical thinking, possibly indicative of latent or pseudoneurotic schizophrenia (Hoch & Polatin, 1949).

"Practice Runs" or the Equivalent

Those people who are "practicing" committing suicide are a high suicide risk. Although they haven't yet done it, their integrative function is deteriorating and their relationship to reality (Frosch, 1964) is diminishing. Aiken's (1974) short story *Silent Snow, Secret Snow* depicts this deterioration artistically, as does Sylvia Plath's (2000) *The Bell Jar.* In clinical practice, people with this degree of ego damage are quite dangerous to themselves and others.

Conscious Refusal to Reveal Details of Suicidal Ideation/Plan

It is a freakish experience to seriously try to evaluate and help people who are suicidal, only for them to tell you that it's none of your business how or when they plan to carry out the suicidal act. The basis for their refusal is most frequently a defense against self–object fusion anxiety, but not as in the "borderline." Here, the self–object problems are complicated by breaks in relationship to reality *and* reality testing. In my experience, people who utilize this gambit tend to be psychotic, and are extremely serious suicide risks. (For a contrasting view, see Akhtar's [1992b] discussion of his treatment of paranoid personality disorders.)

Impossibility of Resolution of Precipitating Conflicts— Especially Interpersonal

When people present for consultation with horrible, tangled problems in their personal lives leading to hopelessness, they are at a high risk for suicide. This is especially the case where there are extremely painful, unresolvable elements.

> Ms. RR, 44, was suicidal. Her husband broke her leg during a beating five years previously, so she was unable to work. She had only completed 9th grade because her mother, a prostitute, had died of syphilis.
>
> At this point, one of her daughters was in jail for felony theft. Ms. RR had been taking care of that daughter's 3-year-old child and receiving AFDC funds, but because she could not walk well and was taking pain medicines, she did not get up one night; the child walked out of the house, was taken in by neighbors, and was eventually removed from her custody due to child neglect.
>
> Her husband was in jail for second degree murder (he had punched a man, while drunk, who died). Ms. RR received social security benefits for mental illness (major depression), was 50 pounds overweight, and had no interests except watching television.

The irreconcilability of her interpersonal problems, at this point in her life, made Ms. RR a high suicide risk.

Breakup of a Marriage That Began Before the Woman Was 19 or the Man Was 23

These are somewhat general ages, plus or minus a couple of years; the point is that people who have not yet completed the second individuation phase of adolescence are prone to form symbiotic relationships. In general, women complete the separation process some years before men (although there are many exceptions both ways).

Symbiotic relationships involve the idea that the two people are "one," and one will or must die without the other's presence. Therefore, adolescent love affairs usually have strong narcissistic elements—the love involves seeing the lover as "part" of oneself. When that "other" part of the self-image is amputated by a breakup of the relationship, massive, violent rage can be liberated toward the previously loved person, resulting in homicidal ideation (what Kohut [1971] refers to as "aggressive breakdown products"). But because of the conflict with loving feelings, the rage may be *turned on the self*. Alternately, the loss of self-esteem due to the breakup may fuel severe fantasies of worthlessness and "nothingness," also a high risk situation.

Even in situations where older people have a history of having married during the second individuation phase, a marital rupture can lead to the above dynamics.

It is useful to express understanding of the symbiotic nature of the relationship and the loss of self-image and self-worth so engendered first. You'll see if the person agrees and begins to associate to the whole issue of identity and self-image. Or, the session may turn to the dynamics of guilt over the rage released. However, because ego strength is typically limited in people who have had persistent symbiotic-style relationships, there is often insufficient integration of these ideas to be therapeutic. Therefore, the suicide risk is high, and measures need to be taken to protect the person.

HIGH RISK CRITERIA FROM DEFENSE THEORY

When someone has just attempted suicide, or contemplated it, it's natural for the evaluator to try to be sympathetic toward the person's sadness and depression. However, it's critical to keep in mind that most of the time, the suicidal person may also be dangerous and possibly even homicidal. Reading the newspaper, you'll find many articles of someone who was trying to stop a suicide, only to be killed by the suicidal person.

In what follows, I recommend that aside from sorting through the above criteria, you may assess the suicidal propensities of a given person from their responses to defense interpretations. Please keep in mind (a) you may not have to do this if you have garnered sufficient data of their danger to themselves by looking at the standard criteria; (b) your tone of voice should be understanding; and (c) to the extent that defense interpretation challenges the suicidal person's beliefs, it is an "aggressive" approach, much like a surgeon using a scalpel—but that type of incursion into people's thinking, although it may momentarily shake them up, can be *life-saving*. To conclude that a person is a high suicide risk, we are looking for **negative or poor responses to initial defense interpretations**. The conflicts and defenses we are most interested in confronting during urgent consultations with suicidal people are as follows:

- *turning on the self* of anger
- *self-punishment* as a defense against guilt
- *minimization* of grief over losses
- *reaction-formations* shielding against guilt over anger
- *socialization* versus shame over rageful suicidal thoughts
- *masochistic provocation* of others to relieve guilt
- *withdrawal* from objects as defense against shame/grief
- *splitting* to avoid shame and mistrust about admitting drug abuse or suicidal fantasies
- *vagueness, withholding, prevarication*
- *identification with aggressor and/or victim*
- *denial* of a painful reality

Turning on the Self of Anger

After you have discovered at whom people are angry, and then explained to them that the anger is getting directed toward themselves to relieve guilt or tension, if people don't "get it," say, "So what!" or show no integrative response, they probably are lacking enough integrative and abstraction ability to utilize the interpretation. This means insight is not readily possible, and the suicide risk is enormous. Hospitalization will no doubt be needed for supportive (see chapter 7), family oriented, and psychopharmacological approaches.

Self-Punishment as a Defense Against Guilt

Related is the mechanism of relieving guilt by getting oneself punished.

> For example, an 18-year-old sailor was humiliated after receiving an administrative punishment for being AWOL (U/A in the Navy). Because he felt he had let his parents down, he then purposely ran his car into a tree (he lived). The admitting resident tried to interpret to him that by driving himself into the tree, he convicted himself and then ordered the death penalty to relieve his guilt. The patient agreed but insisted that he deserved to die for that reason.

During hospitalization, his irrational guilt was ameliorated through a family meeting with his parents (supportive techniques of both introducing reality and reestablishing important object-relations). This was somewhat effective, whereas interpretation had not been.

Minimization of Grief over Losses

When people have had a serious loss of someone they loved, or sometimes of an ability, and they are not grieving, this is a risk. It is not just the history of recent loss that is diagnostic, but the *minimization* (or complete *suppression*) of grief. Grief is a form of depressive affect, and if intense enough, can melt down the ego strength of affect-tolerance and then erode the self-preservation function. The situation is especially dangerous if, after confronting the *minimization*, there is still little affective discharge, so that there is not enough reintegration and adaptation around the loss (Tarachow, 1963).

Reaction-Formations and Rationalizations Shielding Against Guilt over Anger

When a woman becomes suicidal after her husband has beaten her, watch out for these defenses. She is being "too nice" when she says she "still loves" him. This is backward. She actually wants to kill him but is feeling too guilty; so the defense of *reaction-formation* flips her belief around. If, after you point out her reaction-formations to her, she clings to them, you can also try confronting her *rationalizations* ("he had a rough childhood; he can't help himself," e.g.) as relieving guilt over her murderous wishes.

Note: It's better to address her defenses before attempting supportive techniques. If you try to tell her that she *should* get angry, or something like that, it's more likely she'll institute the defenses of *reaction-formation* and *rationalization*. Nevertheless, if interpretations such as these fail to help her recognize the rage and guilt, as well as the reality danger of the husband, hospitalization is advisable, as well as supportive approaches that enter into the woman's life—for example, helping her get a "peace bond" on her husband.

Socialization versus Shame over Rageful Suicidal Thoughts

After a suicide attempt or a confession of suicidal ideation, say, to a spouse, a man begins his evaluation in the emergency room by saying, "Did you catch Tiger Woods in the Open this afternoon?" Here, you are looking at *socialization* as a defense. Alternately, he may say, "I'm sorry they took

you away from your golf game, Doc. Like to be out there myself today."
Socialization mechanisms as defenses are often designed to relieve shame.
The shame can arise over the thought of being mentally ill (having suicidal
thoughts) or over having "lost control."

Try interpreting the socialization as a defense (e.g., "I guess if we
start talking about the Open, we won't have to think you have any mental
problems, although I understand you just tried to kill yourself. Must be
embarrassing for you").

If he responds uncooperatively (e.g., something like, "Hey, Doc, are
you one of those people who reads into everything? I was just making
conversation. There really is nothing much wrong with me; just did a
stupid thing taking that bottle of aspirin. You don't have to worry about
that happening again"), seriously consider hospitalization.

Masochistic Provocation of Others to Relieve Guilt

> Mr. CC, a 27-year-old single man, showed up in the ER thinking of
> hurting himself, asking for help. The psychiatry resident found out
> that Mr. CC was dating a woman who had just told him that she was
> also sleeping with someone else. This situation had occurred several
> times. The resident felt Mr. CC was a glutton for punishment, and
> therefore told him that he seemed to be getting himself punished over
> and over again. Mr. CC agreed and then confessed that he had cheated
> on his girlfriend sometime previously, told her about it, and then sug-
> gested she cheat on him to even the score.
>
> When the resident pointed out to Mr. CC that his suicidal ideation
> seemed to be designed to relieve him of his guilt, and that he also
> seemed to provoke his girlfriend to hurt him to relieve his guilt, Mr.
> CC associated to how he had always felt guilty about sex. He particu-
> larly felt guilty that he had engaged in some sex play during adoles-
> cence with his teenage sister.
>
> The evaluation session seemed to relieve Mr. CC's acute suicidal
> preoccupation. He requested a return visit the next morning with the
> resident, which was arranged. Mr. CC had a fruitful round of short-
> term, intensive psychotherapy as an outpatient. If he had not shown
> the integration and understanding in the ER, along with reduction in
> suicidal ideation, the resident would have admitted him to the hospital
> (see also chapter 5, "Order of Interpretation," Example 2).

Withdrawal from Objects as a Defense Against Shame/Grief

If people have lost all interest in their ties to others, they are at serious risk.
You can interpret to them that avoiding other people seems to allay some
pain, or that it relieves them of feeling guilty over whatever criticism they
harbor toward those they are avoiding.

If this intervention proves productive, people may respond something like, "You know, I never thought of that. My mother always taught me not to be critical of other people, but I guess I've been overdoing it . . . [cries]." If the interpretation goes nowhere, however, the suicidal impulse is more dangerous.

Splitting to Avoid Shame and Mistrust

Wurmser (1987) points out that ". . . many drug abusers use the defense of *splitting* to disavow a drug abusing self-representation that alternates with a non-drug using orientation . . ." Therefore, many who abuse drugs may not present this to you. They similarly may not report suicidal ideation.

If you pick up the slightest suspicion of antisocial activities, such as calling 900 porno numbers, visiting "dungeons" or other S&M parlors, or painting a "too good" picture during sessions, it's wise to confront the splitting mechanism by discussing how things sound too good to be true, or that more upsetting material is not coming into the sessions. If a depressed person is getting "better" too fast, is not sharing disturbed-sounding material, or responds to your confrontation of omitting suicidal thoughts by not discussing any, the suicide risk is increased.

Vagueness, Withholding, Prevarication

One of Akhtar's criteria (above) for assessing seriousness of suicidality is *dishonesty*. Since prevarication is a defense, you can attempt to confront it, either gently or not so gently, as you see fit.

For example, to the man who at first said he fell asleep driving, then later admitted he was angry at his wife, someone could have said, "I see you weren't on the level the first time. What's up?" Or even, "I see you didn't want to admit you were actually having an emotional reaction at first. Is there anything else you're not being completely straight about, because you're afraid or embarrassed?"

(In fact, in that case, the man had also lied about his extensive marijuana and alcohol abuse, which was discovered later during deposition of various family members. That information would likely have led to him being detained for a commitment evaluation in a hospital.) Confronting prevarication is not a guarantee that you will obtain useful data, but it's more likely than if you don't confront it.

If a suicidal person is consciously withholding information, you will soon begin to feel like an interrogator during the evaluation, because the person being evaluated is not giving you much data. You may realize you are frustrated and feel pressure to "dig into" the person. As an alternative to digging, you can try confronting the withholding (*suppression*) defense. If that goes nowhere, the person's secretiveness must be taken as a serious risk factor.

Perhaps most commonly, people being evaluated get vague. You ask about the suicide attempt, where it happened, what they were thinking, and they respond that they don't remember and were just thinking that it was the end. You ask what they were doing, and they say, "Not much." You ask if they drink alcohol much, and they respond, "Not too much. Sometimes." At some point, you can try a confrontation, such as, "I notice you just give me sort of general answers, without much detail." If the person continues to answer vaguely, such as, "Oh, I just don't know . . ." then confrontation is not enough since you are running into an integrative weakness, in addition to a high risk factor.

Identification with the Aggressor and/or Victim

A person's wife has just committed suicide, and he consults you. He is also feeling suicidal. You point out that he seems to be thinking of doing to himself what his wife just did to herself. If he responds with how guilty he feels about her suicide, and can see that the guilt is irrational (which it usually is), he may be amenable to outpatient treatment. However, if he insists that, no matter what, he is the "culprit"—in spite of there being no evidence of such—serious suicide risk is at hand.

Denial of a Painful Reality

A 29-year-old man jumped off a bridge after his wife told him she was leaving him because he was too withdrawn for her. He required considerable surgery, but lived.

When a psychiatry resident interviewed him some weeks later, he claimed he was not suicidal anymore. However, when his views on his marriage were explored, he explained that he was "pretty certain" his wife would return to him if he would just "change" for her. His wife, in a separate interview, had previously confirmed that she had not given him any hope.

In other words, he was using the defense of *denial in fantasy*. On hearing of this situation, I advised the psychiatry resident who had done the evaluation to confront the denial defense, which led to extensive crying on the patient's part, all while he was still on the orthopedics ward. He was eventually transferred to the psychiatry ward and kept in the hospital another couple of weeks while this defense was addressed through interpretation as well as conjoint sessions with his wife. He engaged in painful grieving, and after a period of time was able to accept the reality of his wife's decision without apparent further, active suicidal threats.

SUMMARY

Assessment of suicide risk is complex and difficult, under the best of circumstances. To improve your accuracy, it's useful to evaluate deficiencies in autonomous ego functioning, ego strengths, object relations, and failures to respond to certain defense confrontations. The results of these assessments can then be added to criteria deriving from demographics, diagnosis, and the work of Shneidman, Litman and Tabachnik, Durkheim, Menninger, Jacobs, and Akhtar.

Appendix 1
Schizophrenia:
History of the Development
of Diagnostic Criteria

Eugen Bleuler's Criteria (1908)

- Primary Symptoms
  Association break: disturbance in integration causes loosely organized
    thoughts: blocking, looseness, tangentiality, circumstantiality (lost
    in details), false connections (paralogical), paucity of thought
  Ambivalence: wildly disparate attitudes held simultaneously
  Autism and poor attention: living in own world, not noticing outside;
    negative hallucinations
  Abstraction deficit: not see nuances and symbolism, leading to misin-
    terpretations
  Affect peculiarity: emotionless ("flat") or extreme changeability
- Secondary (Accessory) Symptoms
  Auditory and visual hallucinations: projected sensory perceptions with-
    out the presence of reality testing. Sex, aggression, conscience = usual
    thought content
  Delusions: unrealistic beliefs (and ideas of reference), persecutory, gen-
    der confusion, somatic, grandiose

Sigmund Freud (1914a) Added

- Break with reality
- Withdrawal of interest from the outside world
- *Reconstruction of reality* in an unrealistic way leading to delusions and
  grandiosity

165

Paul Hoch and Philip Polatin (1949) Added

- Pan-neurotic symptoms: obsessions, phobias, anxiety, depression, conversion, and perversion—all together
- Excess sexual thought in consciousness
- Dereistic life approach and derealization phenomena ("world is not real")
- Severe, chronic anxiety

Heinz Hartmann (1953) Added

- Unneutralized aggression may lead to violence and to lack of development of the autonomous ego functions of integration and abstraction

Robert Knight (1954) Added

- Misinterpretation of simple social interactions
- Fracturing of idioms, and other idiosyncratic misuse of language
- Inability to draw reality conclusions from obvious evidence

Kurt Schneider (1959) Added

- Auditorization of thought
- Thought-insertion and thought-broadcasting

Edith Jacobson (1954) Added

- Confusion of properties of self and properties of others (self–object fusion)
- Excess self-destructiveness ("primary masochism")
- Part-object introjects (mental images) of human beings (a nose, finger, or breast, for example)

John Frosch (1964) Added

- Breakdown in both relationship to reality *and* in reality testing

Margaret Mahler (1968) added

- Dedifferentiation of the self from others ("depersonalization." Also see Feigenbaum, 1937)
- Animism (attributing living qualities to the nonhuman)
- Deanimation (people are not people)

John Feighner (1972) Added

• Poor work and social functioning

Otto Kernberg (1975) Added

• Shift from logic and time sense to dreamlike, untimed, condensed, symbolic, displaced thinking, at times resulting in "polymorphous perverse" sexuality
• Failure to develop sublimatory channels (hobbies and interests)
• Concrete fears about body parts (somatic delusions)
• Aggressive-loving defusion (*splitting*)
• Defenses of *omnipotence, devaluation, idealization, denial, projective identification*

Jerome Blackman (2002) Added

In the face of a deficit in the relationship to reality:

• Lack of "Warm-ETHICS"—warmth, empathy, trust, holding environment, identity, closeness, stability
• Multiple ego defects in
  integration and secondary process thinking
  abstraction
  reality testing
  self-care (hygiene)
  self-preservation
  motor control
  +/– speech and memory
• Multiple ego weaknesses in
  containment of primary process fantasy
  impulse control (eating, aggression, and sexuality)
  using fantasy as trial action
  affect-tolerance

Appendix 2
Ego Strengths Assessed
in Diagnosis

Stimulus barrier (Esman, 1983): Ability to concentrate without being overwhelmed.

Impulse control and delay of gratification (Kernberg, 1975): Reining in sexual, oral, and aggressive urges.

Containment of (primary process) fantasy (Hoch & Polatin, 1949): Keeping bizarre condensations and symbols out of consciousness.

Frustration-tolerance: Withstanding ungratified wishes toward the environment.

Affect-tolerance (Kernberg, 1975): Withstanding powerful emotions without breaking down or overusing defensive operations.

Pain-tolerance: Withstanding physical and emotional pain.

Tension-tolerance: Withstanding conflict between urges, conscience, and reality without agitation.

Development of sublimatory channels (Kernberg, 1975): Converting oral, sexual, or aggressive fantasies into productive activities (e.g., the wish to kill a sibling changes into friendly competition).

Fantasy as trial action (Hartmann, 1939): "Thinking through" wishes before acting.

Resistance to libidinal and ego regression (Marcus, 1975): Ability to not act childish in the face of powerful urges or affects.

Mentation over somatic discharge channels (Schur, 1955): Ability to withstand affects without utilizing somatic channels, as occurs in tension headaches or irritable bowel.

Regression in the service of the ego (Kris, 1952; Bellak, 1975, 1989): Ability to allow a bit of primary process (symbolic, condensed fantasy) thoughts into consciousness to play with a child, to create art, or to tell a joke.

Capacity for drive and affect discharge: Ability to manage violent anger or enjoy sexual intercourse without becoming over-whelmed.

APPENDIX 3. Psychoanalytic Diagnostic Developmental Considerations

Autonomous Ego Functions	Ego Strengths	Affects	Drives	Superego	Object Relations	Defenses
Oral phase	*Oral phase*	*Oral phase*	*Oral phase*	*Oral phase*	*Oral phase*	*Oral phase*
consciousness perception memory integration primary process sensorium psychomotor	stimulus barrier	depressive or anxious thoughts from: ego fragmentation annihilation loss of the object fusion mistrust loss of object's love	*physiology:* sucking, rooting *abnormal fixation:* eating disorder oral sex fixation obsessions alcoholism severe dependency mistrust stealing	basic mistrust	*Autism/Symbiosis (0 to 5 months):* part objects self-objects *Separation-Individuation:* differentiation *(5–12months)* practicing *(12–16 months)* *Warmth*	introjection projection hallucination
Anal phase	*Anal phase*	*Anal phase*	*Anal phase*	*Anal phase*	*Anal phase*	*Anal phase*
intelligence speech/language	delay of drive gratification	separation/ autonomy power of drives	*physiology:* excreting sphincter control *abnormal fixation:* messy contentious scatological	"sphincter morality" "No"	*Rapprochement (16–24 months):* unstable self and object constancy *empathy* *trust* *Unstable self and object constancy (25–36 months)*	projective identification, projective blaming, denial (4 types), dedifferentiation, splitting, animism, deanimation, reaction-formation, undoing and rituals, isolation (of affect), externalization, turning on the self, negativism, compartmental-ization, hostile aggression

Autonomous Ego Functions	Ego Strengths	Affects	Drives	Superego	Object Relations	Defenses
First Genital phase	*First Genital phase*	*First Genital phase*	*First Genital phase*	*First Genital phase*	*First Genital phase*	*First Genital phase*
reality sense reality testing reality versus fantasy concentration attention orientation	mentation > somatic discharge fantasy = trial action	objectivity "realangst" castration penetration poor ego function development	*physiology:* pleasure with penis and clitoris with persons *abnormal fixation:* womanizing sexual problems	fear of retaliation for competitiveness	*Self and object constancy (26–48 months):* holding-environment closeness	displacement, symbolization, condensation, illusion formation, prevarication, confabulation, repression, negative hallucination, regression
Latency	*Latency*	*Latency*	*Latency*	*Latency*	*Latency*	*Latency*
self-care secondary process social skills autoplasticity move play to work anticipation ego interests	development of sublimatory channels affect-tolerance frustration tolerance pain tolerance tension tolerance contain primary process thinking	superego social performance unfamiliarity unrealized ideals	*physiology:* growth coordination *abnormal fixation:* sexual inhibition neurosis	internalization of right and wrong; concrete; rules are inflexible; fairness	warmth, closeness, stability	identification (with fantasy, ideal object, aggressor, victim, lost object, introject), seduction of aggressor, sublimation, rationalization, rumination, counterphobic behavior, intellectualization, socialization, instinctualization, inhibition of ego function

Adolescence-Adult	Adolescence	Adolescence	Adolescence	Adolescence	Adolescence	Adolescence
abstraction judgment alloplasticity observing ego self-preservation executive function	impulse control regression in service of ego capacity for drive discharge	identity diffusion sexual function	*physiology:* sex *abnormal fixation:* group functioning masturbation narcissism	abstract rights externalization heightened ideals reliability responsibility punctuality justice	*Rapprochement:* unstable self and object constancy	idealization, devaluation, humor, suppression, concretization, disidentification, group formation, asceticism, ipsisexual object choice
		Adult	*Adult*		*Adult*	
		loss of generativity loss of function sociodystonic character disability	sex and aggression sublimated and controlled		self and object constancy	

Appendix 4
A Bit of History
of Object Relations Theory

Freud, in his paper "On Narcissism" in 1914, and the other papers on instincts following that, codified the idea of a differential in "cathexis": in other words, the intensity of emotional investment one human being makes in another. From a quantitative standpoint, how much *bezetzung* (oomph, or interest) do people direct toward somebody else versus how much toward their own body and their own mental functioning? Lastly, have they regressed—turned all their attention to themselves— if they originally had the capacity to think about others?

Freud initially used this theory to attempt to differentiate psychosis from other disturbances. He thought psychosis involved withdrawal of *bezetzung* (cathexis)—that psychotics did not channel much energy toward others. What we talk about today as empathy and trust did not develop. A self-oriented judgment of reality clouded psychotics' sense of a holding environment. Freud was the first to recognize the mechanism of "reconstruction of reality" in psychotics after they withdrew from people and failed to test reality. Freud's (1914a) formulations about withdrawal of the libidinal cathexis from the outside world evolved partly from his study of *Senatspräsident* (Appellate Court Judge) Daniel Schreber's autobiography (Freud, 1911).

Freud struggled with the concept of character. In one of his later papers, "Libidinal Types" (1932), he looked at narcissistic, erotic, and compulsive types of character functioning, in various combinations. Narcissistic types were more withdrawn and focused on themselves. Erotic types were interested in others. Compulsive types were more defensively oriented. He described combinations of these: narcissistic-erotic, narcissistic-compulsive, compulsive-erotic, and so on. He played with these a bit,

175

struggling to use structural theory to come up with ideas about character.

Hartmann made several important contributions to object relations theory. They include:

1. The concepts formed in the mind of the self and of others are highly influenced by the integrative function.
2. Ego *functions*, like integration, abstraction, and reality testing, are not the same as the self-image, nor are they defense mechanisms.

The capacity to use functions is incorporated in the way you see yourself; but the way you see yourself involves other perceptions that are remembered and integrated by the integrative function. The same is true of the images of objects (usually other people).

Jacobson (1964), in the 1940s and 1950s, elucidated how human beings comprise more than drives and defense mechanisms. Drive activity (which Freud described as urges directed toward people) was actually influenced by perceptions and memories of relationships with people throughout life. The memories were recorded in the brain (to use current ideas) as mental images of themselves and of other people (self and object representations). Jacobson was influenced by Hartmann's concept that the ego functions of integration, reality testing, speech, abstraction, observing ego, and others were included in, but not equivalent to, the self-image.

At different psychosexual phases, children have different feelings and wishes toward their parents, varying perceptions of their parents, and pleasurable and unpleasurable relationships with their parents. Children form images of the relationships with their parents, and those images are integrated over a period of time. So, children develop concepts about who they are and who their parents are.

Moreover, the object image, in other words, the image of any cathected person (one that is important to you), has components of love, hate, superego functioning, ego functioning, and reciprocal capacities for attachment—all of which are conceptualized.

Mahler went many steps further in her study of children. In her long-term study of psychotic, autistic, and "average-expectable" children, she was able to determine the sequence (between birth and age 3 to 3½) of development of the capacities for integrating perceptions about self and other. There are different phases that these capacities go through in order to finally achieve stable, organized, separate concepts, "I" versus "you": what the French call the syncretic versus the non-syncretic "I" and "you." In other words, the "I" and the "you" get separated, understood, stabilized, and cathected (Mahler, 1968; Mahler et al., 1975).

Mahler's first phase of normal autism (0 to 3 months) leads into symbiosis (3 to 5 months) very quickly. The normal symbiosis-like state between mother and child finally is somewhat relinquished during the separation-individuation stage over a several year period: (a) hatching (5 to 12 months), (b) practicing (12 to 16 months), (c) rapprochement (16 to 25 months), and (d) unstable self and object constancy (25 to 36 months). The child is ultimately able to have the stable sense "I am me, you are you": stable self-constancy, stable object-constancy (36 months onward, not without regression). Those of us who have raised or treated children know that there is considerable variation in those stages, even normally.

Blos, in the 1960s and 1970s, reformulated adolescence in similar terms. Adolescents also go through a period of hatching, practicing, and rapprochement with a final establishment of self and object constancy. During adolescence, the self develops even more, including concepts of career, other capacities, and values (superego gets more integrated). Much is happening toward the end of adolescence and early adulthood to construct the self-image.

Akhtar described distancing defenses in people with certain personality disorders. In *Broken Structures* (1992b) and *When the Body Speaks: Psychological Meanings in Kinetic Cues* (1992a), he spent quite a bit of time reviewing the theories of Freud, Hartmann, Jacobson, Mahler, and Kramer (1979).

Appendix 5
Bizet's *Carmen*
on the Couch

Is Carmen simply a shameless, superstitious tramp who plays around with the wrong corporal? And is Don José just an overgrown Boy Scout, overwhelmed by her sex appeal, who goes berserk when she disses him?

Not to this psychoanalyst. Since Freud first offered his thoughts about Leonardo da Vinci, analysts have periodically enjoyed speculating about unconscious factors in historical figures and literary characters. So, although we can't talk to the "patients" directly to confirm or negate our formulations, we can have some fun examining possible unconscious elements in the *personae* of the opera *Carmen*.

First, Don José. He's a shy fellow who doesn't worry himself about the "galanteries" of the soldier/factory-girl trysts. In Act I, before Carmen offers him her flower as a "présent," she asks him what he's doing. José says, "Je fais une chaîne pour attacher mon épinglette" ("I'm making a chain to attach to my firing-pin"—for his gun). Here is the symbolic secret to his character. His sexuality ("firing-pin") gets him attached (chained). Much later, at the end of Act III, when Carmen tries to break up with him, he resists: "Non, non, non, je ne partirai pas!" He insists, "la chaîne que nous lie, nous liera jusqu' au trepas!" ("The chain that binds us will bind us till death!").

So, why didn't he take up with the pretty girl next door ("une perle"), Micaela, and save us the three hours of emotional S&M, to say nothing of the mountain climbing?

When José first encounters Micaela at the post, he looks into her eyes, and what does he see? His mother! In fact, the kiss Micaela gives him was sent by his mother, who had kissed Micaela after church and then told her to deliver it to José (". . . ce besé que je te donne, de ma part tu le lui

179

rendras"). Cute, and José is consciously pleased, singing about how memories of his mother and his hometown ("souvenirs d'autrefois") replenish his heart with strength and courage. But, unconsciously, Micaela is a bit too close to home.

José is ambivalent. He's a chainmaker, but he's trying to break the chain to his mother. That's why he hasn't written, emailed, whatever . . . , why he's so apologetic ("il se repent aujourd'hui"), and why, unconsciously, he is ripe to reject Micaela as soon as Carmen's flower starts to open up, notwithstanding his proclamation, "Ne crains rien, ma mère . . . je la prendrai pour femme . . ." ("Don't worry, Mom, I'll marry her [Micaela].")

How does this young adult male go about separating from his mother? Like the country song, "I like my women a little on the trashy side," José chooses Carmen—the illicit, forbidden, sexual woman—and then forms a symbiotic-style attachment by giving up his identity in order to rebel and be with her. Does this bother his mother? You bet—she sends Micaela back later, in Act III !

After Carmen is arrested for stabbing Manuelita and sentenced to prison for refusing to answer questions by Lt. Zuniga, José's superior officer, she offers José a tit-for-tat seduction. She'll meet him at Lillas Pastia's for a quick séguedille if he'll help her escape from Zuniga, who had tied her up (and who clearly has his own designs on her). José does some time for having abetted Carmen's flight. When he gets out, Carmen begins to make good on her promise, but José is about to leave her ("Adieu pour jamais!") to avoid being AWOL. When Zuniga shows up to put the make on Carmen, though, José goes AWOL, forgoing both his conscience and his identity to avoid the pain of losing her to Zuniga.

Now, what about Carmen, herself? She's supposedly the hottest babe in the Seville metro area. Her opening joke to José is a sexual pun: When she hears he's working on his firing-pin, she calls him "firing-pinner of my soul!" ("épinglier de mon âme!"). (Sort of a 19th century version of Mae West's "Hey, Big Boy, is that a pistol in your pocket. . . .") José is shocked, but turned on by this "effronterie!"

Carmen is first portrayed as sexually and aggressively impulsive. She teases all the soldiers and fights Manuelita. But soon there appears a method in her madness. She tells Zuniga in Act I, ". . . coupe-moi, brûle-moi, je ne te dirai rien . . ." ("cut me, burn me—I won't tell you anything"). Interestingly, she disrespects (and teases) him by using the familiar "tu" verb form. Parenthetically, her mention of masochistic torture seems to capture Lt. Zuniga's attention. He then has her tied up; he sings ". . . elle est gentille vraiment . . ." ("She's really nice . . ."); and he pursues her sexually in Act II.

However, at the same time Carmen is practicing her sorcery on Zuniga, she reveals that her personality has a powerful streak of Fifth Amendment orientation: She wishes to maintain absolute autonomy and freedom of action from everything and everybody, including men and the law. She sings, "Surtout, la chose enivrante: la liberté" ("Above all, the intoxicating thing is Liberty!"). Simultaneously, she wishes to maintain a fantasy-bond to all men who desire her from a distance. Aside from sexual pleasure, she uses her sexuality for several purposes: freedom from societal restraint, fantasy-bond with men, and repetitive separation from the men she ensnares, to reinforce her "enivrante" feeling of independence.

The toreador, Escamillo, may be as narcissistic as Carmen. In Act III, he tells José, who had just shot at him, that it would be a poor companion who would not risk his life to see his love (i.e., Carmen). But Escamillo knows Carmen's type. He sings, "Les affaires de Carmen ne durent pas six moins" ("Carmen's affairs don't last six months").

So Carmen is the "oiseau rebel" (the rebellious bird of the *habañera*). She consciously desires liberty (autonomy). But simultaneously, she enacts her sexual fantasy of passive surrender by chiding José, ". . . sur ton cheval tu me prendrais . . . en croupe tu m'emporterais . . . si tu m'aimais. . . ." ("You'd put me on your horse . . . and steal me away . . . if you loved me"). And José, despite his conscious loyalty ("Dragon d'Alcala . . . fidèle"), is ambivalent about his chain to his mother through Micaela, and unconsciously wishes to be an antiauthoritarian, autonomous sexual brigand, free of them. To solve his conflicts, he shifts his amorous focus to Carmen, becomes as adhesive as his mother, and then won't allow Carmen to break the chain with him.

This wouldn't be a complete psychoanalytic discourse if we left out the oedipus complex of José and Carmen. In other words, sex and violence! The two males, José and Escamillo, fight for possession of the prized female, like male baboons.

José's father is oddly absent, but probably reappears symbolically in the figure of Escamillo. Of course, in Act III, José tries to cut and kill Escamillo ("un coup de návaja") as the "price" for Escamillo's love for Carmen. Carmen prevails in stopping José from killing Escamillo. This oedipal boy does not kill his father.

José has already punished his actual mother by ignoring her and letting her down (although his guilt over this causes him to return to her, in Act III, before she dies). Then, in Act IV, he executes Carmen (symbolically mother), because she has jilted him for the "father," Escamillo. José will now be punished by execution, thereby relieving his guilt over wanting to possess Carmen (mother), wishing to kill Escamillo (father), and finally killing Carmen (mother) so no one else (including father) can have her—a not uncommon variant of disturbed oedipal resolutions.

We know nothing of Carmen's mother or father, although among her "sisters" at the cigarette factory is Manuelita (symbolic of her mother), whom she cuts after Manuelita, through comparison of Carmen to the fly-infested rump of a donkey, implies that Carmen's sexuality makes Carmen a dirty slut. Carmen is punished (executed by José) after she has committed the sin of seducing the father-figure (Escamillo).

Carmen's sexuality is also competitive with other girls (displacements from mother and sisters). She is openly sexually seductive with father-substitutes (all the soldiers panting after her), but practices what she preaches ("Si tu ne m'aimes pas, je t'aime . . ."—"If you don't love me, I'll love you . . .") by picking out the "unavailable" man (symbolically father), José. However, after Carmen emasculates José, he no longer represents the father to her. She denigrates José and sends him home to his mother. She then literally runs after Escamillo, who is macho, older, and not giving up his identity.

But Carmen's guilt over her competitive hostility toward mother-figures (cigarette girls, José's mother, and eventually José), and guilt over her success in obtaining (father-) Escamillo's love ("Si tu m'aimes, Carmen . . .") cause her to provoke her own punishment and death at the hands of the now mother-figure, José.

Carmen is both a morality story for young adults and every parent's worst nightmare. We worry that our sons could get overwhelmed by their sexual desires, needs to separate from mother, and adolescent rebellious urges. They might then fall in with a bad crowd, choose girls of "bad character," and amount to nothing. We worry that our daughters could get fixated on the pleasurable exhibitionistic/narcissistic elements of their adolescent sexuality, fall in with a bad crowd to feel separate, and then get entangled with good-looking, rebellious "bad boys" who hurt them and destroy their lives.

Carmen is a worst-case scenario of sorts, much like a worst-case scenario dream. We're relieved when it's over to find that the awful consequences depicted have not actually happened to us. We, the audience, can then return to our efforts to derive the usual pleasures from living without the need for execution.

Post Script
Some Disclaimers

I have taken as my task the limited goal of describing defenses and giving some information about them that can be useful to the practicing clinician. My theoretical orientation involves elements of ego psychology (Hartmann's, Frosch's, Bellak's, and Kernberg's concepts of ego functions and ego strengths), structural theory (Freud's third theory[1] of drive, superego, and defense), Mahler-based object relations theory (separation-individuation and its vicissitudes), and modern "conflict theory" (C. Brenner, 2002) regarding compromise formations.

You'll see that I don't enter too much into discussion of the controversy about the so-called "Defect-Defense Controversy" (see Frosch, 1990), since I feel that both the concepts of deficiency in function and inhibition of function are important. Some analytic theoreticians are critical of the theories regarding autonomous ego functions developed by Freud-Hartmann-Frosch (and Busch, 1995), and therefore would dispute my description (following Freud, 1926) of defensive inhibition of functions.

The followers of Kohut take issue with much of structural theory (including defenses), preferring to utilize concepts of internal fantasies ("selfobjects") that pertain to self-esteem regulation.

Kleinians, Jungians, Maslowians, Lacanians, and Adlerians use different terminologies and have somewhat different concepts of mental normality and disturbance. I do not attempt to contrast or compare these theories with defense theory in this book.

The controversies *within* psychoanalysis, many unsettled, are at least as numerous and contentious as those *between* psychoanalytic theories and non-analytic theories. Suffice it to say that this book does not attempt a scholarly dissertation on the intra-psychoanalytic theoretical debates nor on the inter-field disputes between analytic theories and non- (or anti-) analytic theories.

Finally, I have not introduced the "biological psychiatry" ideas concerning anxiety, depression, and psychosis, because I don't see a current-day fit for neurobiology and defense theory. (The contributors to the new journal, *Neuro-Psychoanalysis,* are addressing this issue.) I tend to agree with many of Nobel Prize-winner Gerald Edelman's conclusions (e.g., 1992) on the massive complexity of the brain's underpinnings of mental functioning. Although scientific observers, today, believe the brain is the organ of the mind, and we know brain disease can cause mental phenomena, no one has as yet discovered the neuro-electro-chemical basis *for even a single thought.* Even Levin's (2002) masterful summary of Iberhauft's work on the neuroimmune system and learning readiness is, to use his term, "speculative." There are some persuasive statistical correlations between serotonin and norepinephrine levels in the cerebrospinal fluid and some depressions; but we, as yet, don't have the foggiest idea about the brain biochemistry that is responsible for people thinking thoughts that make up half of affects—causing people to feel lonely, unhappy, sorry, or guilty (or happy). Forget about understanding anything anatomo-neuro-physiologically about love, hate, shyness, or regression (the mid-life crisis sportscar, for example).

I have enjoyed seeing some student therapists keep a list of defenses (also ego functions) on the wall over their desks. This book is essentially a bit of an elaboration on that list.

Notes

Preface

1. Steve had had a chromophobe adenoma—a benign, but encroaching, tumor.
2. Numbers in parentheses refer to defense definitions as denoted in Table 2.1 and throughout chapters 2 and 3.

Introduction

1. As noted in chapter 1, following, defenses can also shut other mental functions out of consciousness (such as ego weaknesses, wishes, and other defenses), or even be employed in the development of mental agencies (such as the self-image and the superego). But it's easier and more practical to begin by looking at defenses as operating primarily against affects, since most insight-directed therapeutic work centers on that usage.

Chapter 1

1. Example taken from a lecture by M. Sottarelli, M.D., at L.S.U. Medical School, 1974.

Chapter 2

1. All identifying information has either been removed or extremely disguised.
2. Other defenses that contribute to the formation of prejudicial attitudes include *devaluation* of the other group, *identifications* with the prejudiced group's leader and other members, *generalization* of projected criticisms, *regression* in reality testing, and *displacement* of competitive hostility outside the prejudiced group. These defenses are discussed later.
3. I am using the term *mother* to refer to the mothering individual who cares for the child, rather than using awkward phrasing, such as "primary nurturer and caretaker." In other words, *mother* refers to the *psychological mother*, whomever that may actually be.
4. Volkan (1999) recently expressed a preference to stop using these overlapping technical terms, opting to use vernacular words such as "takes in," "becomes like," or "acts like."
5. Pam Tillis (2000) sings about sticking with a lying, cheating boyfriend:
   ". . . Just call me Cleopatra everybody, 'cause I'm the Queen of Denial."

6. Kernberg (as did Jacobson [1964], Mahler [1968] and Kohut [1971]) also uses Freud's "economic theory" of "object cathexis" to relate *splitting* to "defusion" of sexual and aggressive drive wishes (A. Freud, 1956). This is a very complex theory that essentially involves abrogations of the usual, unconscious ways that sexuality should operate hand-in-hand with aggression in compromise formations when relating to a loved person. The vicissitudes of that theory cannot be adequately covered in this book, and the theory is controversial among psychoanalysts. For views opposing Kernberg's, see Abend, Willick, and Porder (1983).

7. In Wernicke–Korsakoff Syndrome (Medical Council on Alcohol, 2000; Meissner, 1968) is usually due to thiamine deficiency associated with severe alcoholism, but possibly due to other types of brain damage (Weigert-Vowinckel, 1936). The confabulation may be caused entirely by brain damage and not by defense versus the affects engendered by the brain damage.

8. Because we know that thoughts are compromise formations, if a panicky person imagines he or she is going to die in response to the palpitations and hyperpnea, this may be a clue that the repressed thoughts that started the attack involved fearing the death penalty for guilt-ridden hostile or sexual wishes. Alternately, the fantasies of dying during a panic attack may (also) be stimulated by the discomfort of the hypoxia caused by hyperventilation.

9. "You have made my life a misery, and I am yet weak enough to forgive you." (Désirée in a letter to Napoleon after learning of his marriage to Josephine) (Hopkins, 1910).

10 " . . . Thus the desire to go to Rome has in my dream-life became the mask and symbol for a number of warmly cherished wishes, for whose realization one had to work with the tenacity and single-mindedness of the Punic general, though their fulfillment at times seemed as remote as Hannibal's life-long wish to enter Rome. . . ." (Freud, 1900b).

11. It is remarkable that not one of the *DSM*s has included this common personality disturbance in their expansive lists of phenomenological diagnoses.

Chapter 3

1. McDevitt (1985) defines normal aggression as "purposive intentionality"; hostile aggression erupts in response to frustration of normal aggression. Parens (1973) adds that hostile-destructive aggression is only one of four types: nonhostile-nondestructive (studying for a test), nonhostile-destructive (eating), hostile-nondestructive (verbal criticism), hostile-destructive (violence, slander).

2. Although Ms. LM's physical injury was obviously quite minimal, and despite psychiatric testimony that schizophrenic symptoms are not caused by bruised index fingers, the jury awarded Ms. LM $60,000. It's an interesting example of the type of case reported by Howard (1996), where *rationalizations* and the need to blame someone (*projective blaming*) are accepted, somehow, as reality explanations for someone's distress, even if common sense would dictate that there is no connection at all.

3. In the video, a young, attractive woman is first frightened and then eventually charmed by Jackson chasing and threatening her with his sexual gyrations (to compete with his violent male compatriots). She stops trying to run away from him, and when she sees a fire hydrant suddenly gush torrents of water, she supposedly becomes mesmerized by his persistence, and her terror is magically transformed into pleasure. The underlying fantasies that persistence—in the face of a woman's drastic defenses—and symbolic ejaculations will "win" a beautiful girl are quite dramatic. In 2002, 15 years after it was made, this video is still hawked as "classic Michael" and "historical." Its message seems to be the antithesis of modern workplace videos used for "sensitivity training" and prevention of sexual harassment.

4. It is debatable whether her orientation toward "casual sex" could be considered patho-logical if it had not come into conflict with her stated conscious wish to settle down. Some people have no apparent conflicts about staying single and having a series of love relationships without the commitment of marriage and children. I have treated a number of people who had felt guilty about their wishes to stay free and then *gotten married* to defend against the guilt. Once that was clarified in treatment, some of them decided not to pursue further treatment to address their problems with closeness and commitment. Instead, they would simply avoid marrying or promising to marry anyone in the future.

5. Actually, I was not married at the time.

6. On the other hand, it is interesting that some creative writers have been psychotic, at least at times. Ezra Pound is one example of this.

7. One of the advantages of classical psychoanalysis for the treatment of severe character problems is that the use of the couch, with the analyst out of sight behind it, fosters the emergence of analyzable transferences.

8. Abraham (1913) makes the point that the sun (and light) can have a multiplicity of symbolic meanings, and therefore avoiding sunlight is also symbolic. Through the care-ful, lengthy study of several cases he concludes that the light can represent the ". . . ob-servant eye of [the] . . . father" and photophobia, therefore, the "wish to be removed from [it]" (p. 175).

    Regarding a male patient, ". . . at the time of treatment he still shrank from seeing any portion of his mother's body uncovered except her face and hands. Even seeing her in a blouse with an open-work neck used to cause him great distress." Further associa-tions led to the remarkable discovery that ". . . the prohibition of looking at his mother originated in the more particular prohibition of seeing her naked and in especial of seeing her genitals. The idea of not being allowed to look at her was . . . [*displaced* onto] the fear of "not being able to look at the light of the sun" (p. 177).

Chapter 4

1. In other words, countertransference reactions are stirred up in the therapist because of the patient's attitudes and behaviors; other problematic attitudes in the therapist may derive from the therapist's own character functioning. I would add that inexperienced or poorly trained therapists can make mistakes in managing insight-directed therapy that is not based on their unconscious difficulties.

2. The dynamics in this series of interactions were far more complex. I offer the example for the purpose of explicating further the concepts of empathy and countertransference.

3. Delta Dawn, what's that flower you have on?
Could it be a faded rose from days gone by?
And did I hear you say he was a-meetin' you here today,
To take you to his mansion in the sky-eye?

4. McDevitt (1976) quoted Mahler as opining that a minimum of about two hours a day of "quality" time with a consistent mother figure was probably necessary for the toddler to attain adequate self and object constancy, but was clear that research on that subject becomes politicized and difficult to interpret.

5. There are men with this character pathology as well, but we don't usually use this term for them. Also, with the exception of the paid gigolo, most romantic male con artists trade on phony attentiveness to women and less on providing satisfaction of purely sexual fantasies.

6. This type of woman is stunningly portrayed by Kathleen Turner in *Body Heat* (Kasdan, 1981). Her character uses sexual seduction as a shill; the finale reveals her narcissism, orality, and desire for emotional distance.

7. Volkan (1987b), on the contrary, recommends several techniques for analyzing some borderline patients using the couch.
8. The following case material is a bit shocking; however, it is not unusual to be confronted with such reports from people suffering with borderline personality organization.
9. Due to the current mental health climate, I should point out that neither John's sexual orientation nor his profession was relevant to his borderline pathology. Such symptomatic behavior and conflicts occur in borderline heterosexuals and in non-attorneys.

Chapter 5

1. It's not unusual for people being evaluated or treated to respond to an inaccurate or incorrect interpretation with valuable material or even insight. If people feel the therapist is well-intentioned, they often engage in interactions that I think of as "helping the therapist," which additionally has the *transference* meaning of being a good child to the therapist (who unconsciously represents a parent), or a good parent to the therapist (who then represents a needy child).

   For example, some people respond to an ill-timed confrontation of an affect—such as, "You seem angry"—by filling in the conflict and the problematic defenses for themselves, to wit: "Yes, and I felt so guilty I wasn't even going to talk about it!" However, it's usually safer to look at defensive functioning first and get people's observing ego in gear regarding the defenses—perhaps, "You seem a bit guarded today." Otherwise, their response to a confrontation of anger could easily be, "No I'm not. Maybe you've got a problem with it. Why do you want me to be angry?!"

Chapter 6

1. The mnemonic, AORTICS (Abstraction, Observing ego, Reality Testing, Integration, Concentration, Sensorium clear), perhaps gets to the heart of the ego functioning necessary for successful treatment with dynamic techniques.
2. Remarkable variations on this peculiar euphemism include "flaming borderline" and "screaming borderline."
3. She experienced word substitutions—the wrong word would come out of her mouth. This mild dysnomia occurred because of damage, due to the stroke, to Broca's Motor Speech Area in the left temporal lobe of her brain.

Post Script

1. Freud's first theory (1895) was neurological. His second theory (1900 to 1905 or so), sometimes called the hydraulic model, involved psychic energy and the cauldron of "The Unconscious." His third theory was structural theory (1923, 1926). His fourth theory was that of the Life and Death Instincts (1920 to 1939). Theories one, two, and four have mostly been discarded.

   I have retained the concept of "primary process" from the second theory, because excess primary process fantasy in consciousness tends to indicate more severe mental disorder (See Hoch & Polatin, 1949; Kernberg, 1975; Holt, 2002) although Arlow & Brenner (1964) suggest we consider primary process mechanisms only as defensive operations. Mostly, I have utilized *certain* concepts from structural theory, although C. Brenner (2002) argues we should discard it, as well, due to some of its more arcane intra-theoretical incompatibilities.

Bibliography

Aarons, Z. (1958). Notes on a case of *maladie des tics. Psychoanalytic Quarterly, 27*, 194–204.

Abend, S. (1975). An analogue of negation. *Psychoanalytic Quarterly, 44*, 631–637.

Abend, S. (1982). Reality testing as a clinical concept. *Psychoanalytic Quarterly, 51*, 218–238.

Abend, S., Willick, M., & Porder, M. (1983). *Borderline patients: Clinical perspectives.* Madison, CT: International Universities Press.

Aberson, H., & Englander, O. (1941). *Dumbo.* http://us.imdb.com/Title?0033563

Abraham, K. (1913). Transformations of scoptophilia. In *Selected papers on psychoanalysis.* Translated by Bryan, D., & Strachey, A. London: The Hogarth Press, 1948, pp. 169–234.

Ackerman, N., & Jahoda, M. (1948). The dynamic basis of anti-semitic attitudes. *Psychoanalytic Quarterly, 17*, 240–260.

Aiken, C. (1974). *Silent snow, secret snow.* Woodstock, IL: Dramatic Publishing.

Akhtar, S. (1992a). Tethers, orbits and invisible fences: Clinical, developmental, sociocultural, and technical aspects of optimal distance. In S. Kramer & S. Akhtar (Eds.), *When the body speaks: Psychological meanings in kinetic cues.* Northvale, NJ: Aronson.

Akhtar, S. (1992b). *Broken structures.* Northvale, NJ: Aronson.

Akhtar, S. (1994). Object constancy and adult psychopathology. *International Journal of Psychoanalysis, 75*, 441–455.

Akhtar, S. (1996). "Someday . . ." and "If only . . ." fantasies: Pathological optimism and inordinate nostalgia as related forms of idealization. *Journal of the American Psychoanalytic Association, 44*, 723–753.

Akhtar, S. (2001). *Why do patients attempt suicide on Friday nights?* Presentation to Department of Psychiatry, U.S. Navy Medical Center, Portsmouth, VA.

Alexander, F. (1930). The neurotic character. *International Journal of Psychoanalysis, 11*, 292–311.

Almansi, R. (1961). Abstract of Recamier, P. (1957) L'Evolution Psychiatrique III. From anxiety to mania. Clinical and psychological study of mania in its relationship to depression. *Psychoanalytic Quarterly, 30*, 156.

Alpert, A. (1959). Reversibility of pathological fixations associated with maternal deprivation in infancy. *Psychoanalytic Study of the Child, 14,* 169–185.

Alpert, A., & Bernstein, I. (1964). Dynamic determinants in oral fixation. *Psychoanalytic Study of the Child, 19,* 170–195.

Anthony, E. (1961). Panel reports—learning difficulties in childhood. *Journal of the American Psychoanalytic Association, 9,* 124–134.

Arlow, J. (1971). Character perversion. In I. Marcus (Ed.), *Currents in psychoanalysis.* New York: International Universities Press.

Arlow, J., & Brenner, C. (1964). *Psychoanalytic concepts and the structural theory.* New York: International Universities Press.

Armstrong, J. (1994). Reflections on multiple personality disorder as a developmentally complex adaptation. *Psychoanalytic Study of the Child, 49,* 349–364.

AROPA (Asociatia Romana Pentru Promovarea Psihanalizei) (2002). *Sigmund Freud – Biography: I. Childhood.* http://freudnet.tripod.com/biography.html

Asch, S. (1982). Review of Hans Loewald's *Psychoanalysis and the history of the individual.* New Haven, CT: Yale University. Press, 1978. *Journal of the American Psychoanalytic Association, 30,* 265–275.

Balint, M. (1955). Friendly expanses—horrid empty spaces. *International Journal of Psycho-Analysis, 36,* 225–241.

Barglow, P., & Sadow, L. (1971). Visual perception: Its development and maturation from birth to adulthood. *Journal of the American Psychoanalytic Association, 19,* 433–450.

Baruch, D. (1952). *One little boy.* New York: Julian Press. Reviewed by Sperling, M. (1953) in *Psychoanalytic Quarterly, 22,* 115.

Bass, A. (1997). The problem of concreteness. *Psychoanalytic Quarterly, 66,* 642–682.

Bates, J., Bentler, P., & Thompson, S. (1979). Gender deviant boys compared with normal and clinical control boys. *Journal of Abnormal Child Psychology, 7,* 243–259.

Beck, A., & Steer, R. (1988). *Beck Hopelessness Scale (BHS).* The Psychological Corporation-HBJ. http://www.suicide-parasuicide.rumos.com/en/resources/psychological_tests/index.htm, 2002.

Bellak, L. (1989). *Ego Function Assessment* (EFA). Larchmont, NY: C.P.S.

Bellak, L., Hurvich, M., & Gediman, H. (1973). *Ego functions in schizophrenics, neurotics, & normals.* New York: John Wiley & Sons.

Bellak, L., & Meyers, B. (1975). Ego function assessment and analyzability. *International Review of Psycho-Analysis, 2,* 413–427.

Bender, L. (1944). As quoted in Mahler, M. (1944) Tics and impulsions in children: A study of motility. *Psychoanalytic Quarterly, 13,* 430.

Bergmann, M. (1995). The nature and function of a pathological oedipal constellation in a female patient. *Psychoanalytic Quarterly, 64,* 517–532.

Berliner, B. (1947). On some psychodynamics of masochism. *Psychoanalytic Quarterly, 16,* 459–471.

Blackman, J. (1987). Character traits underlying self-neglect and their connection with heart disease. *Journal of the Louisiana State Medical Society, 139*(2), 31–34.

Blackman, J. (1991a). Instinctualization of ego functions and ego defects in male homosexuals: Implications for psychoanalytic treatment. In V. Volkan & C. Socarides (Eds.), *The homosexualities & the therapeutic process.* Madison, CT: International Universities Press.

Blackman, J. (1991b). Intellectual dysfunction in abused children. *Academy Forum, 35,* 7–10.

Blackman, J. (1994). Psychodynamic techniques during urgent consultation interviews. *Journal of Psychotherapy Practice & Research, 3,* 194–203.

Blackman, J. (1997). Teaching psychodynamic technique during an observed analytic psychotherapy interview. *Academic Psychiatry, 35,* 148–154.

Blackman, J. (2000). *Bizet's Carmen on the couch.* Norfolk, VA: Virginia Opera Voice.

Blackman, J. (2001). On childless stepparents. In S. Cath & M. Shopper (Eds.), *Stepparenting: Creating and recreating families in America today* (pp. 168–182). Hillsdale, NJ: The Analytic Press.

Blackman, J. (2002). *DCM: Diagnostic & Clinical Manual of disturbances in mental functioning.* Norfolk, VA: Colley Press.

Blackman, J. (2003). Dynamic supervision concerning a patient's request for medication. *Psychoanalytic Quarterly, 72,* 469–475.

Blatt, S. (1992). The differential effect of psychotherapy and psychoanalysis with anaclitic and introjective patients: The Menninger Psychotherapy Research Project revisited. *Journal of the American Psychoanalytic Association, 40,* 691–724.

Blatt, S., McDonald, C., & Sugarman, A. (1984). Psychodynamic theories of opiate addiction: New directions for research. *Clinical Psychology Review, 4,* 159–189.

Blatt, S., Rounsaville, B., Eyre, S. et al. (1984). The psychodynamics of opiate addiction. *Journal of Nervous & Mental Disease, 172,* 342–352.

Bleuler, E. (1969). *Dementia praecox or the group of schizophrenias.* New York: International Universities Press. (Original work published 1911)

Blos, P. (1962). *On adolescence.* New York: International Universities Press.

Blos, P. (1979). Concretization in adolescence. In *The adolescent passage.* New York: International Universities Press.

Blum, H. (1979) The curative and creative aspects of insight. *Journal of the American Psychoanalytic Association, 27S,* 41–70.

Blum, H. (1981). Object inconstancy and paranoid conspiracy. *Journal of the American Psychoanalytic Association, 29,* 789–813.

Blum, H. (1982). The transference in psychoanalysis and psychotherapy. *Annual of Psychoanalysis, 10,* 117–138.

Blum, H. (1992). Clinical and developmental dimensions of hate. *Journal of the American Psychoanalytic Association, 45,* 359–376

Blum, H. (1994a). The erotic transference: contemporary perspectives. *Psychoanalytic Inquiry, 14,* 622–635.

Blum, H. (1994b). The conceptual development of regression. *Psychoanalytic Study of the Child, 49,* 60–79.

Blum, H. (1996). Seduction trauma: Representation, deferred action, and pathogenic development. *Journal of the American Psychoanalytic Association, 44,* 1147–1164.

Bogdanovich, P., Director. (1971). *The last picture show.* http://www.filmsite.org/lastp.html.

Bornstein, B. (1951). On latency. *Psychoanalytic Study of the Child, 6,* 279–285.

Boyer, B. (1971). Psychoanalytic technique in the treatment of certain characterological and schizophrenic disorders. *International Journal of Psycho-Analysis, 52,* 67–85.

Brenner, C. (1959). The masochistic character: Genesis and treatment. *Journal of the American Psychoanalytic Association, 7,* 197–226.

Brenner, C., Reporter (1975). Alterations in defenses during psychoanalysis. *The Kris Study Group of the New York Psychoanalytic Institute, Monograph VI.* New York: International Universities Press.

Brenner, C. (1982a). *The mind in conflict.* Madison, CT: International Universities Press.

Brenner, C. (1982b). The concept of the superego: A reformulation. *Psychoanalytic Quarterly, 51,* 501–525

Brenner, C. (2002). Conflict, compromise formation, and structural theory. *Psychoanalytic Quarterly, 71,* 397–418.

Brenner, I. (1996). On trauma, perversion, and "multiple personality." *Journal of the American Psychoanalytic Association, 44,* 785–814.

Brenner, I. (2001). *Dissociation.* Presentation to the Annual Meeting of the Virginia Psychoanalytic Society, Charlottesville, VA.

Breuer, J., & Freud, S. (1971). *Studies on Hysteria* (1893–1895). *Standard edition of the complete psychological works of Sigmund Freud, 2,* 1–309. London: MacMillan. (Original work published 1895).

Brown, M. W. (1942). *The runaway bunny.* New York: Harper Collins.

Buie, D. (1981). Empathy: Its nature and limitations. *Journal of the American Psychoanalytic Association, 29,* 281–307.

Busch, F. (1997). Understanding the patient's use of free association: An ego psychological approach. *Journal of the American Psychoanalytic Association, 45,* 407–424.

Calef, V., & Weinshel, E. (1981). Some clinical consequences of introjection: Gaslighting. *Psychoanalytic Quarterly, 50,* 44–66.

Card, O. S. (1991). *Ender's Game.* New York: Tom Doherty Associates. (Original work published 1977).

Carlson, D. (1977). Dream mirrors. *Psychoanalytic Quarterly, 46,* 38–70.

Carlson, R. (2002). *Don't sweat the small stuff* (book series). New York: Don't Sweat Press, Division of Hyperion Books. http://www.crimsonbird.com/books/dontsweat.htm

Cassem, N. (1988). The person confronting death. In A. Nicholi, Jr. (Ed.), *The new Harvard guide to psychiatry.* Cambridge, MA: The Belknap Press of Harvard University Press.

Cath, S. (1986). Fathering, infancy to old age: Overview of recent psychoanalytic contributions. *Psychoanalytic Review, 73,* 469–479.

Cath, S., Kahn, A., & Cobb, N. (1977). *Love and hate on the tennis court: How hidden emotions affect your game.* New York: Charles Scribner's Sons.

Coates, S., & Person, E. (1985). Extreme boyhood femininity: Isolated finding or pervasive disorder? *Journal of the American Academy of Child & Adolescent Psychiatry, 24,* 702–709.

Coen, S. (1981). Sexualization as a predominant mode of defense. *Journal of the American Psychoanalytic Association, 29,* 893–920.

Compton, A., Reporter. (1975). Aspects of psychoanalytic intervention. *The Kris Study Group of the New York Psychoanalytic Institute, Monograph VI.* New York: International Universities Press.

Cukor, G., Director. (1944). *Gaslight.* Warner Brothers. http://www.filmsite.org/gasl.html

Cutter, F. (2002). *Suicide prevention triangle* (Chapter 5: Assessment). http://www.suicidepreventtriangle.org/Suichap5.htm

Davis, T., Gunderson, J., & Myers, M. (1999). Borderline personality disorders. In D. Jacobs (Ed.), *The Harvard Medical School guide to suicide assessment and intervention.* San Francisco: Jossey-Bass.

Dean, J. (1976). *Blind ambition.* New York: Simon and Schuster.

Deutsch, F. (1959). *On the mysterious leap from the mind to the body.* New York: International Universities Press.

Deutsch, H. (1965). Some forms of emotional disturbance and their relationship to schizophrenia. In *Neuroses and character types: Clinical psychoanalytic studies* (pp. 262–281). New York: International Universities Press. (Original work published 1942)

Dorpat, T. (1976). Structural conflict and object relations conflict. *Journal of the American Psychoanalytic Association, 24,* 855–874.

Dorpat, T. (1984). *Denial and defense in the therapeutic situation.* Northvale, NJ: Aronson.

Dorpat, T. (2000). *Gaslighting, the double-whammy, interrogation, and other methods of covert control in psychotherapy and analysis.* Northvale, NJ: Aronson.

Dorpat, T., & Boswell, J. (1964). An evaluation of suicidal intent in suicide attempts. *Comprehensive Psychiatry, 4,* 117.

Easser, R. (1974). Empathic inhibition and psychoanalytic technique. *Psychoanalytic Quarterly, 43,* 557–580.

Edelman, G. (1992). *Bright air, brilliant fire.* New York: Basic Books.

Erikson, E. (1950). *Childhood and society.* New York: W. W. Norton.

Erikson, E. (1968). *Identity: Youth and crisis.* London: Faber & Faber.

Escoll, P. (1992). Vicissitudes of optimal distance through the life cycle. In S. Kramer & S. Akhtar (Eds.), *When the body speaks: Psychological meanings in kinetic cues.* Northvale, NJ: Aronson.

Esman, A. (1983). The "stimulus barrier": A review and reconsideration. *Psychoanalytic Study of the Child, 38,* 193–207.

Everything Preschool. (2002). Review of *The runaway bunny.* http://www.everythingpreschool.com/book/book23.htm

Feder, S. (1974). On being frank. *International Review of Psycho-Analysis, 1,* 277–281.

Feigenbaum, D. (1937). Depersonalization as a defense mechanism. *Psychoanalytic Quarterly, 6,* 4–11.

Feighner, J. P., Robins, E., Guze, S. B., Woodruff, R. A., Winokur, G., & Muñoz,

R. (1972). Diagnositc criteria for use in psychiatric research. *Archives of General Psychiatry, 26,* 57–63.

Ferenczi, S. (1922). The symbolism of the bridge. *International Journal of Psycho-Analysis, 3,* 163–168.

Fogel, G. (1995). Psychological-mindedness as a defense. *Journal of the American Psychoanalytic Association, 43,* 793–822.

Freedman, A., & Kaplan, H. (1967). *Comprehensive textbook of psychiatry.* Baltimore: Williams & Wilkins.

Freeman, T. (1962). Narcissism and defensive processes in schizophrenic states. *International Journal of Psycho-Analysis, 43,* 415–425.

Freud, A. (1936). *The ego and the mechanisms of defense.* New York: International Universities Press.

Freud, A. (1956). The concept of developmental lines. In *Normality and pathology in childhood.* New York: International Universities Press.

Freud, A. (1992). Love, identification, and superego. In J. Sandler (Ed.), *The Harvard Lectures, Anna Freud.* Madison, CT: International Universities Press. (Original work published 1952)

Freud, A., Nagera, H., & Freud, W. E. (1979). Metapsychological assessment of the adult personality: The adult profile. In R. Eissler, A. Freud, M. Kris, & A. Solnit (Eds.), *An anthology of the psychoanalytic study of the child—Psychoanalytic assessment: The diagnostic profile.* New Haven, CT & London: Yale University Press. (Original work published 1965)

Freud, S. (1893). A case of successful treatment of hypnotism. *Standard Edition of the complete psychological works of Sigmund Freud, 1,* 113–128. London: MacMillan.

Freud, S. (1894). The neuro-psychoses of defence. *Standard Edition, 3,* 45–61.

Freud, S. (1895). *Project for a scientific psychology. Standard Edition, 1,* 295–391.

Freud, S. (1900a). *The interpretation of dreams,* Parts I & II. *Standard Edition, 4,* 1–338 & *5,* 339–625.

Freud, S. (1900b). *The interpretation of dreams,* Chapter V-b. *Infantile experiences as the source of dreams.* http://www.psywww.com/books/interp/chap05b.htm.

Freud, S. (1905). Three essays on the theory of sexuality. *Standard Edition, 7,* 130–243.

Freud, S. (1911). Psycho-analytic notes on an autobiographical account of a case of paranoia. *Standard Edition, 12,* 3–82.

Freud, S. (1913). Animism, magic and omnipotence of thoughts. In *Totem and taboo. Standard Edition, 13,* 75–99.

Freud, S. (1914a). On narcissism: An introduction. *Standard Edition, 14,* 73–102.

Freud, S. (1914b). Remembering, repeating and working through. *Standard Edition, 12,* 147–156.

Freud, S. (1916). Some character-types met with in psycho-analytic work. *Standard Edition, 14,* 311–333.

Freud, S. (1917). Mourning and melancholia. *Standard Edition, 14,* 237–258. (Original work published 1915)

Freud, S. (1921). *Group Psychology and the Analysis of the Ego. Standard Edition, 18,* 69–143.

Freud, S. (1923). *The ego and the id. Standard Edition, 19,* 12–66.

Freud, S. (1926). *Inhibitions, symptoms & anxiety. Standard Edition, 20,* 77–178.

Freud, S. (1932). Libidinal types. *Psychoanalytic Quarterly, 1,* 3–6.

Freud, S. (1937). Analysis terminable and interminable. *Standard Edition, 23,* 216–253.

Frosch, J. (1964). The psychotic character: Clinical psychiatric considerations. *Psychiatric Quarterly* 38:1-16.

Frosch, J. (1966). A note on reality constancy. In: R. Loewenstein, L. Newman, M. Schur, & A. Solnit (Eds.), *Psychoanalysis: A General Psychology—Essays in honor of Heinz Hartmann* (pp. 349–376). New York: International Universities Press.

Frosch, J. (1970). Psychoanalytic considerations of the psychotic character. *Journal of the American Psychoanalytic Association, 18,* 24–50.

Frosch, J. (1983). *The psychotic process.* New York: International Universities Press.

Frosch, J. (1990). *Psychodynamic psychiatry: Theory and practice, Vols. 1 & 2.* Madison, CT: International Universities Press

Gabbard, G. (1994). *Psychodynamic psychiatry in clinical practice: The DSM-IV edition.* Washington, DC: The Analytic Press.

Galenson, E., & Roiphe, H. (1971). Impact of early sexual discoveries on mood, defensive organization, symbolization. *Psychoanalytic Study of the Child, 26,* 195–216.

Gardner, R. (1994). You're not a paranoid schizophrenic; you only have multiple personality disorder. *Academy Forum, 38*(3), 11–14.

Garma, A. (1969). Present thoughts on Freud's theory of dream hallucination. *International Journal of Psycho-Analysis, 50,* 485–494.

Gilligan, C. (1980). Effects of social institutions on the moral development of children and adolescents. *Bulletin of the Menninger Clinic, 44,* 498–516.

Gillman, R. (1994). Narcissistic defense and learning inhibition. *Psychoanalytic Study of the Child, 49,* 175–189.

Glasser, M. (1992). Problems in the psychoanalysis of certain narcissistic disorders. *International Journal of Psycho-Analysis, 73,* 493–504.

Glover, E. (1955). *The technique of psychoanalysis.* New York: International Universities Press.

Glover, E. (1964). Aggression and sado-masochism. In I. Rosen (Ed.), *Pathology and treatment of sexual deviation* (pp. 146–162). London: Oxford.

Goldberg, A. (1976). Discussion of the paper by C. Hanly and J. Masson: A critical examination of the new narcissism. *International Journal of Psycho-Analysis, 57,* 67–70.

Goldberger, M. (1988). The two-man phenomenon. *Psychoanalytic Quarterly, 57,* 229–233.

Goldstein, W. (1997). *Beginning psychotherapy.* New York: Brunner/Mazel.

Gorelik, B. (1931). Certain reaction-formations against oral impulses. *International Journal of Psycho-Analysis, 12,* 231–232.

Gray, P. (1994). *The ego and the analysis of defense.* Northvale, NJ: Aronson.

Greenacre, P. (1956). Experiences of awe in childhood. *Psychoanalytic Study of the Child, 11,* 9–30.

Greenson, R. (1949). The psychology of apathy. *Psychoanalytic Quarterly, 18,* 290–302.

Greenson, R. (1965). The working alliance and the transference neurosis. *Psychoanalitic Quarterly, 34,* 155–181.

Greenson, R. (1967). *The technique and practice of psychoanalysis.* New York: International Universities Press.

Greenson, R. (1968). Disidentifying from mother. *International Journal of Psycho-Analysis, 49,* 370–374.

Hamilton, N. G. (1990). *Self and others: Object relations theory in practice.* Northvale, NJ: Aronson.

Harley, M., & Sabot, L. (1980). Conceptualizing the nature of the therapeutic action of child analysis. *Journal of the American Psychoanalytic Association,* 28, 161–179.

Hartmann, H. (1939). *Ego psychology and the problem of adaptation.* New York: International Universities Press.

Hartmann, H. (1981). Comments on the psychoanalytic theory of the ego. In *Essays on ego psychology* (pp. 113–141). New York: International Universities Press. (Original work published 1950).

Hartmann, H. (1953). Contribution to the metapsychology of schizophrenia. *Psychoanalytic Study of the Child, 8,* 177–198.

Hartmann, H. (1955). Notes on the theory of sublimation. *Psychoanalytic Study of the Child, 10,* 9–30.

Hoch, P., & Polatin, P. (1949). Pseudoneurotic forms of schizophrenia. *Psychiatric Quarterly, 23,* 248–276.

Holliman, J. (1996). *McFarlane: Embarrassment may have caused Boorda's suicide.* http://europe.cnn.com/US/9605/17/fatal.flaw/

Holocaust Educational Research. (2002). http://www.nizkor.org

Holt, R. (2002). Quantitative research on the primary process: Method and findings. *Journal of the American Psychoanalytic Association, 50,* 457–482.

Hopkins, T. (1910). *Women Napoleon loved.* Eveleigh Nash. http://www.ddg.com/LIS/InfoDesignF97/aim/desiree.html

Howard, P. (1996). *The death of common sense: How law is suffocating America.* New York: Warner Books.

Jackson, M. (1987). *The way you make me feel.* http://www.michaeljackson.com/video/Way.ram

Jacobs, D. (Ed.). (1999). *The Harvard Medical School guide to suicide assessment and intervention.* San Francisco: Jossey-Bass.

Jacobs, D., Brewer, M., & Klein-Benheim, M. (1999). Suicide assessment: An overview and recommended protocol. In D. Jacobs (Ed.), *The Harvard Medical School guide to suicide assessment and intervention.* San Francisco: Jossey-Bass.

Jacobson, E. (1957). Normal and pathological moods: Their nature and functions. *Psychoanalytic Study of the Child, 12,* 73–113.

Jacobson, E. (1964). *The self and the object world.* New York: International Universities Press.

Jewison, N., Director (1982). *Best friends.* Warner Brothers. http://www.citypaper.com/1999-12-01/rewind.html

Johnson, A., & Szurek, S. (1952). The genesis of antisocial acting out in children and adolescents. *Psychoanalytic Quarterly, 21,* 323–343.

Jones, E. (1942). The concept of a normal mind. *International Journal of Psycho-Analysis, 23,* 1–8.

Jones, R. A. (1986). *Emile Durkheim: An introduction to four major works.* Beverly Hills, CA: Sage. http://www.relst.uiuc.edu/durkheim/Summaries/suicide.html, 2002.

Kanzer, M. (1953). Past and present in the transference. *Journal of the American Psychoanalytic Association, 1,* 144–154.

Kaplan, D. (1990). Some theoretical and technical aspects of gender and social reality in clinical psychoanalysis. *Psychoanalytic Study of the Child, 45,* 3–24.

Kaplan, E. H., & Blackman, L. (1969). The husband's role in psychiatric illness associated with childbearing. *Psychiatric Quarterly, 43,* 396–409.

Karpman, B. (1949). From The autobiography of a liar: Toward the clarification of the problem of psychopathic states, Part II. *Psychiatric Quarterly, 23,* 497–521. Abstracted by Biernoff, J.(1951) in *Psychoanalytic Quarterly, 20,* 151–152.

Kasdan, L. (1981). *Body heat.* http://www.suntimes.com/ebert/ebert_reviews/1999/01/body0929.html

Kaslow, N., Reviere, S., Chance, S., Rogers, J., Hatcher, C., Wasserman, F., Smith, L., Jessee, S., James, M., & Seelig, B. (1998). An empirical study of the psychodynamics of suicide. *Journal of the American Psychoanalytic Association, 46,* 777–796.

Kaywin, L. (1966). Problems of sublimation. *Journal of the American Psychoanalytic Association, 14,* 313–334.

Kernberg, O. (1975). *Borderline conditions and pathological narcissism.* New York: Aronson.

Kernberg, O. (1984). *Severe personality disorders: Psychotherapeutic strategies.* New Haven/London: Yale University Press.

Kitayama, O. (1991). The wounded caretaker and guilt. *International Review of Psycho-Analysis, 18,* 229–240.

Kluft, R. (1985). The natural history of multiple personality disorder. In R. Kluft (Ed.), *Childhood antecedents of multiple personality* (pp. 197–238). Washington, DC: American Psychiatric Press.

Knight, R. (1942). Intimidation of others as a defense against anxiety. *Bulletin of the Menninger Clinic, 6,* 4–14. Abstracted by Greenson, R. (1943) in *Psychoanalytic Quarterly, 12,* 443.

Knight, R. (1986). Borderline states. In M. Stone (Ed.), *Essential papers on borderline disorders: 100 years at the border.* New York: New York University Press. (Original work published 1954).

Kohut, H. (1959). Introspection, empathy, and psychoanalysis: An examination of the relationship between mode of observation and theory. *Journal of the American Psychoanalytic Association, 7,* 459–483.

Kohut, H. (1971). *The analysis of the self.* New York: International Universities Press.

Kramer, S. (1979). The technical significance and application of Mahler's separation-individuation theory. *Journal of the American Psychoanalytic Association, 27*(S), 241–262.

Kramer, S. (1983). Object-coercive doubting: A pathological defensive response to maternal incest. *Journal of the American Psychoanalytic Association, 31S*, 325–351.

Kramer, S. (1992). Nonverbal manifestations of unresolved separation-individuation in adult psychopathology. In S. Kramer & S. Akhtar (Eds.), *When the body speaks: Psychological meanings in kinetic cues.* Northvale, NJ: Aronson.

Kris, E. (1952). *Psychoanalytic explorations in art.* New York: International Universities Press.

Kubie, L., & Israel, H. (1955). "Say you're sorry." *Psychoanalytic Study of the Child, 10*, 289–299.

Lachmann, F., & Stolorow, R. (1976). Idealization and grandiosity: Developmental considerations and treatment implications. *Psychoanalytic Quarterly, 45*, 565–587.

Lampl-de-Groot, J. (1966). Some thoughts on adaptation and conformism. In R. Loewenstein, L. Newman, M. Schur, & A. Solnit (Eds.), *Psychoanalysis— A general psychology. Essays in honor of Heinz Hartmann* (pp. 190–221). New York: International Universities Press.

Langs, R. (1973). *The technique of psychodynamic psychotherapy.* Northvale, NJ: Aronson.

Launer, D. (1992). *My Cousin Vinny.* http://www.foxhome.com/capsule/vinny.htm

Laurents, A., Bernstein, L., Sondheim, S., & Robbins, J. (1956). *West side story.* New York: Random House.

LeRoy, M. (1961). *A majority of one.* http://www.rottentomatoes.com/m/AMajorityofOne-1045419/about.php

Levin, F. (2002). The neuroimmune network and its relevance to psychoanalysis. *Psychoanalytic Quarterly, 71*, 617–627.

Levy, S., & Inderbitzin, L. (1989). Negativism and countertransference. *Journal of the American Psychoanalytic Association, 37*, 7–30.

Lewin, B. (1950). *The psychoanalysis of elation.* New York: Norton.

Lidz, T., Cornelison, A., Fleck, S. et al. (1957). The intrafamilial environment of schizophrenic patients, II: Marital schism and marital skew. *American Journal of Psychiatry, 114*, 241.

Litman, R., & Tabachnick, N. (1967). Fatal one-car accidents. *Psychoanalytic Quarterly, 36*, 248–259.

Loeb, F. (1982). Generalization as a defense. *Psychoanalytic Study of the Child, 37*, 405–419.

Loeb, F., & Loeb, L. (1987). Psychoanalytic observations: Effect of lithium in manic attacks. *Journal of the American Psychoanalytic Association, 35*, 877–902.

Loewenstein, R. (1957). A contribution to the psychoanalytic theory of masochism. *Journal of the American Psychoanalytic Association, 5*, 197–234.

Loewenstein, R. (1969). Development in the theory of transference in the last fifty years. *International Journal of Psycho-Analysis, 50*, 583–588.

Loewenstein, R. (1972). Ego autonomy and psychoanalytic technique. *Psychoanalytic Quarterly, 41,* 1–22.

Lorand, S. (1937). Dynamics and therapy of depressive states. *Psychoanalytic Review, 24,* 337–349.

Lustman, S. (1966). Impulse control, structure, and the synthetic function. In R. Loewenstein, L. Newman, M. Schur, & A. Solnit (Eds.), *Psychoanalysis—A general psychology. Essays in honor of Heinz Hartmann* (pp. 190–221). New York: International Universities Press.

MacGregor, J. (1991). Identification with the victim. *Psychoanalytic Quarterly, 60,* 53–68.

Mahler, M. (1944). Tics and impulsions in children: A study of motility. *Psychoanalytic Quarterly, 13,* 430–444.

Mahler, M. (1968). *On human symbiosis and the vicissitudes of individuation.* New York: International Universities Press.

Mahler, M., Pine, F., & Bergman, A. (1975). *The psychological birth of the human infant.* New York: Basic Books.

Marcus, I. (1971). The marriage-separation pendulum. In I. Marcus (Ed.), *Currents in psychoanalysis.* New York: International Universities Press.

Marcus, I. (1980). Countertransference and the psychoanalytic process in children and adolescents. *Psychoanalytic Study of the Child, 35,* 285–298.

Marcus, I. (1991). Learning disabilities in children. In S. Greenspan & G. Pollock (Eds.), *The course of life.* New York: International Universities Press.

Marcus, I., & Francis, J. (1975). Developmental aspects of masturbation. In I. Marcus & J. Francis (Eds.), *Masturbation from infancy to senescence.* New York: International Universities Press.

Mason, J. (2001). *Munchausen Syndrome by Proxy.* http://www.emedicine.com/emerg/topic830.htm

McCullers, C. (1936, December). Wunderkind. *Story 9,* 61–73.

McDevitt, J. (1976). *Lecture.* Louisiana State University Medical School Department of Psychiatry.

McDevitt, J. (1985). The emergence of hostile aggression and its defensive and adaptive modifications during the separation-individuation process. In H. Blum (Ed.), *Defense and resistance* (pp. 273–300). New York: International Universities Press.

Medical Council on Alcohol. (2000). *Prevention and treatment of Wernicke-Korsakoff Syndrome (WKS) in accident & emergency departments (A&E).* www.medicouncilalcol.demon.co.uk/wks.htm.

Meers, D. (1975). Masturbation and the ghetto. In I. Marcus & J. Francis (Eds.), *Masturbation from infancy to senescence.* New York: International Universities Press.

Meissner, W. (1968). Notes on dreaming: Dreaming as a cognitive process. *International Journal of Psycho-Analysis, 49,* 699–708.

Meissner, W. (1970). Notes on identification. *Psychoanalytic Quarterly, 39,* 563–589.

Meissner, W. (1971). Notes on identification II: Clarification of related concepts. *Psychoanalytic Quarterly, 40,* 277–302.

Menninger, K. (1933). Psychoanalytic aspects of suicide. *International Journal of Psycho-Analysis, 14,* 376–390.

Molière, J. de. (1992). *The misanthrope*. Mineola, NY: Dover Press. (Original work published 1666)

Molière, J. de. (1994). *Le Misanthrope ou L'Atrabilaire Amoureux*. Paris, France: Classiques Bordas. (Original work published 1666)

Moore, B., & Rubinfine, D. (1969). The mechanism of denial. *The Kris Study Group of the New York Psychoanalytic Institute, Monograph III*. New York: International Universities Press.

Niederland, W. (1981). The survivor syndrome: Further observations and dimensions. *Journal of the American Psychoanalytic Association, 29*, 413–426.

Novick, J., & Novick, K. (1996). *Fearful symmetry: The development and treatment of sadomasochism*. Northvale, NJ: Aronson.

Oliver, J. (1988). Successive generations of child maltreatment. The children. *British Journal of Psychiatry, 153*, 543–553.

Paniagua, C. (1997). Negative acting in. *Journal of the American Psychoanalytic Association, 45*, 1209–1223.

Paniagua, C. (1999). Personal communication.

Parens, H. (1973). Aggression: A reconsideration. *Journal of the American Psychoanalytic Association, 21*, 34–60.

Parens, H. (1990). Girls' psychosexual development. *Journal of the American Psychoanalytic Association, 38*, 743–772.

Parens, H., Pollock, L., Stern, J., & Kramer, S. (1976). On the girl's entry into the oedipus complex. *Journal of the American Psychoanalytic Association, 24S*, 79–107.

Pine, F. (1990). *Drive, ego, object, self*. New York: Basic Books.

Plath, S. (2000). *The bell jar*. New York: Harper Collins.

Pullman, P. (1996). *The golden compass*. New York: Alfred A. Knopf.

Racker, H. (1953). A contribution to the problem of countertransference. *International Journal of Psycho-Analysis, 34*, 313–324.

Ramis, H.., Director. (1998). *Analyze this*. http://www.rottentomatoes.com/m/AnalyzeThis-1084884/reviews.php

Raphling, D. (1996). The interpretation of daydreams, I. *Journal of the American Psychoanalytic Association, 44*, 533–547.

Reddy, H. (1973). *Delta dawn*. Capitol Records. http://ww.superseventies.com/1973_7singles.html

Renik, O. (1978). The role of attention in depersonalization. *Psychoanalytic Quarterly, 47*, 588–605.

Renik, O. (1999). Playing one's cards face up in analysis. *Psychoanalytic Quarterly, 68*, 521–540.

Rexford, E. (1978). *A developmental approach to problems of acting out*. New York: International Universities Press.

Rochlin, G. (1965). *Griefs and discontents: The forces of change*. Boston: Little, Brown.

Rosegrant, J. (1995). The anal world of a six-year-old boy. *International Journal of Psycho-Analysis, 76*, 1233–1243.

Rosenbaum, M. (1980). The role of the term schizophrenia in the decline of diagnoses of multiple personality. *Archives of General Psychiatry, 37*, 1383–1385.

Rothstein, A. (1979). An exploration of the diagnostic term "narcissistic personality disorder." *Journal of the American Psychoanalytic Association, 27,* 893–912.

Sandler, J. (1960). On the concept superego. *Psychoanalytic Study of the Child, 15,* 128–162.

Sandler, J. (1990). On the structure of internal objects and internal object relationships. *Psychoanalytic Inquiry, 10,* 163–181.

Sandler, J., & Freud, A. (1983). Discussion: *The ego & the mechanisms of defense. Journal of the American Psychoanalytic Association, 31*(S), 19–146.

Schafer, R. (1977). *Aspects of internalization.* New York: International Universities Press.

Schilder, P. (1939). The relations between clinging and equilibrium. *International Journal of Psycho-Analysis, 20,* 58–63.

Schilder, P., & Wechsler, D. (1935). What do children know about the interior of the body? *International Journal of Psycho-Analysis, 16,* 355–360.

Schneider, K. (1959). *Clinical psychopathology.* New York: Grune & Stratton.

Schur, M. (1955). Comments on the metapsychology of somatization. *Psychoanalytic Study of the Child, 10,* 119–164.

Schur, M. (1966) *The id and the regulatory principles of mental functioning.* New York: International Universities Press.

Sederer, L., & Rothschild, A. (1997). *Acute care psychiatry: Diagnosis & treatment.* Baltimore: Williams & Wilkins.

Settlage, C. (1977). The psychoanalytic understanding of narcissistic and borderline personality disorders: Advances in developmental theory. *Journal of the American Psychoanalytic Association, 25,* 805–833.

Settlage, C. (1993). Therapeutic process and developmental process in the restructuring of object and self constancy. *Journal of the American Psychoanalytic Association, 41,* 473–492.

Shneidman, E. (1999). Perturbation and lethality: A psychological approach to assessment and intervention. In D. Jacobs (Ed.), *The Harvard Medical School guide to suicide assessment and intervention.* San Francisco: Jossey-Bass.

Slavson, S. (1969). *A textbook in analytic group psychotherapy.* New York: International Universities Press.

Spencer, T. (2002). Pharmacologic treatment of attention-deficit hyperactivity disorder in children. *CME.* http://www.medscape.com/viewprogram/1927.

Sperling, M. (1957). The psycho-analytic treatment of ulcerative colitis. *International Journal of Psycho-Analysis, 38,* 341–349.

Sperling, O. (1963). Exaggeration as a defense. *Psychoanalytic Quarterly, 32,* 533–548.

Spiegel, R. (1985). Faces of truth in the psychoanalytic experience. *Contemporary Psychoanalysis, 21,* 254–265.

Spruiell, V. (1989). On blaming: An entry to the question of values. *Psychoanalytic Study of the Child, 44,* 241–263.

Stewart, R., & Levine, M. (1967). Individual psychotherapy. In A. Freedman & H. Kaplan (Eds.), *Comprehensive textbook of psychiatry* (pp. 1212–1214). Baltimore: Williams and Wilkins.

Stone, L. (1961). *The psychoanalytic situation: An examination of its development and essential nature.* New York: International Universities Press.

Sutherland, J. (1980). The British object relations theorists: Balint, Winnicott, Fairbairn, Guntrip. *Journal of the American Psychoanalytic Association, 28,* 829–860.

Symonds, P. (1946). *The dynamics of human adjustment.* New York & London: D. Appleton-Century.

Tarachow, S. (1963). *An introduction to psychotherapy.* New York: International Universities Press.

Target, M. (1998). The recovered memories controversy. *International Journal of Psycho-Analysis, 79,* 1015–1028.

Tillis, P. (2000). *Cleopatra, queen of denial.* http://www.arracis.com.ua/Pam/cleopatra.htm.

Tolpin, M. (1971). On the beginnings of a cohesive self: An application of the concept of transmuting internalization to the study of the transitional object and signal anxiety. *Psychoanalytic Study of the Child, 26,* 316–352.

Treece, C., & Khantzian, E. (1986). Psychodynamic factors in the development of drug dependence. *Psychiatric Clinics of North America, 9,* 399–412.

Turow, S. (1977). *One L.* New York: Warner Books.

U.S. Public Health Service. (1999). *The Surgeon General's call to action to prevent suicide.*Washington, DC. http://www.surgeongeneral.gov/library/calltoaction/calltoaction.htm

Vaillant, G. (1992). *Ego mechanisms of defense: A guide for clinicians and researchers.* Washington/London: American Psychiatric Press.

Volkan, V. (1976). *Primitive internalized object relations: A clinical study of schizophrenic, borderline, and narcissistic patients.* New York: International Universities Press.

Volkan, V. (1987a). *Linking objects and linking phenomena.* New York: International Universities Press.

Volkan, V. (1987b). *Six steps in the treatment of borderline personality organization.* Northvale, NJ: Aronson.

Volkan, V. (1999). *Presentation to the Virginia Psychoanalytic Society,* Richmond, VA.

Volkan, V., & Corney, R. (1968). Some considerations of satellite states and satellite dreams. *British Journal of Medical Psychology, 41,* 283–290.

Waelder, R. (1936). The principle of multiple function: Observations on overdetermination. *Psychoanalytic Quarterly, 5,* 45–62.

Wagner, R. (1870). *Die Walküre.* http://www.metopera.org/synopses/walkure.html.

Waugaman, R. (1996). Experiences of schizophrenia: An integration of the personal, scientific, and therapeutic. *Journal of the American Psychoanalytic Association, 44,* 395–939.

Weigert-Vowinckel, E. (1936). A contribution to the theory of schizophrenia. *International Journal of Psycho-Analysis, 17,* 190–201.

Weiss, R., & Hufford, M. (1999). Substance abuse and suicide. In D. Jacobs (Ed.), *The Harvard Medical School guide to suicide assessment and intervention.* San Francisco: Jossey-Bass.

Weiss, S. S. (1987). The two-woman phenomenon. *Psychoanalytic Quarterly, 56,* 271–286.

Werman, D. (1985). Suppression as a defense. In H. Blum (Ed.), *Defense and resistance* (pp. 405–415). New York: International Universities Press.

White House. (2002). *Theodore Roosevelt.* http://www.whitehouse.gov/history/presidents/tr26.html

Whitmer, G. (2001). On the nature of dissociation. *Psychoanalytic Quarterly, 70,* 807–837.

Willick, M. (1985). On the concept of primitive defenses. In H. Blum (Ed.), *Defense and resistance* (pp. 175–200). New York: International Universities Press.

Willick, M. (1993). The deficit syndrome in schizophrenia: Psychoanalytic and neurobiological perspectives. *Journal of the American Psychoanalytic Association, 41,* 1136–1157.

Wilson, C. P., Hogan, C., & Mintz, I. (1992). *Psychodynamic technique in the treatment of the eating disorders.* Northvale, NJ: Aronson.

Wimer, L. (1989). Understanding negative hallucination: Toward a developmental classification of disturbances in reality awareness. *Journal of the American Psychoanalytic Association, 37,* 437–463.

Winnicott, D. (1969). The use of an object. *International Journal of Psycho-Analysis, 50,* 711–716.

Wolf, E. (1994). Narcissistic lust and other vicissitudes of sexuality. *Psychoanalytic Inquiry, 14, 519–534.*

Wurmser, L. (1974). Psychoanalytic considerations of the etiology of compulsive drug use. *Journal of the American Psychoanalytic Association, 22,* 820–843.

Wurmser, L. (1977). A defense of the use of metaphor in analytic theory formation. *Psychoanalytic Quarterly, 46,* 466–498.

Wurmser, L. (1987). Flight from conscience: Experience with the psychoanalytic treatment of compulsive drug abusers, I: Dynamic sequences, compulsive drug use. *Journal of Substance Abuse Treatment, 4,* 157–168.

Zetzel, E. (1956). Current concepts of transference. *International Journal of Psycho-Analysis, 37,* 369–375.

Zetzel, E. (1968). The so-called good hysteric. *International Journal of Psycho-Analysis, 49,* 256–260.

Zwerling, I. (1955). The favorite joke in diagnostic and therapeutic interviewing. *Psychoanalytic Quarterly, 24,* 104–114.

Index

Index note: page references with a *t* indicate a table on designated page.

reaction-formation
case examples, 9, 31
defenses associated with, 41, 45, 72
defined, 13*t*
suicide risk, 159
Reagan, Ronald, 52
reality, 52–53
reality sense, 51–52, 68
reality testing, 52, 144
reconstruction of reality, xiv, 16*t*, 63–64, 75
"recovered memories," 77
Reddy, Helen, 97
regression in the service of the ego, 169
relationships, intrapsychic foundations of, 97
Renik, O., xiii, 31, 35, 64, 124, 148
repression
case examples, 2, 9
defenses associated with, 4, 65, 77
defined, 14*t*, 33–34, 186*n*8
"resistance to resistance," 8
"resonance," 95
reticence, definition and case examples, 4, 15*t*, 27–28, 64, 122
Rexford, E., 38
rituals, definition and case examples, 5, 9, 13*t*
Rochlin, G., 150
Roiphe, H., 30
Roosevelt, Theodore, 7
Rosegrant, J., 81
Rosenbaum, M., 77
Rothschild, A., 149, 150
Rothstein, A, 65
Rubinfine, D., 22
rumination, definition and case examples, 14*t*, 46
"Runaway Bunnies," 101, 103–4
running away, 104

Sabot, L., 146
Sadow, L., 50
Sandler, J., xiii, 6, 13*t*, 14*t*, 19, 40, 41, 99
"satellite state," 102
Schafer, R., 19
Schilder, P., 68, 71
schizoid personality, 100
schizophrenia

development of diagnostic criteria for, 165–66
disrupted ego functions in, xiv, 77, 90–91, 92
high risk for suicide, 150
Schneider, K., 166
Schur, M., 92, 100, 169
secondary process, disruptions of, 53, 81, 102–3
second genital phase
asceticism, 15*t*
concretization, 15*t*
defenses during, 15*t*
disidentification, 15*t*
group formation, 15*t*
humor, 15*t*
ipsisexual object choice, 15*t*
Sederer, L., 149, 150
seduction of the aggressor, definition and case examples, 14*t*, 41–42, 45, 67
self-aggrandizement, 7
self-care, *inhibition of,* 53, 91, 140
self-object fusion, 23–24
self-preservation
disruption of, 57, 92, 140–41
suicidal activity, 141
therapy for disruptions, 144
self-punishment, risk of suicide with, 158–59
sensations, as component of affects, xiii–xiv, 4
sensorium, disorders of, 51, 90
Settlage, C., 92
sexual abuse
defenses in victims, 67–68
dissociation in victims, 76
ego meltdown in victims, 91
memories of, 119
sexual intercourse as a defense, 10
Shepherd, Cybill, 58
Shneidman, E., 150–51, 163
Shneidman's high risk criteria for suicide, 150–51
short-term therapy, defenses in and case examples of, 132–35
"shoulds," in therapistss, 124
signal affect, 3–4
"Silent Cal'", 64
Silent Snow, Secret Snow (Aiken), 155
simple defenses, 7
Slavson, S., 7, 64